NATURE WRITING

THE PASTORAL IMPULSE IN AMERICA

STUDIES IN LITERARY THEMES AND GENRES

Ronald Gottesman, Editor
University of Southern California

NATURE WRITING

THE PASTORAL IMPULSE IN AMERICA

Don Scheese

Twayne Publishers
An Imprint of Simon & Schuster Macmillan
NEW YORK

Prentice Hall International
LONDON • *MEXICO CITY* • *NEW DELHI*
• *SINGAPORE* • *SYNDNEY* • *TORONTO*

Studies in Literary Themes and Genres No. 7

Nature Writing: The Pastoral Impulse in America
Don Scheese

Copyright © 1996 by Simon & Schuster Macmillan

Twayne Publishers
An Imprint of Simon & Schuster Macmillan
1633 Broadway, New York, NY 10019-6785

Library of Congress Cataloging-in-Publication Data

Scheese, Donald.
    Nature writing : the pastoral impulse in America / Donald Scheese.
      p.   cm.—(Twayne's literary themes and genres ; 7)
    Includes bibliographical references and index.
    ISBN 0-8057-0964-9
    1. Pastoral literature, American—History and criticism.
  2. Natural history—United States—Historiography. 3. Country life
in literature. 4. Landscape in literature. 5. Nature in
literature. I. Title II. Series.
PS163.S34   1996
810.9'321734—dc20   96-2399
                                           CIP

"A Homecoming" from *The Country of Marriage,* copyright © 1971 by Wendell Berry, reprinted by permission of Harcourt Brace & Company.

"The Place for No Story" from *The Selected Poetry of Robinson Jeffers,* by Robinson Jeffers, copyright © 1932 and renewed 1960 by Robinson Jeffers. Reprinted by permission of Random House, Inc.

10 9 8 7 6 5 4 3 2 1 (hc)

Printed in the United States of America

In memory of my father and mother.

General Editor's Statement

G enre studies have been a central concern of Anglo-American and European literary theory for at least the past quarter-century, and the academic interest has been reflected, for example, in new college courses in slave narratives, autobiography, biography, nature writing, and the literature of travel, as well as in the rapid expansion of genre theory itself. *Genre* has also become an indispensable term for trade publishers and the vast readership they serve. Indeed, few general bookstores do not have sections devoted to science fiction, romance, and mystery fiction. Still, genre is among the slipperiest of literary terms, as any examination of genre theories and their histories will suggest.

In conceiving this series we have tried, on the one hand, to avoid the comically pedantic spirit that informs Polonius's recitation of kinds of drama and, on the other hand, the equally unhelpful insistence that every literary production is a unique expression that must not be forced into any system of classification. We have instead developed our list of genres, which range from ancient comedy to the western, with the conviction that by common consent kinds of literature do exist—not as fixed categories but as fluid categories that change over time as the result of complex interplay of authors, audiences, and literary and cultural institutions. As individual titles in the series demonstrate, the idea of genre offers us provocative ways to study both the continuities and the adaptability of literature as a familiar and inexhaustible source of human imagination.

Recognition of the fluid boundaries both within and among genres will provide, we believe, a useful array of perspectives from which to study the complex development of literature. Genres, as traditional but open ways of understanding the world, contribute to our capacity to respond to narrative and expressive forms and offer means of discerning the moral significance embodied in these forms. Genres, in short, serve ethical as well as aesthetic purposes, and the volumes in this series attempt to demonstrate how this double benefit has been achieved as these genres have been transformed over the years. Each title in the series should be measured against this large ambition.

Ron Gottesman

Contents

List of Illustrations   xi
Acknowledgments   xiii
Chronology   xvii

Chapter 1
Overview   1

Chapter 2
Walden, Ktaadn, and Walking   39

Chapter 3
My First Summer in the Sierra   61

Chapter 4
The Land of Little Rain   75

Chapter 5
A Sand County Almanac   90

Chapter 6
Desert Solitaire   106

Chapter 7
Pilgrim at Tinker Creek   120

Chapter 8
Conclusion   133

Bibliographic Essay   137
Recommended Titles   167
Notes and References   183
Index   223

List of Illustrations

Figure 1: View from Mount Holyoke (The Oxbow) 2

Diagram 1: Polar Forces in American Pastoralism 5

Diagram 2: Wilderness-Landscape Spectrum 7

Diagram 3: Major Tributaries of Nature Writing 12

Figure 2: Twilight in the Wilderness 25

Figure 3: The Rocky Mountains, Lander's Peak 26

Figure 4: North and Half Domes from Sentinel Dome 27

Figure 5: The Earth from the Moon 33

Figure 6: El Capitan, Sunrise, Yosemite Valley, 1968 34

Figure 7: Lackawanna Valley 45

Figure 8: Mount Ktaadn 57

Figure 9: Looking Up Yosemite Valley 70

Figure 10: Alkali Flat, Alabama Hills and
Sierra Nevada in Distance 88

Figure 11: Leopold and His Dog in Wisconsin
Farm Country 104

Figure 12: Early Morning in Chesler Park 118

Figure 13: South Lookout, Hawk Mountain 131

Books are for the scholar's idle times. When he can read God directly, the hour is too precious to be wasted in other men's transcripts of their readings. But when the intervals of darkness come, as come they must—when the sun is hid and the stars withdraw their shining—we repair to the lamps which were kindled by their ray, to guide our steps to the East again, where the dawn is. We hear, that we may speak.

Ralph Waldo Emerson, "The American Scholar"

Acknowledgments

To employ some familiar tropes of ecocriticism, this study has involved a long and arduous trek in wild places where sometimes no trail existed. Sigurd Olson once said, "My life has been a series of campfires," and I wish to thank many people who helped illuminate the way and in the process added a touch of human warmth.

Various friends during my life were a source of insight and good times on The Trail: George, the Roach-Man, the Vickster, Q-Ball, Nina and Johnny-B, Z-Man, and Charlie the Jackpine Savage.

Students in courses I taught over the years at the University of Iowa, Santa Clara University, and Gustavus Adolphus College inspired and educated me about the relationship between humans and the nonhuman world. In particular, for the examples they set of informed passion about the wilderness experience, I thank: Eric Syverud, Kathleen Tonry, Nancy Piepho, Jig Wiley, Andrew Leider, Becky Romsdahl, Denise Kiecker, Robyn Bipes, Kari Bisbee, Meg Lojek, Kim Lindell, Kristin Fisher, and Patrick Haugen.

At the University of Idaho and the University of Iowa I had the good fortune to work with professors who became my friends as well as my teachers; and who, through their belief in me and their continual questioning of my ideas, confirmed what the literary critic Karl Kroeber once said: "Opposition is true friendship." Walter Hesford helped legitimize for me the study of nature writing by offering the first course I ever took on nature and literature, and by subjecting my early work on Edward Abbey to trenchant examination. Bob Sayre, Wayne Franklin, and the late Sherman Paul encouraged and cajoled me over the years, helped me find my way, and instilled in me the confidence to make my own path. Dan Peck, another Iowa graduate and subsequent mentor, provided the same kind of intellectual and emotional support, especially during an NEH Summer Institute on Landscape Art and Literature at Vassar College, at which he served as director. Sayre and Peck also offered insightful criticism of a late version of the manuscript.

Throughout my career I have been fortunate in being able to follow the pathbreaking work in ecocriticism done by various members of the Western Literature Association and, later, the Association for the Study of Literature and the Environment (ASLE). The work of Ann Ronald, Glen Love, and Tom Lyon guided me at an early stage in my career and validated my belief that nature writing could be a serious and fruitful focus of literary criticism. From the following members of ASLE I have received support, criticism, and encouragement (occasionally over cigars and whiskey into the wee hours of the morning): Ralph Black, Mike Branch, Douglas Burton-Christie, SueEllen Campbell, Michael Cohen, Nancy Cook, Chris Cokinos, Terrell Dixon, Elizabeth Dodd, Cheryll Glotfelty, Verne Huser, Mike Kowalewski, Ian Marshall, Sean O'Grady, Rebecca Raglon, Suzanne Ross, Stephanie Sarver, Scott Slovic, Stan Tag, John Tallmadge, David Taylor, David Teague, Allison Wallace, and Kathy Wallace.

At Gustavus Adolphus College I have been blessed by colleagues who not only have supported my interest and work in fields traditionally viewed as outside the normal purview of an English department, but have read my work with engagement and enthusiasm. With Mark Johnson, Bob Moline, and Tim Sipe I have had a number of insightful conversations about the contributions of nature writing as viewed from the disciplines of geology, geography, and biology, respectively. Linnea Wren helped me to make connections between literature and landscape painting in 19th-century American culture. Florence Amamoto, Deane Curtin, and John Rezmerski offered critiques of various chapters of this book in the early stages of its evolution. Dean Elizabeth Baer and the Development Committee at the College supported my field-work with two summer Research, Scholarship, and Creativity grants. My research assistant Jean Merrill read the entire manu-script and offered many useful suggestions. I thank the English Department secretary Janet Fredlund for organizing, at the eleventh hour, the keyboarding of the entire manuscript; and the students who typed it: Stacy Antonovich, Melissa Bodle, and Tricia Turk. My greatest debt is to Claude Brew, who believed in me and my work from the first, supported me during some diffi-cult times, and read the entire manuscript with characteristic rigor and zeal. It goes without saying that any persisting errors or ques-tionable interpretations are solely my responsibility.

Ron Gottesman, the General Editor of the Twayne Series on Literary Themes and Genres, has been a delight to work with from the outset, offering suggestions which clarified my approach early on and close readings of the manuscript in later stages. I also thank Sylvia Miller, my former editor, for early sup-port and for an incisive critique of the introduction; my current editor, Anne Davidson, for timely official acceptance of the man-uscript and much-needed advice to a first-book author; and pro-duction manager Dawn Lawson, editorial assistant Mary Reed, and production supervisor Susan Gamer for their patience and expert assistance in seeing the book through to publication. Finally, my most heartfelt thanks go to Peg, who has always believed in and supported me in so many ways; and who has saved me from that greatest of academic afflictions: taking myself or my work too seriously.

Chronology

Circa 30,000 B.C.E.	Images of horses, elk, bears, and other animals are drawn in caves in France, the beginning of an artistic record of the nonhuman world—and the beginning of natural history.
4th century B.C.E.	Aristotle compiles *Historia Animalium,* the first work of written natural history; in his grand scheme of classification, he divides the animal kingdom into two categories, creatures with and without blood.
200–1 B.C.E.	Pastoral poetry originates in ancient Greece in the work of Theocritus and Virgil, who celebrate the bucolic life of shepherds.
1200–1800 A.C.E.	Native American cultures pay homage to their dependence on the nonhuman environment through oral traditions: prayers, songs, chants, stories, and creation myths.
1492	Columbus's expedition lands in the Bahamas, marking the European "discovery" of (in F. Scott Fitzgerald's words) the "fresh green breast of the New World."
1678	John Bannister begins a natural history collection of plants and insects to send back to England. It is the first attempt in the new world to catalog nature purely for the sake of information.

1691   "Broad arrow" policy of the English Crown—that
        trees tall enough for ship masts are to be pre-
        served in the Massachusetts colony—becomes the
        first enforced conservation law in America.

1720   Gilbert White is born in the vicarage of
        Selbourne, England.

1735   The Swedish botanist Carolus Linnaeus publish-
        es *Systema Naturae*, which imposes systematic
        terminology and nomenclature on natural histo-
        ry. The tenth edition of the work (1753) becomes
        the definitive version.

1788   Gilbert White's *The Natural History and Antiquities
        of Selbourne, in the County of Southampton* is pub-
        lished.

1791   *Travels* by William Bartram is published; it is
        based on the author's four years (1773–1777) of
        natural history exploration from the Carolinas to
        Florida to the mouth of the Mississippi River. The
        work is later hailed as one of the first appreciative
        aesthetic responses to American wilderness.

1793   Gilbert White dies.

1804   Meriwether Lewis and William Clark, under
        orders from Thomas Jefferson, begin their explo-
        ration of the Louisiana Territory. One of their
        purposes is to catalog natural history informa-
        tion about the American west.

1817   Henry David Thoreau is born in Concord,
        Massachusetts.

1820s   The artist Thomas Cole becomes well-known in
        America for his celebration of wilderness.
        Subsequently he is recognized as the founder of
        the Hudson River school of landscape painting.

1831   John James Audubon begins publication of his
        Ornithological Biography.

1832   The painter and ethnographer George Catlin pro-
        poses a "magnificent park" in the Great Plains to
        preserve resident Native American tribes and the
        bison on which they depend. This is believed to
        be the first call for a national park.

1836   Emerson's *Nature* is published. Thomas Cole writes in "Essay on American Scenery": "The most distinctive, and perhaps the most impressive, characteristic of American scenery is its wildness."

1838   John Muir is born in Dunbar, Scotland.

1839   *The Voyage of the Beagle* by Charles Darwin is published; it is based on Darwin's worldwide cruise from 1831 to 1836. It becomes the basis of his landmark theory of natural selection.

1845–1847   Thoreau lives at Walden Pond.

1849   John Muir's family emigrates to Wisconsin.

1854   *Walden* is published.

1859   *On the Origin of Species* by Darwin is published.

1862   Thoreau dies.

1864   United States government cedes to the state of California some 100 acres in Yosemite "for public use, resort, and recreation . . . inalienable for all time." A precedent is thus set for governments to preserve nature for recreational purposes. In effect, Yosemite becomes the first national park.

1868   Mary Austin is born in Carlinville, Illinois.

1869   John Muir spends his first summer in the Sierra Nevada, as a sheepherder.

1872   The first official national park is created in Yellowstone.

1887   Aldo Leopold is born in Burlington, Iowa.

1890   Yosemite, Sequoia, and General Grant national parks are created. United States Census declares that the frontier is officially (statistically) closed.

1891   Sierra Club is founded by John Muir and several other influential men in California. Forest Reserve Act is passed, authorizing the president to designate portions of the public domain "national forests."

1901   National Association of Audubon Societies for the Protection of Wild Birds and Animals is created, the forerunner of the Audubon Society.

1903   *The Land of Little Rain* by Mary Austin is published.

1906   United States Forest Service is established.

1911   *My First Summer in the Sierra* by John Muir is published.

1912   Congress authorizes construction of a dam in Yosemite National Park that will flood Hetch Hetchy Valley, despite national opposition led by Muir of the Sierra Club.

1914   Muir dies.

1916   National Park Service is established.

1924   Gila Primitive Area is set aside in New Mexico, in part as a result of the efforts of Aldo Leopold. It is the forerunner of the wilderness preservation system.

1927   Edward Abbey is born in Home, Pennsylvania.

1934   Austin dies.

1935   Wilderness Society is founded.

1945   Annie Dillard (née Doak) is born in Pittsburgh, Pennsylvania.

1948   Leopold dies.

1949   *A Sand County Almanac* by Aldo Leopold is published.

1951   *The Sea Around Us* by Rachel Carson, the second book of her sea trilogy, is published; it becomes a best-seller.

1955   *The Edge of the Sea* by Rachel Carson is published.

1956   Congress opposes construction of a dam on the Colorado River that would flood part of Dinosaur National Monument. The defeat of the dam is a major victory for conservationists.

1957   *The Immense Journey* by Loren Eiseley is published.

1962   *Silent Spring* by Rachel Carson is published.

1964   Wilderness Act becomes law, establishing a national wilderness preservation system.

1968   *Desert Solitaire* by Edward Abbey is published. National Wild and Scenic Rivers Act is passed, creating the equivalent of wilderness areas on and along certain rivers.

1970   First "Earth Day" is celebrated worldwide.

1973   Endangered Species Act becomes law.

1974   *Pilgrim at Tinker Creek* by Annie Dillard is published. It wins the Pulitzer Prize for nonfiction.

1977   *The Unsettling of America* by Wendell Berry is published.

1980   Alaska National Interest Lands Conservation Act becomes law. It more than quadruples the size of national wilderness and more than doubles the size of the national park system.

1989   Abbey dies.

1990   *The Norton Anthology of Nature Writing* is published. The 20th anniversary of Earth Day is celebrated worldwide.

1994   California Desert Protection Act becomes law, preserving more land in the lower 48 states (7 million acres) than any other single measure since the passage of the Wilderness Act.

1995   *The Environmental Imagination: Thoreau, Nature Writing, and the Formation of American Culture* by Lawrence Buell is published—a landmark in ecocriticism.

Chapter 1

Overview
Pastoralism:
Ilustration and Definition

I n 1836, at the National Academy of Design in New York City,
the artist Thomas Cole exhibited a landscape painting based
on a sketch he had first done in 1833: *View from Mount
Holyoke, Northhampton, Massachusetts, after a Thunderstorm (The
Oxbow)* (Figure 1). The work features a view from a vantage
point that was fast becoming one of the most popular sites on the
American "grand tour." In 1833 Cole first made a pilgrimage to
the summit of Mt. Holyoke, 1,070 feet above the Connecticut
River, from which point observers were struck by the natural
curiosity of a river appearing to nearly double back on itself.

But it was not only the oddity of the oxbow that attracted
spectators. The view provided an outstanding example of the
sublime—a phenomenon, according to the 17th-century English
philosopher Edmund Burke, "productive of the strongest emotion which the mind is capable of feeling." In delineating a theory of the sublime Burke adds that "astonishment . . . is the effect
of the sublime in its highest degree; the inferior effects are admiration, reverence, and respect." In the 19th century, significant
numbers of middle- and upper-class Americans, self-conscious

Figure 1: *The Oxbow (The Connecticut River near Northampton)*, by Thomas Cole (1801–1848).
Courtesy of the Metropolitan Museum of Art. Gift of Mrs. Russell Sage, 1908. (08.228).

about the newness and alleged inferiority of our country's art, sought out local examples of the sublime, determined to prove to Europe that we as a nation could produce creative work that was commensurate with our magnificent natural environment. That the oxbow was seen in these terms is confirmed in its description by a tourist in 1833, who wrote that the view of the river was a "scene of sublime beauty . . . one of the most magnificent panoramas in the world."[1]

Cole's depiction of the river in 1833 underwent a significant transformation by the time the large canvas (51.5 by 76 inches) was executed three years later. He exaggerated the panoramic qualities of the scene, increased the spatial depth, heightened the elevation of the mountains, and contrived to divide the canvas in half by introducing a thunderstorm on the left side. A viewer of *The Oxbow* (which since 1908 has hung in New York's Metropolitan Museum of Art) gazes at the following landscape: in the left foreground stands a weather-blasted tree, rendered in minute detail; behind it a thunderstorm passes over a forested

ridgeline and, one assumes, the river valley; a flock of large birds
hovers in front of the rain falling from the clouds. In the right
rear are forested mountains; closer are cultivated clearings
marked by farmhouses with smoking chimneys. In the right
lower corner are signs of humans along the river, perhaps part of
a ferryboat operation. In the right foreground is an artist, turned
toward the viewer of the painting, with an easel and canvas; to
his right on a rock outcropping is his parasol.[2]

How are we to interpret this panorama, which is now re-
garded as "probably the most renowned of all Hudson River
school landscape paintings," "the most meaningfully devised
American landscape work up to that time," "one of the established icons of American art"? First of all, the painting clearly sets
up a number of tensions or polarities: light versus dark, civilization versus wilderness, a rural versus a wild landscape. The presence of the artist in the painting suggests further possibilities for
interpretation. He is well-ensconced in the wilderness portion of
the scene, but he also functions as a mediator between view and
viewer, nature and art. In nature but also dwarfed by nature, relatively inconspicuous, he appears to be conscious of his dual role
as dweller in and creator of nature.[3]

The mountain in the center of the canvas, on whose forested
slopes are carved the Hebrew letters for *Shaddai*, or "the
Almighty," adds further to the interpretive possibilities. Is Cole
coyly suggesting the existence of a new covenant between God
and America, "nature's nation"? Overall, is the artist alluding to
the process of "manifest destiny," since the painting follows the
classic pattern of domesticating the wilderness as America pro-
ceeds westward?[4]

The painting's ambiguity is enhanced if one also considers
that the river itself forms a question mark, suggesting that this
rendering of a page from the "book of nature" is open to endless
interpretation.

It may seem odd to open a study of nature writing with an
analysis of a painting. But this methodology is appropriate, I
think, for a number of reasons. Cole himself was a nature writer
of sorts, recording his thoughts and impressions in writing while
out in the field. He was also an influential spokesperson for the
concept of wilderness in American culture, as I will demonstrate

subsequently in a reading of his famous "Essay on American Scenery." Furthermore, *The Oxbow* was exhibited at a critical time in the history of landscape aesthetics: that same year, Ralph Waldo Emerson's *Nature* was published, a work now seen as the cornerstone of the transcendental movement in America and widely recognized as a major influence in the development of modern nature writing. Also at this time, landscape tourism was becoming firmly established as a middle-class economic activity, thanks to the completion of the Erie Canal in 1820 and the emergence of tourist sites in the northeast—the Catskills Mountain House, the White Mountains of New Hampshire, Niagara Falls. There was a significant overlap in the audiences for the paintings of the Hudson River school and the writings of Emerson, Henry David Thoreau, Henry Wadsworth Longfellow, James Fenimore Cooper, and others.[5]

Most important, I open with an examination of Cole's painting because it is a visual representation of the pastoral, a tradition integral to the development of nature writing. The pastoral as a literary type harks back to ancient Greece and the poetry of Theocritus and Virgil, featuring herdsmen (typically shepherds) in a bucolic setting caring for their animals and singing of the benefits of rural over urban life. It evolved over the centuries into a complex form, especially during the 1800s, when romantic writers confronted the forces of modern industrialization. One of the foremost scholars of modern pastoralism is Leo Marx, who defines it as "the desire, in the face of the growing complexity and power of organized society, to disengage from the dominant culture and to seek the basis for a simpler, more harmonious way of life 'closer' (as we say) to 'nature.'" At the heart of the pastoral, no matter what its historical context, is a preference for the apparently "simple" world of "nature" (traditionally understood as the nonhuman realm) over the complicated life of "civilization." Writers (and artists) of this tradition have typically represented or constructed nature as a retreat or sanctuary, as Arcadian garden or wilderness refuge.[6]

As *The Oxbow* illustrates, pastoralism also entails a process of containment which, according to another important critic, Herbert Lindenberger, "defines itself through the forces with which it sets up tensions." Once the protagonist has completed the move from civilization to nature, pastoralist writing "takes the form of an isolated moment, a kind of island in time, and one which gains its meaning and intensity through the tensions it creates with the historical world." In Cole's painting, for example, the artist—from his idyllic mountainside retreat in the liminal space bordering the dark, wild terrain and the sunlit, cultivated landscape—can witness (in an allegorical reading) a collision of the forces of wilderness and civilization, symbolic of the transformation of nature that was occurring on a wide scale in 19th-century America. The presence of both wilderness and farmland in *The Oxbow* pertains to another important point made by Lindenberger. He distinguishes between two different kinds of pastoral: "the 'soft' pastoral of cultivated landscapes and social communion and the 'hard' pastoral of wind-swept slopes and total solitude." Though his focus is on Shakespearean and European romantic examples of pastoral, Lindenberger's discussion has been applied to the American tradition as well.[7]

In fact, I would argue that American pastoralism presents the fullest, most compelling version of the tradition, both in the number and kinds of forces it contains and in the diversity of "soft" and "hard" pastoral versions it has represented. Diagram 1 shows some of the more important tensions or polarities to be found in the works of nature writing that I will discuss individually.

Pastoralism has flourished as a genre and a cultural activity because it contains and, through a dialectic, attempts to resolve

---

Diagram 1: Polar forces in American pastoralism.

Wilderness	Civilization
Nature	Culture
Wildness	Domestication
Re-creation	Recreation
Unconsciousness	Self-consciousness
Biocentrism	Anthropocentrism
Native American cultures	Euramerican culture
Traditional environmentalism	Radical environmentalism
Antimodernism	Progress

---

key tensions manifest in the culture at large. One of these tensions is the conflict between civilization and wilderness, the result of society's traditional definition and encouragement of "progress" at the expense of the nonhuman world. At heart pastoral writers are antimodernists who employ the pastoral to tell of their "escape to"—a less pejorative way to put it might be "quest for"—a particular place in order to celebrate a return to a simpler, more harmonious way of life "closer to nature"; and to present to their audience, from the vantage point of the predominantly nonhuman world, the pleasures and privileges of living a kind of border life.

PASTORALISM AND NATURE WRITING

What is the relationship between pastoralism and nature writing? As I will detail shortly, modern nature writing—the primary focus of this study—emerged in response to the industrial revolution of the late 18th century and has become without question the most popular form of pastoralism. The typical form of nature writing is a first-person, nonfiction account of an exploration, both physical (outward) and mental (inward), of a predominantly nonhuman environment, as the protagonist follows the spatial movement of pastoralism from civilization to nature. In its key emphases, nature writing is a descendant of other forms of written discourse: natural history, for its scientific bent (the attempt to explain the workings of the physical universe over time); spiritual autobiography, for its account of the growth and maturation of the self in interaction with the forces of the world; and travel writing (including the literature of exploration and discovery), for its tracing of a physical movement from place to place and recording of observations of both new and familiar phenomena.[8]

THE GEOGRAPHY OF NATURE WRITING

How to describe the place to which nature writers escape is a problem fraught with ethnocentric implications. "Wilderness" has been the traditional designation, connoting land unaffected by humans. However, given the insights provided recently by environmental historians, the standard term—or at least what it has come to signify—no longer suffices, for archaeological and historic evidence indicates that portions of the North American continent were manipulated by Paleo-Indians at least 10,000 years prior to European discovery and settlement. It is no coincidence that the popularity of wilderness grew during the 19th century even as "wild" lands and Native American populations drastically shrank; "wilderness" thus became an invention, a social construction, to suit the ideology and policies of the dominant postcolonial culture. Yet wilderness retains such resonance that a satisfactory synonym is difficult to find. In part this has to do with legal authorization (namely the Wilderness Act of 1964): the very word "wilderness" is now officially recognized. I use the term, then, to distinguish it from what we generally understand as rural, urban, and suburban space.[9]

The cultural geographer J. B. Jackson has clarified the debate over nomenclature by distinguishing between wilderness and landscape. He defines "landscape" as "synthetic space, a man-made system of spaces superimposed on the face of the land." As Diagram 2 illustrates, the inner city, with its totality of built environments and minimum of space unaffected by humans, qualifies as the ultimate form of landscape; the suburbs constitute a form of the soft pastoral with managed vegetation and modicum of green space; the farm, with its manipulation of land through cultivation but with remnant trees and plants along the agricultural margins, stands for a "middle landscape" and another form of the soft pastoral; while terrain with little or no historic evidence of human manipulation, whether it be "virgin" forest, desert, or alpine summit, constitutes wilderness. (Granted, in reality the distinctions between these domains are not so clearcut.) I follow Jackson's lead in my classification of the habitats of nature writers along this spectrum, with "wilderness" at one end

---

Diagram 2: Wilderness-landscape spectrum.

WILDERNESS			LANDSCAPE
"Wild" terrain	Farm	Suburb	Inner city
"Hard" pastoral	"Soft" pastoral		

---

and "landscape" at the other; corresponding terms are "hard" and "soft" pastoral, respectively.[10]

Of the six writers who are the focus of this study, I argue that Thoreau (at times), John Muir, Mary Austin, and Edward Abbey inhabited and visited wilder terrain, the hard pastoral; whereas Aldo Leopold and Annie Dillard chose to live in the soft pastoral, in landscape as opposed to wilderness.

It should be recognized, however, that all nature writers, regardless of where they live, whether it be the New Jersey suburbs or the old-growth forests of Oregon, are able to find and celebrate *wildness:* the existence of nonhuman elements—whether they be geological, botanical, or zoological—in spite of the forces of modernity. In this regard it is worth invoking Thoreau's oft-cited (and misquoted) declaration from "Walking": "In Wildness [not "wilderness"] is the preservation of the World."[11]

THEORETICAL APPROACHES

A few words are in order regarding my critical approach, which I characterize from the outset as eclectic. Ecocriticism is the most important perspective informing my reading of pastoralism. This critical movement arose recently in response to anxiety over the state of the environment and a growing disenchantment on the part of many scholars with contemporary literary criticism, which fails to acknowledge a "real" world outside the text. An important essay in the history of ecocriticism is William Rueckert's "Literature and Ecology: An Experiment in Ecocriticism," which issues this challenge: "How can we resolve the fundamental paradox of [the English] profession and get out of our heads? . . . how can we do something more than recycle WORDS? *Free us from figures of speech.*"[12]

There are no fixed definitions or unanimously accepted principles of ecocriticism, though the scholarly output that has emanated from this perspective has been prodigious (a point I develop in the Bibliographic Essay). Like other ecocritics, I hold that the nonhuman environment is a dominant character in the worlds both inside and outside the text; that the authors themselves subscribe to this belief; and that an important interaction occurs between nonhuman environment and author, place and text, which can result in a paradigmatic shift in the consciousness of the protagonist from an ego-centered (anthropocentric) view of the world to an eco-centered (biocentric) perspective. Ecocritics do not ignore or play down a central argument of post-structuralism: that everything—institution, building, rock—is a psychological, verbal, or social construct. Among the most eloquent of ecocritics is Belden Lane, who reaffirms this very point: "Landscape is first of all an effort of the imagination—a construed way of seeing the world. . . . Landscape is never simply something 'out there.' . . . The very choice and framing of the scene is itself a construction of the imagination." But what distinguishes ecocriticism as a theoretical perspective is its insistence on the primacy of a physical world that forms the basis of the construct: No ideas but in things. Ecocriticism rejects absolutely and considers absurd and dangerous the claim of poststructuralism that "there is no nature."[13]

In addition to these principles of ecocriticism, I maintain that fieldwork—personal investigation of the place inhabited by a particular nature writer—is helpful in understanding the dynamics that develop between author and locale. This point deserves elaboration, in that the English profession has enjoyed a long and venerable tradition of scholarship carried out, in the main, indoors. Why should English professors now engage in fieldwork, embarking on costly junkets to out-of-the-way locales? This is a question skeptical administrators pose to would-be ecocritics seeking funding for research trips to Walden Pond and camping outings for students enrolled in courses on nature writing. My responses are several. First, I think it important to experience the primacy of the nonhuman environment firsthand, as nature writers do. Second, fieldwork can serve as a check or inspection of the accuracy of a writer's descriptions of a place, taking into account the natural and cultural evolution that may have taken place over time. Third, it does ecocritics no harm and may in fact do them a great deal of good to get out of the office, study, or classroom in order to be recharged, physically and spiritually, by the nonhuman world, and to be reminded that what we call nature contains a civilization other than our own.

In fact, literary scholars have been making a case for fieldwork for a number of years. But when I first became seriously interested in the study of literature and the environment in the late

1970s, I was initially unaware of scholarship informed by outdoor research, acknowledged as such, and incorporated into traditional criticism. Michael Cohen's book on John Muir, *The
Pathless Way* (1984), was the first secondary study I discovered to
include accounts of a critic's own explorations of a nature
writer's locale. One passage in particular moved me profoundly:

> A great danger awaits the student of the environmental movement
> in America: he may be too good a student, too well-read. Emerson
> had to remind the American scholar that 'books are for the scholar's
> idle times. When he can read God directly, the hour is too precious to
> be wasted in other men's transcripts of their readings.' So we are in
> danger of that failing today. I, for instance, have had to put on my
> pack and spend several days in the Grand Canyon of the Tuolumne
> to remind myself of what I am talking about. Even late in the season,
> when the oaks are flaming and the aspens are dropping their yellow
> leaves, one needs to sit by a campfire and remind oneself that the
> real research library of Yosemite lives in its canyons, rivers, lakes,
> meadows, forests, and mountains.

More recently, Jonathan Bate has cited the importance of hiking
through landscape familiar to Wordsworth and Ruskin as a vital
source of insight in his own "green study" of the English
Romantic poets, and he quotes Keats to this effect: "Keats said
that we may read fine things but we never feel them to the full
until we have gone the same steps as the author." Thoreau himself endorses the belief in the supremacy of world over word
when he writes in *Walden* that "instead of calling on some
scholar, I paid many a visit to particular trees. . . ."[14]

In sum, I would say that ecocriticism is a way of reading both
texts and the land itself, of trying to comprehend both the word
and the world that inspired it, on their own terms. So to know
better the worlds inhabited and created by nature writers I
include my own "foot notes" when analyzing major works of
Thoreau, Muir, Austin, Leopold, Abbey, and Dillard. For centuries we have employed the metaphor of the "book of nature"—
nature as text. Why not the text as nature?

On occasion I refer to landscape art as part of my methodology. The strategy in this case is to emphasize that nature writers
have always operated out of a larger cultural-historical matrix
that is vital to consider in order to understand better the cultural
work performed by the writing. I use landscape art as well to

represent visually the tensions I identify in the writings (as in *The Oxbow*). And because we are a visually oriented species I use images of the landscapes and wilderness inhabited by nature writers as aids to help the reader envision the writers' textual and physical worlds.[15]

My critical approach also draws on the New Historicism, which emphasizes the "textuality of history and the historicity of texts" (to use the phrase most often invoked as a definition of this critical theory). By this is meant the inevitable subjectivity of any interpretation—including, of course, my own interpretation—and the inevitable influence of history on any writer, including literary and cultural critics. We see through the lenses of our own historical era that blur and distort, reflect and refract, and tell our stories acccordingly.[16]

In New Historicist fashion, I analyze my subject in terms of key historic moments or paradigmatic encounters—as the collision of two forces in opposition to each other when a nature writer arrives at an "island in time." Thoreau sits in his cabin doorway near Walden Pond at dawn, listening to the sounds of nature, only to have his revery disturbed by the whistle of a train; or he attempts to reach the summit of Mt. Katahdin but is engulfed by clouds and repulsed by hostile forces of nature. John Muir in the valley of Yosemite rejects the Calvinist view of a harsh and angry God in favor of a benevolent deity. Mary Austin, raised in the humid midwest, moves to the Mojave Desert and discovers a new kind of pastoral terrain. Aldo Leopold elegizes sandhill cranes in the marshes of Wisconsin, their habitat nearly eliminated by government conservation agencies. Edward Abbey confronts hordes of motorized tourists on Labor Day as a ranger in a national park. Annie Dillard watches in fascinated horror as a frog is sucked dry by a giant water bug. It is at moments such as these, whether they occur in "soft" or "hard" pastoral environments, that polar forces collide and nature writers attempt to reconcile them in epiphanic prose.

THE EVOLUTION OF NATURE WRITING

Nature writing appeared as a particularly forceful form of pastoralism in the 19th century in response to the industrial revolution. Before focusing on this important manifestation of pastoralism, however, it would be instructive to map the major precursors or tributaries of nature writing in order to better understand the genre's evolution and the development of essential elements and significant streams of influence. Diagram 3 indicates these major branches; I shall take up each one in turn as they occur, combine, separate, overlap, and (in some cases) recombine over time. I should also state at the outset of this history that my focus will be mainly on Euramerican traditions, as I see the influence exerted almost exclusively in a westerly direction.[17]

Diagram 3: Major tributaries of nature writing.

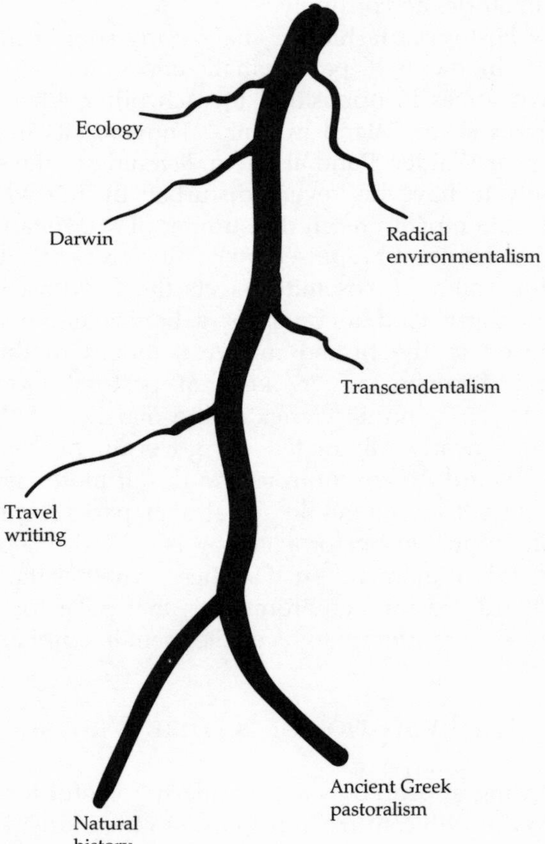

NATURAL HISTORY: ANCIENT FORMS

Although nature writing harks back to the ancient literary tradition of the pastoral, its roots are traceable to an even older form of discourse: natural history, the systematic observation and recording of natural phenomena. Aristotle (384–322 B.C.E.) stands as the first natural historian, according to William Beebe in *The Book of Naturalists*. Beebe points out that the realism and comprehensiveness of Aristotle's observations mark him as the "greatest naturalist of all time." Whether remarking on the hunting techniques of the octopus, the predatory nesting habits of the cuckoo, or the sleeping patterns of mammals, Aristotle practiced natural history with care and circumspection. Although he made errors in his observations and conclusions, he was the first to attempt a grand classification system for nature, beginning with a fundamental division of the animal kingdom into two categories, those with and those without blood. He also contributed to natural history by advancing teleological arguments, holding that all species are directed toward an end or purpose. This view anticipated the emergence of natural theology in later years.[18]

An important successor to Aristotle, Pliny the Elder (A.C.E. 23–79), represented both the best and the worst aspects of natural history. In preserving and synthesizing hundreds of remnants of natural history writing by his predecessors while compiling his *Natural History* (published in 77 A.C.E.), and in dealing with more than 20,000 subjects, Pliny established a reputation for indefatigable work in the tradition. But his own natural history is marred by his willingness to rely on hearsay rather than direct observation. For example, in conjecturing that the pearl of an oyster is formed when the mollusk drinks dew, he reveals his faulty methodology. Natural history, like pastoralism, contains its own set of tensions, in this case negotiating the difficult course between maintaining high standards of accurate observation and striving for literary effect. Yet Pliny's work was considered authoritative for more than 1,000 years and in 1469 became the first "scientific" study ever printed.[19]

ANCIENT GREEK PASTORALISM

Pastoralism, as Raymond Williams illustrates in *The Country and the City*, dawned with the writing of such classic Greek poets as

Theocritus (3d century B.C.E.) and Virgil (70–19 B.C.E.), who celebrated what they saw as the benefits of bucolic life. In the *Eclogues* Virgil pointed to the advantages of rural existence in Italy:

Ah fortunate old man, here among hallowed springs
And familiar streams you'll enjoy the longed-for shade, the cool shade.
Here, as of old, where your neighbor's land marches with yours,
The sally hedge, with bees of Hybla sipping its blossom,
Shall often hum you gently to sleep. On the other side
Vine-dressers will sing to the breezes at the crag's foot;
And all the time your favourites, the husky-voiced wood pigeons
Shall coo away, and turtle-doves make moan in the elm tops. . . .

Several salient points should be made in analyzing this venerable form of pastoralism as a precursor to modern nature writing. Pastoral poetry called attention to the shepherd, a simple rustic type, as its hero. Pastoralism was an urban phenomenon, composed by poets in the city; only when urban space threatened the rural landscape did the pastoral tradition grow in reputation. The rural scene was deemed morally and physically healthier than the city, and so virtue became associated with nature. Arcadia, the Greek version of paradise, epitomized bucolic contentment and simplicity.[20]

NATURAL HISTORY AND TRAVEL WRITING

Natural history lapsed into a true dark age for many centuries following the pioneering efforts of Aristotle and Pliny the Elder. John Ray at the end of the 17th century finally raised the status of natural history with *The Wisdom of God Manifested in the Works of the Creation* (1691). But Ray was more a synthesizer than an innovator; his main purpose, as the title of his work suggests, was to employ natural history in the service of natural theology in order to prove God's existence through revealing the intricate patterns of nature: the "argument from design."[21]

Not until the 18th century, with the development by Carl Linnaeus of a simple binomial system to classify natural phenomena, did the discipline make a methodological breakthrough to emerge from the chaos of classification in which it had been mired for over a thousand years. Coinciding with the discovery by Europeans of the new world, which greatly increased the body of knowledge about nature to be categorized and studied, natural history as practiced by Linnaeus and his successors became increasingly important in European culture. During the struggle over the empire of the Americas from 1500 to 1800, the imperialistic agendas of the crowns of England, France, and Spain became a significant part of the cultural work performed by natural history. It became important to know and catalog the botanical, zoological, and mineral resources of North and South America. Thus travel writing, especially in the form of exploration and discovery literature, merged with natural history to become an important subgenre in its own right. Christopher Columbus, as the first European to record his impressions of the new world, was in the vanguard of American natural history, though like many other early European explorers he mistakenly associated American species with European ones if they even remotely resembled any he was familiar with in the old world.[22]

A better-informed and more objective observer was William Wood, an Englishman who spent the years 1629–1633 in Massachusetts. His writings provide a representative case study of natural history carried out mainly for utilitarian reasons. *Prospect* (1634) is an attempt to catalog the land, rivers, flora, and fauna of New England, always with an eye to their commodity values. Consider this passage from Wood's work on the beaver: "Their wisdom secures them from the English who seldom or never kills any of them, being not patient to lay a long siege or to be so often deceived by their cunning evasions, so that all the beaver which the English have comes first from the Indians whose time and experience fits them for that employment." The utilitarian aspects of natural history were never more important than during the age of exploration. This emphasis on utility would have repercussions for the debate over the nature of natural history and the rise of conservation in the late 19th century.[23]

LOCAL NATURAL HISTORY

Gilbert White, an English prelate, was unquestionably the most famous and important natural history writer in England prior to Darwin. White's *The Natural History and Antiquities of Selbourne, in the County of Southampton* was published in 1788. (Most editions have subsequently omitted the "Antiquities" section, as it is mainly a religious history of local clerics.) Like important natural historians before him, White stressed the theological purposes of the discipline. He also placed a renewed emphasis on the importance of fieldwork, criticizing many of his contemporaries for inaccurate armchair speculations about the behavior of animals. Overall, White made two crucial contributions to the genre. First, he devoted himself to the study of natural history in and around a particular place, namely the parish of Selbourne in southern England. For 23 years he faithfully kept a natural "Kalendar" or phenology based on his observations of the seasonality of natural phenomena in the vicinity of his parish, believing that "every kingdom, every province, should have its own monographer." Second, he transformed his fieldwork observations and notes into concise, precise, and well-turned writing—which is to say, he was a creator of literature. Virtually all commentators on White are sure to remark on the literary qualities of *Selbourne*.[24]

The work was written in epistolary form, from 1767 to 1787. The first 44 letters are to the English naturalist Thomas Pennant, the last 66 to Daines Barrington, an English explorer. From the outset White emphasizes the "parochial" qualities of his observations, urging the reader to see them as a merit rather than a defect, because "it is . . . in zoology as it is in botany: all nature is so full, that that district produces the greatest variety which is the most examined" (55). He also argues for and anticipates specialization in natural history in order to reduce errors in observation: "for, as no man can alone investigate all the works of nature, these partial writers may, each in their department, be more accurate in their discoveries, and freer from errors, than more general writers; and so by degrees may pave the way to an universal correct natural history" (80).

White looked backward as well as forward as part of the natural history tradition. Like John Ray, he practiced natural history primarily to prove the existence of God. One of his monographs, on the fallow deer, illustrates this point. This mammal, White observes, possesses the ability to plunge its head deep into water for a long time in order to drink, breathing through a vent at the inner corner of each eye while its nostrils are submerged. Thus the fallow deer, according to White, exemplifies "a new instance of the wisdom of God in the creation" (42–43, 57). He also exhibits

16

his rationalist tendencies by repeatedly claiming to find evidence of order in nature and championing the Linnaean system of taxonomy because "without system the field of nature would be a pathless wilderness" (208). His pejorative use of the "pathless wilderness" metaphor reveals that, unlike many nature writers to come in the next century, White preferred that his pastoral retreat remain "soft" rather than "hard," landscape as opposed to wilderness.

The rationalist, Baconian trademark—seeking empirical proof—characterizes White's methodology. This leads him to rebut some of the observations of his predecessors and contemporaries. One of the tensions contained and resolved in *Selbourne* has to do with the conflict between "old" and "new" schools of natural historians: those who are content to pronounce "truths" of natural history without doing thorough fieldwork versus those whose investigations are exhaustive. He takes John Ray to task for holding that there are no species of web-footed rats; White makes a discovery to the contrary in his Selbourne district. He also disputes a claim by an Italian naturalist, Giovanni Scopoli, that house martins do not feed their young on the wing, an assertion he knows is false on the basis of repeated observations of his own. Yet White himself is guilty of errors; probably the most obvious is his insistence that birds hibernate rather than migrate during the winter. Though he meets with evidence to the contrary, he cannot relinquish this particular piece of conventional wisdom of his time.

White anticipates an important element of nature writing when he laments the disappearance of red deer from his district: "another beautiful link in the chain of beings is wanting" (22). By invoking the "chain of Being," a theological concept of the 17th and 18th centuries that placed humans near the top of a physical and moral hierarchy, White is perhaps implying that we as a species are obligated to manage nature like husbandmen. He thus confirms his anthropocentrism while at the same time demonstrating his nascent conservationist sentiments. It is for this reason that the environmental historian Donald Worster sees White as a key figure in the strain of ecological writing he calls "Arcadian."[25]

The most severe limitation of *The Natural History of Selbourne* is that, ironically, little history, especially human history, figures in the work. Humans play virtually no role in White's vision of nature. He mentions Gypsies mainly to describe their superstitious and inaccurate nature reporting. Overall, his neglect of the human species is more than a little curious, for White wrote when the industrial revolution was beginning to accelerate in London, not 50 miles away. Yet, though he occasionally complains of his rural isolation, he also turns it to his advantage, effectively secluding himself from larger political developments that might disturb the quietude of his pastoral enclave. In a 1793 letter to a fellow naturalist who lived in London, he points out that "the reason you having [sic] so many bad neighbors is your nearness to a great, factious manufacturing town. Our common people are more simple-minded and know nothing of Jacobin clubs." That White ignores the industrial revolution and the political radicalism embroiling Europe at the time marks him as a classic pastoralist writer who seeks to preserve his version of an arcadian garden. Even if one grants that White had no reason to address urban concerns, it remains true that the agricultural upheaval of the day—resulting from the Acts of Enclosure passed by Parliament to transform farmland into grazing districts, which created a large group of landless laborers—did affect the rural landscape of districts such as Selbourne. About this White has nothing to say in *Selbourne*. His version of natural history is just that: "natural" in the common sense of the term, meaning (largely) nonhuman.[26]

These limitations notwithstanding, the provincial charm of *Selbourne* helped make it "the fourth most published book in the English language." American readers turned to it during the hectic 19th century, when White's vision of a rational, orderly, benevolent nature offered solace and comfort. Subsequently, the industrial revolution, the Darwinian revolution, and the threat of overexploitation of natural resources would profoundly alter the kind of natural history practiced by writers like White, marking its transformation into nature writing.[27]

THE POLITICS OF NATURAL HISTORY

Natural history writing in America during the 18th century did not shy away from political engagement. In fact, some of the more important works embraced politics, especially during the Revolutionary era. Part of the agenda of writers such as Thomas Jefferson, J. Hector St. John de Crèvecoeur, and William Bartram was to forward their program of cultural nationalism and celebrate things American, as Thomas Cole did in *The Oxbow*. In *Notes on the State of Virginia* (1784–1785), which Jefferson wrote in France while serving as a diplomat there, natural history emerges in response to the French naturalist Count Buffon's charges that animal species in Europe are larger, more diverse, and greater in number than their American counterparts. Jefferson refutes Buffon's European chauvinism using empirical proof, supplying detailed lists demonstrating the superiority in size and diversity of American quadrupeds. And as president, Jefferson linked natural history and manifest destiny in the 19th century by commissioning the expedition of Meriwether Lewis and William Clark into the Louisiana Territory.[28]

Crèvecoeur similarly puts natural history at the service of nationalism in *Letters from an American Farmer* (1782). His claim that America is the "most perfect society now existing in the world" rests largely on the argument that the transformation of wilderness into productive farmland would result, in the long run, in moral, virtuous, hardworking English colonists. However, in the last of the letters the allegorical Farmer James is expelled from his arcadian garden because of the American Revolution (Indians who sympathize with the British raid the settlement). Crèvecoeur thus initially endorses but ultimately rejects the fundamental premise of pastoralism: that it is possible to escape from society and enjoy a bucolic existence.[29]

To classify *Letters* as natural history is problematic, however, for propaganda, not science, is Crèvecoeur's main concern. He helps perpetuate a number of what might be called natural history fables—such as the piece of folklore in which a Dutch farmer and his son are "bitten" by a rattlesnake when they don boots in which the reptile broke off its fangs. As "science," then, the work's credibility obviously suffers. This certainly is not true of William Bartram's *Travels* (1791), detailing a journey during the Revolutionary War from the Carolinas to the mouth of the Mississippi River. In remarking on the varied biogeography of the region, in recording more than 200 species of birds, in observing the land-use practices of American Indians, Bartram created a document that still stands as the premier work of natural history in America up to 1800. *Travels* manages to be both a political and an apolitical document, promoting America through a celebration of its ecological diversity, yet ignoring the most important political issue of the day: the colonists' war with England for independence. That Bartram embarked on his expedition during the Revolution yet made virtually no mention of the conflict clearly qualifies his work as pastoral.[30]

ROMANTIC NATURAL HISTORY

Bartram's *Travels* also represents the first sustained appreciation of wilderness in America, marking the transition from rationalism to romanticism in American culture. Unlike Gilbert White, who avoided the "pathless wilderness," Bartram sought it out. The geography of the pastoral thus shifted from garden to wilderness. The meaning of the term "wilderness," once considered "the place of wild beasts," "a tract of solitude and savageness," became more complex and multivalent, taking on arcadian overtones. It was around this time, as historians such as Raymond Williams, Paul Shepard, and Roderick Nash have demonstrated, that a paradigmatic shift in attitude among intellectuals and artists toward nature became noticeable. This was partially in response to the industrial revolution, which began in England in the late 1700s and materialized in America by the 1820s. As the factory system proliferated and cities grew in size, as more laborers were drawn from rural areas, a nostalgic pastoral longing for nature became common. For the first time in world history, significant numbers of writers and painters began to express concern over the rate at which wilderness was being consumed by western civilization. (That this "wilderness" had been inhabited by indigenous cultures for thousands of years was of course largely ignored.) Writers from Wordsworth to Thoreau made pleas for nature's preservation, and the tension between civilization and wilderness began to come to a head.[31]

The romantic preference for the primitive, then, was one important influence on the way in which natural history began to change around the beginning of the 19th century. Another romantic influence on the genre was the increasing tendency to celebrate the self: natural history writing became more autobiographical. (The first documented use of the word *autobiography* occurred in 1797.) Whereas Gilbert White shied away from using the first person, John James Audubon put himself in the foreground. In writing of his natural history travels in the south, for example, Audubon devotes significant attention to his rivalry with another important ornithologist of the time, Alexander Wilson, who, he complains, failed to give him adequate credit for sketches he donated to his rival. This preference for the personal did not come at the expense of scientific accuracy, however; Audubon became famous mainly because his art appeared to be more realistic than that of his predecessors. He also enhanced the readability of the genre by including human foibles.[32]

THE DARWINIAN REVOLUTION

Perhaps more than any other single figure, Charles Darwin transformed perspectives about nature with his theory of natural selection. The foundation of the theory was laid during Darwin's circumnavigation of the globe aboard the *Beagle* from 1831 to 1836. In *The Voyage of the Beagle* (published in 1839) Darwin effectively melded travel literature and natural history. He also helped restore history to natural history by underscoring the importance of evolutionary—that is, temporal—changes in nature. He notes, for instance, how animals have adapted over the years to changing environmental conditions through the development of different physiological characteristics. The most famous example of this phenomenon is the different-sized beaks of finches he observed on the Galápagos Islands, a result (he theorized) of genetic responses to radically varied environments within close proximity. By studying the evolution of species within a particular environment, Darwin became a key figure in the emergence of ecology, the study of interrelationships among organisms in a given locale. *On the Origin of Species* appeared in 1859, publicly announcing the theory of natural selection. In 1866 the word *ecology* was first coined by the German zoologist Ernst Haeckel, and in defining the term Haeckel made specific reference to Darwin as one who contributed significantly to the understanding of the interactions of complex organisms.[33]

Darwin was among the last of the great amateur natural historians to practice in the field. In America the tradition became professionalized with the opening of the Smithsonian Institution in the 1840s, and more specialized as science itself was divided into various disciplines. Taxonomy was replaced by laboratory anatomy as the epic efforts of naturalists to catalog natural phenomena concluded with the final phase of the discovery and exploration of the world's land masses. Increasingly, naturalists were employed by federal or state governments. Universities began to form specialized schools to train natural historians in particular disciplines such as botany, geology, and zoology. Yale University created the first School of Science in the country, Sheffield, in 1859. The result: a generalist such as Bartram was replaced by specialists like the botanist Asa Gray, the geologist Clarence King, and the (proto-) anthropologist Lewis Henry Morgan.[34]

TRANSCENDENTALISM

Out of this welter of cultural developments emerged Ralph Waldo Emerson and Henry David Thoreau, the progenitors of modern nature writing and the authors most responsible for the transformation of natural history into nature writing. Emerson was a transcendentalist, an American version of the Romantic, who imported and recast key ideas from German idealism and the English romantic poets Wordsworth and Coleridge. *Nature*, written and privately published by Emerson in 1836, became the key text of the transcendental movement, and Thoreau, an early disciple of Emerson, read it during his college years at Harvard. Among its many influential claims is Emerson's belief in the possibility of transcending our physical senses through a heightened awareness of the world beyond the scope of the senses. Perhaps the work's most famous image is of the speaker "Standing on the bare ground,—my head bathed by the blithe air, and uplifted into infinite space,—all mean egotism vanishes. I become a transparent eye-ball. I am nothing. I see all. The currents of the Universal Being circulate through me; I am part or particle of God." But even as Emerson emphasizes the possibility of attaining oneness with the nonhuman other, which he calls the "Oversoul"—thus moving from egocentrism toward ecocentrism—he insists on the anthropocentricity of all that humans observe: "Nature always wears the colors of the spirit." For, according to Emerson, "Particular natural facts are symbolic of particular spiritual facts." This belief in a correspondence between facts and spiritual truths, perceiver and nature, lies at the heart of the difference between natural history and nature writing. Although the genre had not yet fully shed its anthropocentrism, it nonetheless was moving further toward biocentrism, a philosophy and way of living realized more fully by nature writers of the 20th century. Emerson inherited this human-centered conviction from the Puritans, who looked to the natural world for signs or emblems of religious salvation—a religious quest ultimately traceable to Augustine, whose *Confessions* was the first spiritual autobiography. The literature of transcendentalism represented a confluence of autobiography and natural history, combining to form a new genre, nature writing.[35]

Another way Emerson effected the transformation of natural history into nature writing was through his criticism of natural historians for their narrow focus on taxonomy and specialization. In the final chapter of *Nature,* Emerson writes:

> It is not so pertinent to man to know all the individuals of the animal kingdom, as it is to know whence and whereto is this tyrannizing unity in his constitution, which evermore separates and classifies things, endeavouring to reduce the most diverse to one form. When I behold a rich landscape, it is less to my purpose to recite correctly the order and superposition of the strata, than to know why all thought of multitude is lost in a tranquil sense of unity. I cannot greatly honor minuteness in details, so long as there is no hint to explain the relation between things and thoughts.

By stressing the need for nature reporting that is holistic and multifaceted (what we would today call "ecological"), Emerson anticipated and inspired the more complex, intense, and far-reaching kinds of nature observation that emerge in the writings of his chief disciple, Thoreau.[36]

Thoreau resembled Gilbert White (whose *Selborne* he admired) in his lococentrism, his attachment to the home place. But he alternated between the two poles of residence and travel by writing works that qualify as both inhabitation literature in the tradition of *Selborne*—most obviously *Walden* but also much of his fourteen-volume Journal—and travel writing (based on a popular form of writing in the 19th century, the excursion essay): *The*

Maine Woods and *Cape Cod*. He also differs from White in his attention to environmental history, the way landscape is shaped and changed by different cultures. That is, Thoreau underscores the role of humans as agents of change in the dynamics between nature and culture, while White seems to ignore it. The project of natural history takes on a significantly broader scope; as Thoreau once put it in his Journal, "Properly speaking, there can be no history but natural history."[37]

His accentuation of the ways in which humans affect the biotic environment led to another critical element in nature writing: the polemic. Thoreau engages in cultural criticism because he wrote when the industrial revolution was peaking in New England, and when the term "manifest destiny" was coined and the United States was expanding westward at a furious pace. The tension between civilization and wilderness grew more acute, and Thoreau is seen as a godhead in the environmental movement today precisely because he was one of the earliest nature writers to criticize the profligate exploitation of natural resources and to call on the government to preserve nature and on landowners to engage in more ethical (as opposed to economic) land-use practices. His pleas for preservation also include American Indians, to whom he devoted many years of study and whom he saw as victims of America's modernization and expansion. For Thoreau the attenuation of the pastoral realm was alarming, and nature writing is transformed by the possibility that a wilderness retreat might no longer exist.[38]

THE ROLE OF LANDSCAPE ART

Landscape painters played an important role in raising the public's consciousness of the diminishing wilderness. Thomas Cole, Asher Durand, Frederic Church, Jasper Cropsey, and other artists painted in what later came to be known as the Hudson River school, focusing on sublime scenes mainly in the East and helping to popularize an American grand tour of sites along the Hudson River and in New England. One painting stands for the popularization of a wilderness aesthetic particularly well. In *Twilight in the Wilderness* (Figure 2), Frederic Church portrays a scene totally free of human influence; even the stump in the foreground, which in the 19th century had become an icon of

Figure 2: *Twilight in the Wilderness*. Oil on canvas, 1860, 101.6 by 162.6 centimeters. Frederic Edwin Church, American, 1826–1900.
© *The Cleveland Museum of Art, 1995, Mr. and Mrs. William H. Marlatt Fund, 65.233*.

progress and manifest destiny, is natural. Cole, in his "Essay on American Scenery," argues that nature appreciation is a cultural universal and urges his countrymen to engage in wilderness worship. In crafting a nationalist mythology he points out that in Europe the natural environment had been conquered for hundreds of years, while America possessed a unique attribute that writers and artists should exploit: "The most distinctive, and perhaps the most impressive, characteristic of American scenery is its wildness." Yet Cole concludes his essay with the lament, and warning, that "the beauty of such landscapes [is] quickly passing away—the ravages of the axe are daily increasing—the most noble scenes are made desolate, and oftentimes with a wantonness and barbarism scarcely credible in a civilized nation." Like the Greek pastoral poets, like White, like Crèvecoeur, the Hudson River painters constructed their own version of the pastoral; like Thoreau and other romantics, Cole favored the "raw elemental wilderness."[39]

As America extended westward, the Hudson River school experienced an expansionist phase, with artists such as Albert

Figure 3: *The Rocky Mountains, Lander's Peak,* by Albert Bierstadt (1830–1902).
Courtesy of the Metropolitan Museum of Art, Rogers Fund, 1907. (07.123).

Bierstadt and Thomas Moran applying similar formulas and aesthetic criteria to the mountains of Colorado and California. In *The Rocky Mountains, Lander's Peak* (1863; Figure 3), Bierstadt creates a representation of the romantic sublime, with heavenly, ethereal light shining on the lofty summits, suggesting God's presence in the wild. Following the gold rush, San Francisco emerged as the most important city in the west, and soon Yosemite Valley became the locus of visual and verbal art. Photographers actually preceded other artists; C. L. Weed and Carleton Watkins were among the earliest to document the sublimity of Yosemite's granite walls. Watkins, in *North and Half Domes from Sentinel Dome* (1863; Figure 4) calls attention to the raw elemental wilderness of the High Sierra with the foreground diagonal of monolithic rock and the dome-dominated horizon. As in Church's painting, there is no sign of human presence: wilderness is valued over landscape as a pastoral retreat. The imagery of such artists helped popularize Yosemite Valley and make it the first site in America to be preserved for aesthetic reasons; in 1864 the federal government, which owned the region as part of the public domain, ceded 100 acres to the state of California with the provision that it be preserved for scenic

Figure 4: *North and Half Domes from Sentinel Dome.* Photograph by Carleton Watkins, *Photographs of the American West.*
  Courtesy of the Boston Public Library, Print Department.

appreciation "for all time." In effect, the idea of the national park, initially called for by the artist and ethnographer George Catlin in the 1830s on the Great Plains, was realized. Yellowstone became the world's first official national park in 1872.[40]

THE ROMANTIC EXPLORERS

In response to the official closing of the frontier in 1890 and the widespread abuse of natural resources and overexploitation of public lands, nature writing became more overtly political as writers sought to resolve the growing conflict between wilderness and civilization. A work of international scope calling attention to environmental degradation by humans is George Perkins Marsh's *Man and Nature* (1864). In the same period a series of explorers (many of them government-sponsored) led scientific and resource reconnaissance expeditions into the American west and wrote popular accounts of their journeys. Two noteworthy works of exploration, travel, and nature writing are *The Explor-*

ation of the Colorado River and Its Canyons (1869) by John Wesley Powell and *Mountaineering in the Sierra Nevada* (1872) by Clarence King. The popularity of these works testified to the public's continued desire for the pastoral in an era of diminishing wilderness.[41]

Another romantic explorer of the late 19th century, and the most influential nature writer of the period, was John Muir, who combined scientific interests, natural theology, and political activism to bridge the genres of natural history and nature writing. Muir was born in Scotland in 1838 and spent his boyhood in Wisconsin before embarking on a long trek from Indiana to Florida. During this epic journey, as he reports in *A Thousand-Mile Walk to the Gulf* (1916), Muir arrived at a life-transforming revelation: the world was not made for humans alone. In the swamps of the south he observed creatures that had no obvious utilitarian value yet seemed to have a place in the larger scheme of things. Muir then traveled to California to see Yosemite Valley, spending his first summer there as a sheepherder in 1869. A largely self-educated geologist and botanist, he devoted much of the rest of his life to a tireless campaign for the creation of national parks throughout the west, including in Alaska. Raised by a Bible-thumping fundamentalist father, Muir transferred his religious devotion to nature and became the leading secular prophet in a new spiritual movement that flourished at the turn of the century. Although he admired Emerson and Thoreau (leading the former on a tour of Yosemite in 1871), he moved beyond their lingering anthropocentrism in arguing "What the earth does is right."[42]

BACK TO NATURE

One historian has called 1880–1920 the age of the "back to nature" cult. Nature study was formally incorporated into many educational curricula; the term "nature writing" appeared with considerable frequency in popular magazines; and the writings of Muir, George Bird Grinnell, Florence Hyde Bailey, Mary Austin, and John Burroughs, among others, were widely circulated. An "Indianist" movement (in which Austin played a significant role) gained momentum, urging Anglo-Americans to learn from and preserve the culture of Native Americans rather than assimilate them into extinction. The Audubon Society was formed in response to the mass killing of shorebirds, whose feathers were used to decorate ladies' hats. A national controversy involving President Theodore Roosevelt ensued over the issue of "nature faking." Some nature writers, Ernest Thompson Seton among them, were accused of falsifying nature reports, excessively anthropormorphizing the behavior of animals to enhance the drama of their stories. Burroughs and Roosevelt argued that this threatened the very foundation of nature writing—accurate scientific reporting.[43]

In an age when nature writing was becoming increasingly politicized, it is ironic that John Burroughs, who claimed to be the most apolitical of artists, was the most popular nature writer. Yet Burroughs's popularity is explainable exactly because he embodied the modern urbanite's desire to flee the complexities and frenzies of fin de siècle society. Much of his writing is based on rambles from his literary retreat at Slabsides, in the Catskill Mountains of New York. He was a prolific author, producing more than 20 volumes of nature writing by the time he died in 1921. As a critic and a practitioner of the genre, he distinguished himself from Thoreau, whom he characterized as an ethical writer; Burroughs, in contrast, is more concerned with aesthetics. Readers were generally charmed by his self-deprecating style. He characterizes his own writing in this way: "It has been all play. I have gone a-fishing, or camping, or canoeing, and new literary material has been the result." His aim was not to preach one word. During an era of manifold social change—rampant urbanization, industrialization, internal expansion, immigrant infusion—readers were drawn to Burroughs's alluring rambles in the countryside as a way of experiencing vicariously a pastoral haven secure from change.[44]

The polemical tradition largely disappeared from nature writing until the 1960s. Despite the appearance and growth of conservation groups and outdoor clubs—in addition to the Audubon Society, the Sierra Club, the Boone and Crockett Club, and the Boy Scouts of America were established around this time—the genre from 1920 to 1960 consisted in the main of genteel, leisurely reflections on natural history, with occasional autobiographical asides. This renewed conservatism, perhaps traceable to Gilbert White, manifested itself in England in the works of such writers as Richard Jeffries (*The Life of the Fields*, 1884; and *The Open Air*, 1885) and W. H. Hudson (*Hampshire Days*, 1903; and *The Life of a Shepherd*, 1901). In America *The Outermost House* (1928) by Henry Beston, a seasonal account of life on Cape Cod, is also of this type. So is Sally Carrighar's *One Day at Beetle Rock* (1994), in which animals (Weasel, Coyote, Deer, Grouse) are the major characters on a June day in the vicinity of an outcrop of rock in the Sierra Nevada. Donald Culross Peattie was another popular writer, reaching a wide audience with works such as *An Almanac for Moderns* (1935) and *The Road of a Naturalist* (1941); again, observation, not cultural criticism, is the primary desideratum.[45]

In Canada a nature writing tradition emerged along a similarly classic pastoral pattern. The works of Ernest Thompson Seton, R. M. Patterson, Theodora Stanwell-Fletcher, and Farley Mowat all feature animals of various kinds to a significant degree; also predominant is the harsh and interminable winter of the far north. Seton and Mowat became famous writers whose popularity crossed international borders, while Patterson and Stanwell-Fletcher remain less well-known authors of relatively "undiscovered" classics of nature writing.[46]

ECOLOGICAL PRESERVATIONISM

Two historical developments occurred during 1920–1960 that did transform the genre, however. Ecology emerged as a legitimate scientific discipline, and a campaign for wilderness preservation was mounted. Fieldwork once again became a significant component of scientific study as ecologists explored wetlands, prairies, and forests, studying individual species and their roles in ecosystems. As species and habitat continued to diminish, a renewed push was made for preservation of natural areas, led by such newly formed groups as the Wilderness Society, founded in 1935. The "dust bowl" of the 1930s was dramatic evidence of how much abuse and overexploitation of land had occurred in America; conservationists began to recognize that national parks and primitive areas visited by tourists were inadequate protection from overexploitation. Since private property now constituted the majority of land ownership, landowners themselves had to be taught and encouraged to practice ethical land use over the long term.[47]

A *Sand County Almanac* (1949) by Aldo Leopold addresses these issues in a way that has led to its description as "the Bible of the conservation movement." Leopold trained as a forester at Yale and then began a career with the Forest Service in the American southwest. Early on he took note of the abusive land-use practices of ranchers who cared little about the erosion caused by overgrazing. Later in his career, as the first professor of wildlife management in the country at the University of Wisconsin, Leopold observed further land abuse in the upper midwest—and indeed wherever he went in America. In the 1930s he and his family purchased some abandoned farmland in southern Wisconsin and constructed a cabin from a chicken coop to use as a weekend retreat. Although the vacation home in the woods was becoming a popular form of the 20th-century pastoral, on a deeper level the Leopolds undertook an experiment in wilderness restoration. They planted prairie flowers and grasses and thousands of trees in an attempt to restore the native ecosystem. Part I of *Almanac* recounts these efforts and the satisfaction the family derived from the ironic process of re-creating wilderness. In writing of wildland reclamation, Leopold advanced nature writing with a philosophy he calls the "land ethic," which he defines as land-use practices that "preserve the integrity, stability, and beauty of the biotic community"; and by focusing on the landowner as opposed to the tourist.[48]

Although an anthropologist rather than an ecologist, Loren Eiseley contributed to the increasingly holistic enterprise of nature writing. Eiseley helped popularize appreciation of nature by recognizing it a cultural universal: "It is a commonplace of all religious thought, even the most primitive, that the man seeking visions and insight must go apart from his fellows and live for a time in the wilderness." Recording his observations of nature in locales as multiform as the Badlands of the Dakotas and New York City in essay collections such as *The Immense Journey* and *The Night Country*, Eiseley reminds readers of the primitive roots of the human species, and of the connections among all living things.[49]

NATURE WRITING IN THE NUCLEAR AGE

Three events since 1960 have been recognized as paradigmatic moments in the rise of modern environmentalism resulting in further transformation of the genre of nature writing. The first was the publication of *Silent Spring* by Rachel Carson in 1962. Initially appearing in *The New Yorker* and then published as a book, *Silent Spring* is a scientific monograph by a marine biologist and author of a best-selling nonfiction trilogy on the sea. Carson attacks the chemical industry for its production of pesticides and herbicides used indiscriminately, resulting in the deaths of countless animals as the chemicals work their way up the food chain. The hallmark of the book is its lucid and authoritative style; Carson knew that to make an impact she had to write for the layperson and make clear the ecological relationships affected by broadcast chemical applications. Though she was declared a "mad, hysterical woman" by her opponents in the chemical industry, Carson eventually won at least a partial victory: commercial use of DDT was banned in 1971. *Silent Spring* also initiated a new kind of nature writing, one that would proliferate in the late 1980s: the literature of environmental apocalypse.[50]

The second landmark event occurred in the late 1960s and early 1970s, when the Apollo astronauts took a series of photographs of Earth from space (Figure 5). As the ecologist Daniel Botkin observes, "Perhaps more than any other single image or any single event these photographs of the Earth have done more to change our consciousness about the character of life, the factors that sustain it, and our role in the biosphere and our power over life. Those images from space have radically altered our myths about nature." This change in the way we see our planet was officially recognized in April 1970 with the designation of the first Earth Day, the third major event in the emergence of modern environmentalism. The widespread recognition that environmental problems were ultimately global, transcending artificial national boundaries, was both sobering and energizing; international environmental organizations and government agencies formed to help solve the ecological crises of global warming, toxic waste, depletion of the ozone layer, and destruction of rain forests.[51]

The visual arts once again acted as a catalyst in promoting environmental awareness. Photographers such as Ansel Adams popularized wild places and helped transform them into American icons; often photographers joined their images with the words of nature writers. Adams became both nature photographer and writer. *El Capitan, Winter Sunrise, Yosemite Valley, 1968* (Figure 6) from *Celebrating the American Earth: A Portfolio by Ansel*

Figure 5: *The Earth from the Moon.* December 29, 1968.
  Courtesy of NASA.

Adams, recalls Bierstadt's *The Rocky Mountains* with its ethereal light, here cast on the world's largest monolith, and the ascription of benevolence to the alpine environment. The Sierra Club began to publish books of photography by Adams and other photographers in coffee-table format; one of the earliest of these was a book on Glen Canyon, a little-known area along the Colorado River in Utah. *The Place No One Knew,* with photographs by Eliot Porter and prose by David Brower, president of the Sierra Club, brought to the public's attention the government's flooding of a canyon in order to produce hydroelectric power from a dam, and celebrates the area as a little-known pastoral refuge. Both writers and visual artists, in focusing on the central tension between wilderness and civilization, continued to question the notion of "progress."[52]

RECENT DEVELOPMENTS

Nature writing has continued to evolve since the 1960s in response to cultural dynamics. Changes include radicalization;

Figure 6: *El Capitan, Winter, Sunrise, Yosemite National Park, California, 1968. Photograph by Ansel Adams.*
  Courtesy of the Ansel Adams Publishing Rights Trust.

expansion of its focus to include rural (agricultural), suburban, and urban environments; adoption of postmodern theories about the nature of knowledge; and renewed attention (since Thoreau and Austin) to aboriginal peoples as a model of how to interact with nature.

Edward Abbey is the main figure responsible for the radicalization of nature writing. In *Desert Solitaire* (1968), a nonfiction narrative about his experiences as a park ranger in Utah, Abbey protests the paving of roads within a national park by uprooting surveyors' stakes marking the route of a new road, and fantasizes about the destruction of Glen Canyon Dam. In his subsequent novel *The Monkey Wrench Gang* (1975) he heroizes four eco-raiders in the southwest who level billboards, incapacitate construction equipment devoted to building highways in roadless areas, and blow up portions of a strip-mining operation. These and other works by Abbey helped inspire the creation of the radical environmental group Earth First!—which has become notorious for such acts as tree-spiking to save old-growth forests in the American west and the attempted sabotage of a nuclear power plant in Arizona. In effect, Abbey and other radical environmentalists have taken biocentrism to an extreme by insisting on the parity of all species and by defending species threatened by humans. The mantle of radical nature writing has been worn more recently by Terry Tempest Williams in *Refuge* (1992). Williams, a naturalist at Great Salt Lake in Utah, is also a Mormon whose female family relatives have developed cancer from atomic testing conducted by the American military in the 1950s. Borrowing from the Thoreauvian tradition of civil disobedience, she writes of protesting the continued testing of nuclear weapons in the "empty" deserts of the Great Basin. Williams warns that pastoral refuges may ultimately disappear as a result of dangerous government activity.[53]

In nearly 30 works of fiction, nonfiction, and poetry, Wendell Berry also performs the role of an American Jeremiah; his emphasis is on the American farm and what has come to be known as "sustainable" agriculture. In nonfiction such as *The Unsettling of America* (1977) he attacks agribusiness for promoting monoculture—production of single crops at the expense of ecological diversity—and for impoverishing family farmers as well as drastically reducing their number. In fiction such as *A Place on*

Earth (rev. ed. 1983) he offers an alternative, self-sustaining vision of agriculture based in the fictional setting of Port William, Kentucky. And in the poems of *Farming: A Handbook* (1973) he captures the grace and beauty of simple chores on the farm. [54]

With the 1990 census revealing that for the first time in American history more people lived in suburbs than in cities or rural areas, it is appropriate that nature writers celebrate the pastoral retreat to what one historian has called the "crabgrass frontier." The emergence of suburb-based nature writing may also have to do with the growing phenomenon of "loving wilderness to death," as visits to official wilderness areas and parks increase exponentially; more and more people seem to prefer exploring the "undiscovered country of the nearby." Michael Pollan's *Second Nature* (1991) tells of the author's complex discoveries of the nature of nature, wilderness, and garden as he tries to re-create a wild landscape in his small backyard in Connecticut. The title of the book is polysemous: it suggests that the suburb and garden have traditionally been seen as "inferior" to wilderness, and that gardening, i.e., restoring wilderness to the landscape, can become "second nature" to those who immerse themselves deeply in the organic process. The publication of Pollan's work coincides with the increasing popularity of gardens and gardening business—one more sign that another "back to nature" cult is growing at this end of the 20th century. The renascence of love of nature in popular culture is illustrated also by the emergence of urban nature writing. One recent title suggests the oxymoronic possibilities of this subgenre: *Snowshoeing through Sewers* (1995). The author, Michael Aaron Rockland (1995), chooses to *"adventure not where no one has been but where no one wishes to go."* Whether circumnavigating Manhattan by canoe or walking across Philadelphia, Rockland's rationale for his urban explorations is that "a weed-and-trash-filled city lot or even a hillside above an interstate may be a better place than the wilderness to contemplate one's relationship to nature."[55]

Annie Dillard points nature writing in yet another new direction with her most famous work to date, *Pilgrim at Tinker Creek* (1974). Citing Heisenberg's principle of uncertainty, and prepossessed by her own self-consciousness, she questions whether she can ever really know and become one with the microcosmic world she lives in—and indeed mentally constructs—along a small creek in the Blue Ridge Mountains of Virginia. Dillard returns nature writing to its ancient roots in natural history—citing such authors as Aristotle, Pliny, and Edwin Way Teale—and reminds us, through her anguish over questions of ontology and theodicy, that natural history and natural theology were once synonymous. *Pilgrim at Tinker Creek* ultimately delivers the message that the journey taken by so many nature writers is as much a mental and spiritual journey as it is a physical pilgrimage.[56]

Pilgrimage is very much the theme of N. Scott Momaday's *The Way to Rainy Mountain* (1969). Part Kiowa, Momaday decided to journey to his grandmother's burial site in Oklahoma. The pilgrimage is reported through ancient stories of his people related in the oral tradition, historic accounts of ethnohistorians and ethnographers, and his own reflections on the stages of his vision quest. From this moving memoir comes a passage frequently cited in environmental literature, one that testifies to the power of place in the pastoral tradition:

> Once in his life a man ought to concentrate his mind upon the remembered earth, I believe. He ought to give himself up to a particular landscape in his experience, to look at it from as many angles as he can, to wonder about it, to dwell upon it. He ought to imagine that he touches it with his hands at every season and listens to the sounds that are made upon it. He ought to imagine the creatures there and all the faintest motions of the wind. He ought to recollect the glare of noon and all the colors of the dawn and dusk.[57]

Momaday's incorporation of ancient tribal creation stories makes us realize that the oral traditions of indigenous cultures across the world represent a barely tapped resource of vast proportions. Recognizing this, contemporary nature writers such as Gary Snyder (*Turtle Island,* 1974), Barry Lopez (*Arctic Dreams,* 1986), Gary Paul Nabhan (*The Desert Smells Like Rain,* 1982), and Richard Nelson (*The Island Within,* 1989) have turned to AmerIndian cultures not only as alternative models of coexistence with the nonhuman environment, but also for the indigene's reliance on stories to emphasize the sacredness of place. We would do well to remember that before the decline of "primitive" cultures and the emergence of agricultural and then industrial societies, before the alienation of the human species from its wilderness condition, there was a time when people felt no need to retreat to a pastoral haven because where they lived was where they wanted to be—they were at home in nature and felt no separation from it. The recently discovered cave art of Chauvet, France, radiocarbon-dated at more than 30,000 years old, dramatically illustrates an environmental integrity that postmodern denizens know only atavistically as blurred, distorted images deeply embedded in their subconscious.[58]

In concluding this overview, I would like to stress that nature writers seek to recoup a "oneness" with the nonhuman world that harks back in certain ways to the mind-set of primitive cultures. The project of nature writers should not be dismissed as neoprimitivism, however, for as creatures of the 19th and 20th centuries, they bring to bear their modern and postmodern sensibilities. Their task has become increasingly pressing in this age of environmental apocalypse. Combining the place-consciousness of pastoralism and the scientific curiosity of natural history, the religious quest of spiritual autobiography and the peregrinations of travel writing, the lyricism of nature enthusiasts and the polemical tone of cultural criticism, nature writing as a cultural activity is more vital than ever as we enter the 21st century. This bears keeping in mind as I engage in a closer examination of particularly important works in the tradition, identifying and analyzing key tensions in the dialectic of nature writing.

Chapter 2

Walden, Ktaadn, and Walking: Henry David Thoreau

Many visitors to Walden Pond participate in a form of pilgrimage. There is no more famous literary site in America, and Thoreau himself, according to one scholar, is "the closest approximation to a folk hero that American literary history has ever seen." Given all the fanfare surrounding Thoreau and the pond, and all the layers of testimony and homage that have accumulated over the years, the question confronting the ecocritic becomes: how to realize an unmediated, original experience with the universe of Walden Pond?[1]

This is the challenge I faced when I visited Walden for the first time a few years ago. Virtually everyone I informed of my proposed visit warned that any hope of encountering a "pristine wilderness" would meet with disappointment. I should expect the profanation of the pond—an overcrowded swimming hole and congested paths. Frankly, I was surprised by the concern many people expressed over the inevitable disappointment a Thoreauvian pilgrim must suffer when visiting Walden. Those who have read *Walden* closely know that the area was not a wilderness when Thoreau lived there from 1845 to 1847; the locale had been settled by Anglo-Americans for more than 200 years, and as Thoreau reveals in the opening paragraph, he lived but "a mile from any neighbor." I was also well aware that in the late 20th century some 5,000 people visit the pond on a typical summer day, and approximately 750,000 come annually.[2]

Still, these warnings about an overcrowded Walden made me determined to somehow avoid the crowds. This seemed even more difficult given that I was visiting the pond during the 4th of July weekend (while attending the annual Thoreau Society meeting, held in Concord). So I conceived a plan that I hoped would guarantee, if not complete solitude, then at least a modicum of serenity.

I got up before dawn, borrowed a canoe, and put in on water that to me was as sacred as the Ganges. As it turned out, there was only one other person on the water, a fisherman. I paddled around the perimeter, listened to the calls of the birds, observed a few people walking along the shore, and read from *Walden*: the chapter called "The Ponds." For several hours, then, I experienced, if not an unmediated or even original relationship with Walden, a thoroughly satisfactory and fulfilling first acquaintance. The pilgrimage continued later, when I walked around the area with Walter Harding, the dean of Thoreau scholars, and joined an early-morning group of a few other pilgrims who listened to the "living history" actor David Barto give his impersonation of Thoreau. For all the warnings I'd received about the desecration of Walden, my experience included some elements of the sacred essential to any pilgrimage: a meaningful measure of relative solitude, a feeling of awe in the presence of the sacred site, a sharper understanding of the historical and cultural significance of the place.[3]

In fact, my experience was richer for the tensions that persist in and around the Walden environs. As I said, the pond was serene in the early morning, but always in the background was the hum of traffic on State Highway 2. Birds sang from the forest surrounding Walden, but their calls were periodically drowned out by the rattling of a commuter train that runs along the southwest corner of the pond. As I paddled around, read *Walden*, lay back in the canoe, and drifted with the breeze that morning, more visitors appeared, mostly swimmers and sunbathers, hardly "pilgrims" in the strict sense of the term. Then there was the fact of the reserve itself, with its annoying regulations on maximum number of cars in the parking lot, signs warning hikers to stay on the trails to prevent erosion, and list of dos and don'ts on the beach. As in parks everywhere, national, state, and local, nature has become, through the legal process of preservation, one more artifact of civilization. Thoreau went to Walden Pond, among other reasons, to escape society; but even in his own time the human world impinged to a significant degree, and in the late 20th century it impinges all the more.

There is a long history of critics of *Walden* carping about the "tameness" of Thoreau's pastoral retreat, pointing out how domesticated and civilized a landscape Walden really was in the mid-19th century. Even John Muir, a devotee of Thoreau and Emerson, had this to say about his pilgrimage to Concord in 1893: "[Walden Pond] is only about one and a half or two miles from Concord, a mere saunter, and how people should regard Thoreau as a hermit on account of his little delightful stay here I cannot guess."[4]

But to devalue the work and the experience because Thoreau did not live in a bona fide wilderness is to miss the point. *Walden* is justly famous and seminal because it resolves a central conflict in American culture: the tension between wilderness and civilization. Like Cole in *The Oxbow,* Thoreau presents the two forces in opposition. From this central dialectic arise other tensions: the savage versus the civilized, wildness versus domestication, leisure versus work, biocentrism versus anthropocentrism. Conflicts figure prominently in Thoreau's other writings, too, and I will discuss two essays that have been widely anthologized: "Ktaadn" from *The Maine Woods* and "Walking." Overall, Thoreau contributed significantly to the development of modern pastoralism by both dramatizing and resolving key tensions in American culture at a critical time in the nation's history. A self-styled chanticleer, he sought to alert his readership to the dangers of modernization, as well as to the pleasures and privileges of a pastoral retreat.

Thoreau's continual quest for a vocation has been well documented. Having failed to hold a permanent job as a schoolteacher after graduating from Harvard, he chose to live at home with his parents and siblings in Concord for much of his life, finding periodic employment as a surveyor, a worker in his father's pencil factory, a lecturer, and a writer. The challenge of living became, he once wrote in his Journal, how to respire and aspire at the same time.[5]

In 1845 he decided to conduct an experiment with this goal in mind. He was responding to his mentor, Ralph Waldo Emerson, who in *Nature* (which Thoreau had read while at Harvard) called for finding an original relationship with the universe in order to establish a closer connection with God. Believing that "the richest vein is somewhere hereabouts," he built a cabin on land owned by Emerson just west of the shore of Walden Pond. Thoreau lived at the pond for more than two years and then used his Journal notes to write seven drafts of *Walden*. He contined to revise the manuscript after he returned to live with his parents in 1847, until the book was published in 1854.[6]

By building his own house in the woods, Thoreau engaged in a form of homesteading similar in some respects to the "log cabin in the wilderness" that had virtually become an American ritual by the 1850s. But early in *Walden* he declares that he has in mind a kind of frontier different from the frontier that confronted the typical pioneer. "It would be some advantage to live a primitive and frontier life, though in the midst of an outward civilization, if only to learn what are the gross necessaries of life and what methods have been taken to obtain them" (13). From the outset he makes clear that his homestead is not in the hinterlands; to relocate to the west is unnecessary. The frontier he wishes to penetrate is figurative, not literal, a liminal space that will allow him to escape from "profane social structures" and institutions and enter a realm where the natural and the cultural are not so much at odds. The opening chapter, "Economy," lays down his principles of home economics and explains how to minimize one's material needs: food, shelter, clothing, and fuel. It is also a critique of how civilization has distorted and exaggerated our material wants, and a manual on how to simplify or resimplify our lives. The question Thoreau seeks to answer is this: "Is it impossible to combine the hardiness of . . . savages with the intellectualness of the civilized man?" (11)[7]

Of the several paradigmatic moments of conflict I will identify and discuss in *Walden,* one of the more striking occurs in the chapter "Visitors." Thoreau befriends a Canadian woodchopper (identified in his Journal as Alek Therien). He is attracted to the woodchopper because the fellow seems to embody certain characteristics of the "simple life." With few wants and needs, Therien has largely divorced himself from the market economy that Thoreau sees as corrupting, entangling, and encumbering. There is nothing artificial about Therien—"His mirth was without alloy" (146)—and he strikes one as a totally "natural man." But as Thoreau enumerates his qualities, it becomes clear that Therien in important ways resembles the unthinking, unreflective pioneer. "The intellectual and what is called spiritual man in him were slumbering as in an infant" (147). "Yet I never, by any manoeuvring, could get him to take the spiritual view of things" (150). Much to Thoreau's regret, the woodchopper, finally, does not represent an effective synthesis of the savage and the civilized.[8]

Part of the problem with Therien is congenital: he is a simpleton, lacking subjectivity and self-consciousness, and thus cannot make effective intellectual use of his leisure time. Earlier, in the chapter called "Sounds," Thoreau presents himself as a counterexample to Therien, an exemplary instance of self-culture—a concept integral to the transcendental program of self-reform—as he sits on the doorstep of his cabin in the early morning, "rapt in a revery," and listens to the sounds of nature and the nearby village. It is an archetype of the pastoral "island experience," an isolated moment during which the protagonist succeeds in divorcing himself from human distractions and is able to experience a sense of otherness: to move from egocentrism to ecocentrism. Though Thoreau's leisure is (he projects) "sheer idleness" to his fellow townspeople, he defends his physical inactivity and defiance of the work ethic by explaining that his life improves in quality in proportion to the less work he performs, for he has more time for contemplation. He has succeeded in escaping the "restless, nervous, bustling, trivial nineteenth century" (329) not by traveling outward but by journeying inward, exploring his inner shores.[9]

What he contemplates this particular summer afternoon becomes one of the key resolutions of conflict in *Walden*. Thoreau lived a kind of border life at the pond, straddling an imaginary line between wilderness and civilization, attempting to capitalize on the advantages of both. Although he "left" civilization in part because he was alienated from the people of Concord, he knows he must be reconciled with the civilized world, or at least minimize his differences with it, because he cannot exist without it.[10]

Thus, although many students are surprised by or refuse to accept Thoreau's apparent accommodation with the railroad in "Sounds," this is what occurs. Thoreau opens this section with an account of the nonhuman activities he witnesses around his clearing: pigeons, an osprey, a mink, and "reed-birds" are all active. Last he mentions the "rattle of railroad cars." Then follows a series of similes, each one an obvious attempt to incorporate what Leo Marx has identified as a major motif in American literature: the "machine in the garden." The Dopplerian rattle of the railroad cars is like "the beat of a partridge" (114); the whistle of the locomotive sounds "like the scream of a hawk" (115); the engine and train of cars remind him of a comet with its orbit of returning curve (116); the steam cloud of the engine appears "like many a downy cloud which I have seen" (116); and the "iron horse . . . snort[s] like thunder" (116). Thoreau's strategy here may be to accept the artifacts of civilization, but on nature's terms, for these similes reverse the anthropocentrism inherent in the pathetic fallacy; the nonhuman world becomes the dominant frame of reference.[11]

Later he praises the train for its heroic workers, its punctuality, and its cosmopolitan commerce, but he also tempers his enthusiasm with a parallel series of subjunctive caveats:

> If all were as it seems, and men made the elements their servants for noble ends! If the cloud that hangs over the engine were the perspiration of heroic deeds, or as beneficent to men as that which floats over the farmer's fields, then the elements and Nature herself would cheerfully accompany men on their errands and be their escort. (116)

In the next paragraph he further qualifies his enthusiasm for the railroad with two more cautionary statements: "If the enterprise were as innocent as it is early! . . . If the enterprise were as heroic and commanding as it is protracted and unwearied!" (117).

Confusion often results over how to deal with an apparently blatant contradiction: How can Thoreau appreciate both nature and the machine? The problem is compounded when, later in *Walden*, he unequivocally condemns the "Devilish Iron Horse" for being the cause of logging in the surrounding forest (to fuel the engine's appetite). It helps, I think, to contextualize the reading. The railroad was introduced to America in the 1820s; by the 1840s it had become a fixture in the more populated portions of the eastern seaboard. Thoreau may be resigned to the fact that the railroad is here to stay: one might as well make the best of it. As Leo Marx observes, Thoreau realizes that Walden "cannot provide a refuge, in any literal sense, from the forces of change."[12]

This interpretation is reinforced by a comparison with a landscape painting by the American artist George Inness executed about a year after *Walden* was published in 1854. *Lackawanna Valley* (Figure 7) presents a rural viewer reclining with his back to us in a meadow dotted by tree stumps, watching an oncoming train in the middle distance, around which animals continue to graze peacefully; farther away are a railroad roundhouse and a village, backed by distant mountains. What is going on in the mind of the viewer? Is he angry about the machine's abrupt intrusion into his idyllic reverie, or is he mesmerized by this latest piece of technology? Perhaps he is noticing how the machine

Figure 7: *The Lackawanna Valley*, by George Inness, c. 1856, oil on canvas, .860 by 1.275. Gift of Mrs. Huttleston Rogers.
© *1995 Board of Trustees, National Gallery of Art, Washington, D. C.*

has been assimilated into the landscape, signified by the matching puffs of smoke from the railroad engine, the roundhouse, and the village factories. When one learns that Inness's painting was commissioned by a railroad company, the inference may well be that the railroad represents a benign force in the landscape. Like advertisements in the 1990s that feature Jeeps in the rugged wilderness, the painting serves as corporate propaganda—the incorporation of the machine in the garden indeed.[13]

But the artist, like the writer, has brilliantly complicated the scene with elements of ambivalence. The stumps are ugly, the train is no doubt noisy. From the point of view of a 20th-century observer, certainly, the pastoral idyll has been disrupted. As Thoreau observes near the conclusion of the railroad passage in "Sounds," "So is your pastoral life whirled past and away" (122).

In "Spring," Thoreau harmonizes the technological and the organic once again when he finds in the thawing sand and clay of the railroad cutbank "not a mere fragment of dead history . . . but living poetry like the leaves of a tree . . . not a fossil earth, but a living earth" (309). The land, rejuvenated by the warmth of spring, is reborn and renewed, and Thoreau, in a classic transcendental episode—linking natural facts and spiritual truths—is likewise renewed. The cutbank is actually an artifact, a piece of landscape created by the construction of the railroad, "a phenomenon not very common on so large a scale, though the number of freshly exposed banks of the right material must have been greatly multiplied since railroads were invented" (304). Thoreau is able, through his transcendental hermeneutics, to transform it into a compelling symbol. Civilization and wilderness are reconciled once again: "There is nothing inorganic" (308).[14]

I shall focus on three other key moments of pastoral conflict and containment in *Walden*. First, recall a portion of a passage quoted above: "If the cloud that hangs over the engine were the perspiration of heroic deeds, *or as beneficent to men as that which floats over the farmer's fields*, then the elements and Nature herself would cheerfully accompany men on their errands and be their escort" (italics mine). In opening a discussion of the conflicts present in "The Bean-Field," one might well ask why the cloud produced by the farmer's labor is "beneficent." Thoreau mythologizes the farmer to justify his practice and mode of agriculture, and to reconcile the tensions between wilderness and civilization through a "middle landscape" of farming.[15]

46

It may seem odd that Thoreau castigates local farmers in "Economy"—"The better part of the man is soon ploughed into the soil for compost" (5)—even though he himself farms. But he quickly establishes that his is a different kind of agriculture from that practiced by his neighbors around Concord. Agriculture is part of his self-culture. He is interested in cultivating more than just beans; in fact, he writes that he doesn't want to eat the beans, he wants to make beans speak! He farms "as some must work in fields if only for the sake of tropes and expression to serve a parable-maker one day" (162). It is not literal but figurative profit or harvest he seeks. Once again, the transcendental theory of correspondence—"Particular natural facts are symbols of particular spiritual truths"—is operative.[16]

The literary tropes blossom on close reading. Planting, hoeing, harvesting beans, Thoreau is attached to the earth; this allows him to get closer to nature. Implicitly, Thoreau criticizes the alienation of the worker from his labor that occurred in the factory system appearing in Massachusetts at this time. As he hoes, he uncovers Indian relics and so participates in the ongoing history of the landscape. And as he farms, he stops from time to time to observe and meditate on the phenomena of nature: "When I paused to lean on my hoe, these sounds and sights I heard and saw any where in the row, [are] a part of the inexhaustible entertainment which the country offers" (160).

Perhaps most important, his agricultural labors restore farming to the status it held during the era of the classical Roman writers Cato and Varo (whose works he admired). The opposition central to "The Bean-Field," that of ancient and modern agriculture, gets to the heart of Thoreau's antimodernism: the meaning of "progress" in the 19th century. Thoreau, with his little farm, represents the "connecting link between wild and cultivated fields" (158). In this instance, though, a curious reversal takes place, as modern farmers become the barbarians and ancient ones civilized citizens:

> Ancient poetry and mythology suggest, at least, that husbandry was once a sacred art; but it is pursued with irreverent haste and heedlessness by us, our object being to have large farms and large crops merely. . . . By avarice and selfishness, and a grovelling habit, from which none of us is free, of regarding the soil as property, or the means of acquiring property chiefly, the landscape is deformed, hus-

bandry is degraded with us, and the farmer leads the meanest of
lives. He knows Nature but as a robber. (165–66)

In the earlier portion of this passage Thoreau implicates himself
in the decline of agriculture, but at the end "the farmer"
becomes the culprit. This self-exoneration occurs because
Thoreau recognizes what the average farmer does not—that
there is a wildness to agriculture that ought to be cultivated.
The cultivation of the wild—a seemingly contradictory
phrase—anticipates the work of the 20th-century ecologist Aldo
Leopold, who sought to restore wildness to a tract of worn-out
farmland he purchased in Wisconsin (though Leopold planted
wild species rather than domesticated crops). Thoreau admits
feeling guilty about disrupting the previous elements of the
field—wildflowers—and argues that woodchucks have a right
to eat his beans and weeds have a right to grow amidst his
crop. His thinking on the need to preserve wildness around his
plot of land prefigures the ideas of another 20th-century nature
writer, Wendell Berry, a proponent of "sustainable" agriculture.
Thoreau seeks to avoid the marginalization of wildness that
typically occurs on farms. Wildness and agriculture can coexist;
they are, ideally at least, complementary.[17]

The promotion of wildness continues in "Higher Laws," a
chapter crucial to understanding Thoreau's pastoral ideology. It
represents a brilliant strategy to contain key oppositions. He now
has a sudden urge to devour raw the woodchuck he previously
wanted to feed. One evening, walking home with a string of fish
he has caught, he spots the animal and experiences an epiphanic
moment of self-revelation: "I found in myself, and still find, an
instinct toward a higher, or, as it is named, spiritual life, as do
most men, and another toward a primitive and savage one, and I
reverence them both. I love the wild not less than the good" (210).

The question that Thoreau confronts here is this: in practical
terms, how does one actually live a life that attempts to synthe-
size the savage and the civilized? He has found Therien wanting
as an example. In his own case, he admits that he has hunted
and fished, and he feels inadequate as a result, for "I believe that
every man who has ever been earnest to preserve his higher or
poetic faculties in the best condition has been particularly
inclined to abstain from animal food, and from much food of any

kind" (214–15). He proposes an anthrogenesis, an evolution of the human species in which man "goes thither at first as a hunter and fisher, until at last, if he has the seeds of a better life in him, he distinguishes his proper objects, as a poet or naturalist it may be, and leaves the gun and fish-pole behind" (212–13). Thoreau confesses that he himself has not yet attained this "higher" stage of evolution.[18]

He resorts once more to the theory of correspondence to reconcile or at least contain the tensions that constitute the source or his ambivalence toward hunting and fishing. We are what we eat; the purer our diet, the purer our lives will be; and Thoreau has no doubt "that it is part of the destiny of the human race, in its gradual improvement, to leave off eating animals, as surely as the savage tribes have left off eating each other when they came in contact with the more civilized" (216). In this conflict between the epicurean and the ascetic, Thoreau resolves it in favor of the latter. The simple life dictates an austere diet as part of one's program of self-reform.[19]

Thoreau's vegetarianism is also justifiable in terms of his biocentrism. As a final example of the reconciliation of polarities in *Walden*, consider an often neglected chapter, "Winter Animals," in which several conflicting themes come to the fore: society versus solitude, natural history versus nature writing, anthropocentrism versus biocentrism. Ostensibly a bestiary of the creatures Thoreau regularly encounters on his winter walks—owls, foxes, squirrels, jays, chickadees, partridges, hounds, rabbits—the inventory of animals is really an attempt to redefine "society" so as to include nonhuman species: "for if we take the ages into our account, may there not be a civilization going on among brutes as well as men?" (273). Thoreau even goes so far as to suggest that certain animals like rabbits and partridges outlive human cultures. The way he records animal behavior—not by shooting and stuffing animals, as natural historians were wont to do in his time, but through careful and prolonged observation of their habits in the field—illustrates the humanitarianism he brings to his outdoor studies. He desires to go beyond mere classification, to attach mythic significance to the lives of these animals. In the process he develops a sense of otherness for the rest of the biotic world that ultimately leads, in the "Conclusion," to a radical reenvisioning of the human species:

As I stand over the insect crawling amid the pine needles on the forest floor, and endeavoring to conceal itself from my sight, and ask myself why it will cherish those humble thoughts, and hide its head from me who might perhaps be its benefactor, and impart to its race some cheering information, I am reminded of the greater Benefactor and Intelligence that stands over me the human insect. (332)[20]

Elsewhere in the "Conclusion," Thoreau urges his readers to "Be rather the Mungo Park, the Lewis and Clark and Frobisher, of your own streams and oceans . . . be a Columbus to whole new continents and worlds within you, opening new channels, not of trade, but of thought" (321). He implores us to follow his example and make not only an outward but, more important, an inward exploration, to be an expert in (quoting the British poet William Habington) "home-cosmography" (321).[21]

Thoreau's advocacy of lococentrism poses yet another paradox within *Walden*. Even as he urges readers to stay at home, he travels; even as he resides at Walden, he leaves the pond to journey to other locales. Midway through his Walden retreat, in late summer of 1846, he traveled to the Maine woods to attempt an ascent of Mt. Katahdin, at 5,271 feet the highest peak in Maine and the second-highest in New England. He later published an essay about the experience, "Ktaadn" (adopting the Indian spelling for the title). It is one of Thoreau's best travel pieces, and I turn to it here as another example of his pastoral impulse. Whereas his Walden retreat represents inhabitation of the middle landscape between wilderness and civilization, the journey to Mt. Katahdin stands for his attempt to visit and "subdue" (verbally) a bona fide wilderness. He moves from the "soft" pastoral of the bean field and the pond's serene surface to the "hard" pastoral of Katahdin's wind-blasted, treeless, granitic summit. One of the lessons of the Maine woods is that the human-centered perspective of transcendentalism cannot prevail in all environments.[22]

Thoreau kept notes in the form of an outline of the trip, which took 12 days, and then composed a rough draft on his return from Maine in mid-September 1846. In January 1848 he gave a lecture at the Concord lyceum on his Katahdin experience. The revisions he made between the initial rough draft and the published version that appeared in serial form in *Union Magazine* from July through November 1848 suggest that he was revising with two seemingly conflicting goals in mind: to write in a "pot-boiler" style (at times) to increase the appeal to a popular audience (his audience at the lyceum as well as readers of popular literature), and to engage issues of transcendentalism in order to redefine the relationship between humans and the nonhuman world.[23]

Thoreau made the journey into the Maine woods with five other men. The entire trip, some 60 miles into the interior—up the West Branch of the Penobscot River by bateau, then along a ridge of the mountain now known as the Abol Slide, to near the summit, and back—occurred in several stages. The first stage involved making the trip to Maine, hiring guides to lead them into the wilderness, and poling upstream to the base of Katahdin. Whenever I read Thoreau's account, I am struck by his curious ambivalence toward human artifacts the group encounters, even as he seeks out wilderness. Thoreau records without fail (with varying degrees of inaccuracy, it must be said) how many miles from the last town they have journeyed, as well as a list of vestiges of civilization. Successively, he notes a large public house, a small store and a clearing, a lumber mill and railroad, cabins, a dam, logging booms, a brick, a pork barrel, an advertisement for clothing nailed to a tree, scratch marks on rocks from the spikes of loggers' boots, and logs marked with their owners' symbols. Everywhere he observes that the white pine, the tree most coveted by lumbermen, has been cut; and the portages the group makes between lakes and around rapids are on well-worn paths tramped out over the years by loggers and Indians. Yet he continues to insist that each artifact represents the "last trace of civilization" the party will encounter. Clearly, Thoreau is trying to separate himself from civilization and enter the wilderness— the wilderness he could not hope to find at Walden.[24]

Only when they reach the base camp, near the confluence of the Aboljacknagesic Stream and the West Branch of the Penobscot River, are Thoreau and company able to put behind them evidence of human activities (thought they know that five or six others have climbed the mountain before, the earliest in 1804). As they enter the seemingly impenetrable forest, Thoreau observes that "there was not the slightest trace of man to guide us further in this direction." The paths (what few that exist for short stretches) and an occasional clearing have been created by moose. At this point a geographical transition has occurred—the party has proceeded from landscape to forest wilderness. They take a compass bearing and proceed to follow it, but the going is slow and tedious. By late afternoon they decide to camp along a stream. Thoreau writes that it "was the worst kind of travelling" (59), and it doesn't improve as he sets off alone in an attempt to climb the mountain. He ascends a steep ravine over rocks and krummholz (dwarf spruce shrunken by the fierce subalpine climate): "certainly the most treacherous and porous country I ever travelled"(61).[25]

Thoreau is turned back by clouds and impending darkness, having gotten near the Table Lands, the summit plateau from which the final peak of the mountain rises. In the morning the entire party attempts the climb, but Thoreau quickly leaves everyone behind.

The second stage of the journey begins as Thoreau approaches the summit. He reaches the Table Lands this time for certain. In the remaining 20 pages of the essay are three critical passages, two of them well worked over by critics. I will argue that these two have often been misread, and that all three have not yet been adequately examined and synthesized. By employing a rhetorical analysis of Thoreau's varying audiences, by considering the revisions he made over a two-year period, and by engaging in fieldwork (actually climbing Katahdin and camping on its slopes), I hope to demonstrate that Thoreau crafted a coherent essay which effectively melds travel literature and transcendental philosophy. In the process, he both confirms and rejects certain Emersonian principles in his pastoral theory of containment.[26]

When Thoreau reaches the Table Lands, he is whited out— that is, he finds himself immersed "deep within the hostile ranks of clouds," caught inside a "cloud factory" (63, 64; the second metaphor here suggests the pervasiveness of the industrial revolution). He becomes disoriented, and a process of destabilization and disembodiment ensues. In the first of the two most famous passages of the essay (which appear in the initial draft), Thoreau writes of the rocks and crags of the summit, which he occasionally glimpses through windows in the clouds: "It was vast, Titanic, and such as man never inhabits. Some part of the beholder, even some vital part, seems to escape through the loose grating of his ribs, as he ascends" (64). Now he emphasizes, in contrast to most of the journey up to this point, that there is no evidence of civilization. "The tops of mountains are among the unfinished parts of the globe" (65). He has effectively moved from forested wilderness to subalpine wilderness.[27]

Thoreau decides to return to his party, reasoning that little would be gained in terms of taking in the vistas. Upon descending, he finds the five others berrying on the side slope, where they are just below the clouds and able to see for a hundred miles. In contrast to his earlier emphasis on the many traces of civilization in the forest—including the extensive logging of the white pine—he now sees "no clearing, no house. It did not look as if a solitary traveller had cut so much as a walking-stick there" (66). This passage is not in the original draft. But in verbal space—that is, long after the actual physical experience—he mythologizes his travels, directly contradicting earlier evidence, creating a mythic Maine woods in which he figures as a transcendental hero.[28]

The second famous passage occurs a few pages later. Thoreau describes the party's descent along an alpine stream and then into the "Burnt Lands," the thick, nearly impenetrable regrowth that sprang up following a wildfire some 50 years earlier. It begins, "Perhaps I most fully realized that this was primeval, untamed, and forever untameable *Nature*, or whatever else men call it, while coming down this part of the mountain" (69–70). This passage appears in the first draft, as does the next: "It is difficult to conceive of a region uninhabited by man. We habitually presume his presence and influence everywhere" (70). That Thoreau remains preoccupied with the distinction between landscape and wilderness is confirmed by the addition of the following passages sometime after he completed the first draft (presumably when preparing his lecture and the manuscript for publication in the magazine):

Here was no man's garden, but the unhandselled globe. It was not lawn, nor pasture, nor mead, nor woodland, nor lea, nor arable, nor waste-land. It was the fresh and natural surface of the planet Earth . . . . It was Matter, vast, terrific, not his Mother Earth. . . . There was here felt the presence of a force not bound to be kind to man. . . . not even the surface had been scarred by man, but it was a specimen of what God saw fit to make this world. (70–71)

He has returned to the forest wilderness in which no prospects are available. In the discourse of ecocriticism, he arrives at the biocentric realization that anthropocentrism is misplaced. Contrary to Emerson's belief, nature does not always wear the colors of the spirit.[29]

Then comes, in another passage added after the first draft, what has been called the "metaphysical climax of the essay." After contrasting the palimpsest of the Concord landscape worked over by generations of Indian and Yankee farmers with the "virgin" surface of Katahdin, Thoreau again writes of experiencing alienation, destabilization, disembodiment:

> I stand in awe of my body, this matter to which I am bound has become so strange to me. I fear not spirits, ghosts, of which I am one,—*that* my body might—but I fear bodies, I tremble to meet them. What is this Titan that has possession of me? Talk of mysteries!— Think of our life in nature,—daily to be shown matter, to come in contact with it,—rocks, trees, wind on our cheeks! the *solid* earth! the *actual* world! the *common sense! Contact! Contact!* Who *are we?* where *are we?* (71)

It is this passage in particular that some critics have called the most frenzied Thoreau ever wrote. For one of the few times in his life, language fails him—or he fails to find a language that can express his state of mind.[30]

This assessment, however, fails to consider Thoreau's composition process, his various audiences, and his previous mountaineering experience. As I have mentioned, Thoreau added this potboiler passage long after the experience. Why? I agree with Stephen Fink that Thoreau was much more astute about the literary marketplace than has been recognized, particularly in the case of "Ktaadn," his first major foray into popular writing. That the essay was initially conceived as a lecture also had to have influenced its style and substance, especially considering that his previous philosophical lectures had not gone over well with audiences.[31]

I shall discuss the six-paragraph conclusion in a moment. First, though, some insights into "Ktaadn" based on my fieldwork. I climbed Mt. Katahdin in late July 1993, in conditions remarkably similar to those experienced by Thoreau. I, too, was whited out; clouds prohibited any expansive views. Unlike Thoreau, I did reach the true summit (along with perhaps 50 others that day). The mountain, with its plateau-like, windswept, treeless summit formed of boulders, rocks, and talus, can be quite formidable—especially when thick clouds disorient the climber. I empathized with Thoreau's sense of disembodiment.

Further insight came a few days later. I was reminded while climbing in the Presidential Range and in southern New Hampshire that Thoreau had had previous mountaineering experience that should have prepared him to some extent for the ascent of Katahdin. In 1839 Thoreau climbed a higher peak, Mt. Washington (at 6,247 feet the tallest in New England), but he makes little mention of it in *A Week*, the book that contains the account of the ascent, or in his Journal. Given this previous experience, he had little reason to "freak out" (as some critics have claimed he did) on Katahdin. Both peaks are subject to sudden and extreme weather—mountains are their own storm makers, as Thoreau found out in Maine. Prior to 1846 Thoreau climbed other mountains as well: Mt. Monadnock in southern New Hampshire and Mt. Greylock in western Massachusetts— "lesser" mountains than Katahdin, to be sure; but with their weathered, exposed summits (which I have also climbed), still providing a modicum of alpine experience. Yet, after reviewing the voluminous criticism on "Ktaadn," I am aware of no critic who considered Thoreau's previous mountaineering experience. I find this more than curious; I think it is symbolic of the academy's, particularly the English profession's, general neglect and ignorance of the nonhuman environment, and its emphasis on nature as a social construct rather than physical reality.[32]

If Thoreau deliberately exaggerates certain aspects of the trip to appeal to a popular audience, does this mean that he must totally revise his transcendentalism? I think not. A clue to his pastoral strategy occurs in both the original and the final drafts when he writes about some extraordinary luck the party had while fishing for dinner one evening: "how all history, indeed, put to a terrestrial use, is mere history; but put to a celestial, is mythology always" (54). Thoreau is interested in transforming the facts of experience into metaphysical truths, and the

"Contact!" passage, as well as the six-paragraph paean to the Maine wilderness that ends the essay, is a stunning example of this transcendental formula.

For much of the journey Mt. Katahdin remains obscured by clouds. It remains aloof, unobtainable, *celestial*. Even when Thoreau nears its summit, he cannot grasp its ultimate meaning. He has an awesome experience; he encounters, as a number of critics have pointed out, the romantic sublime. Thoreau experiences an overwhelming sense of terror on the Table Lands. It is only during his descent over the Burnt Lands that he can make sense of what has happened. Contact with the terrestrial establishes a connection with the mysteries of nature; before, while in the clouds, he could not make this connection. He may not be able to figure out the mystery—obscured by clouds as the celestial is—but simply to experience it is a boon. The corresponding truth he arrives at—much later, to be sure, back in Concord—is that the clouded summit symbolizes nature's unfathomable qualities. Mystery, not mastery, must be our relation to nature. Transcendentalism is thus both rejected and confirmed; correspondence between matter and spirit can be inferred, but the transcendentalist's belief in a human-centered perspective is disproved. There are parts of nature that remain beyond human comprehension.[33]

Thoreau's mythologizing continues in the conclusion. This section, also added after the first draft, constitutes part of the third stage of the journey, after he returns to Concord: "What is most striking in the Maine wilderness is the continuousness of the forest. . . . I am reminded by my journey how exceedingly new this country still is. . . . the country is virtually unmapped and unexplored, and there still waves the virgin forest of the New World" (80–83). How can Thoreau conclude this way, after devoting much of the essay prior to the climb to describing the inescapable vestiges of civilization? He effectively escapes society and the forces of history and progress by reenvisioning a "virgin" nature, a view of Maine that he recalls from near the summit, from which he saw "no clearing, no house." He has a pastoral island experience near the summit of Katahdin after all.

It is a vision of Maine that I too retain after having returned from the clouded summit of Katahdin. What stands out in the recollection of the climb is not the trail bridges, the cabins, the signposts—all the artifacts of 20th-century wilderness preservation culture (the mountain and range are now enclosed within and protected by Baxter State Park). No, what I recall most vividly is the descent from the summit to Thoreau Spring, the area on the Table Lands believed to be the highest point of Thoreau's ascent. It is now marked by a signpost. As I scribbled in my field journal after reaching the site, a hawk suddenly emerged from the thick clouds. Its mystical appearance made me think of a passage from the chapter in *Walden* called "Spring," one of several that Thoreau added after the Katahdin experience emphasizing the wildness of his surroundings at the pond. The flight of a hawk he saw near Walden was, he writes, the "most ethereal" he had ever witnessed.

Thoreau's resolution of the tensions between wilderness and civilization is much more artful, imaginative, and successful than that of a visual artist who also ventured to Maine seeking material for his work. The landscape painter Frederic Church exhibited *Mount Ktaadn* (Figure 8) in 1853, following his visit to Maine and successful ascent of the mountain in 1852. The painter presents an image essentially without conflict—a viewer in the left fore-

Figure 8: Frederic Edwin Church, *Mount Ktaadn.*
   Yale University Art Gallery. Stanley B. Resor, B.A. 1901, Fund.

ground, reclining against a tree, observes cows grazing in front of a tranquil pond; a mill is inconspicuously inserted along a stream on the verge of the woods; the mountain itself stands tall but unthreatening. Indeed, the writer and the painter appear to have engaged in processes opposite in composition and theme. When Church first sketched the mountain scenery he included little evidence of civilization (only a trapper's hut); Thoreau, in contrast, calls attention to many traces of civilization in the first two-thirds of his essay. But in the conclusion, as we have seen, Thoreau emphasizes wilderness over civilization. Elision and occlusion occur in each artistic process, but with different results. Church, at least in this instance, capitulates to the forces of "progress" by accommodating the machine in the garden (recalling the similar strategy of "Sounds," in *Walden*), while Thoreau here resolves the tension in favor of wilderness.[34]

In effect, Thoreau ventured west figuratively when he traveled northeast to the frontier of Maine in 1846. West versus east is another important set of polar forces in his thought and writing, another way of representing the conflict between wilderness and civilization. In "Walking," he articulates this tension in a memorable way. "Walking" was first given as a lecture entitled "The Wild" in April 1851, and later combined with another lecture entitled "Walking" and published in *Atlantic Monthly* in 1862. I would like to conclude my treatment of Thoreau with a brief analysis of "Walking," because I see it as a summation of much of his strategy of pastoral containment.[35]

This essay is a philosophical defense of the need to walk, to engage in the rite of pastoral pilgrimage. Thoreau's Journal of 1851 indicates that he was preoccupied with thoughts about the wild and walking at this time, as he continued to revise *Walden* while living at home with his parents, seeking to combine vocation and occupation. His first book, *A Week on the Concord and Merrimack Rivers*, published in 1849, had been a failure (he had to pay back the publisher for hundreds of copies that went unsold, ruefully remarking in his Journal that "I now have a library of nearly nine hundred volumes, over seven hundred of which I wrote myself"). But he persevered in writing what he hoped would be his next book, adding Journal material to it as he revised. "Walking" and *Walden*, written and revised simultaneously, contain similar messages: wildness can be found almost anywhere; it represents a psychic state as much as a physical realm. Walking is a means of discovering wildness, and through this discovery it becomes possible to create mythology, both personal and national. Living in or near civilization, one can still without much effort cross a border into wildness, the psychic equivalent of the physical wilderness. In *Walden,* in a great peroration near the end of "Spring," Thoreau insists that civilization needs the "tonic of wildness" (317). In "Walking" he opens with the declaration, "I wish to speak a word for Nature, for absolute freedom and wildness."[36]

Thoreau elevates walking to an art, and to form of pilgrimage, by giving the word a fanciful etymology, linking walking to "sauntering," from "Sainte-Terrer," someone in the Middle Ages who traveled to the holy land. "Every walk is a sort of crusade" (94). Where does he walk? Westward, to the literal and symbolic west. "An absolutely new prospect is a great happiness, and I can still get this any afternoon. Two or three hours' walking will carry me to as strange a country as I ever expect to see" (99). He finds himself inevitably heading southwest, in the direction of the afternoon sun, the time of day when he usually chooses to walk. "Eastward I go only by force; but westward I go free" (105). East is symbolic of the past and the old world, and Thoreau, following Emerson's call to experience an original relationship with the universe, chooses the opposite direction. "I must walk toward Oregon, and not toward Europe. And that way the nation is moving, and I may say that mankind progress from east to west" (106). Though at times he is critical of manifest destiny and cultural nationalism, here he champions both, in a special sense: he calls on America to live up to its initial promise as a new world arcadia, a pastoral paradise.

I first read "Walking" in 1980, when I was an eastern expatriate firmly ensconced in northern Idaho. I took Thoreau's words quite seriously—"the west is but another name for the wild"— and, surrounded by officially designated wilderness, felt that I was carrying out the manifesto of "Walking" by literally living in the west and exploring its wild, unoccupied lands. But after moving to the midwest a few years later, I realized that I had been guilty of western chauvinism. As Thoreau makes clear, and as I came to understand, wildness can be found almost anywhere—even if large tracts of its geographical equivalent, wilderness, cannot. In his Journal Thoreau maintains that wildness *within* is a prerequisite to the existence of wildness *without*: "It is vain to dream of a wildness distant from ourselves. There is none such. It is the bog in our brains and bowels, the primitive vigor of Nature in us, that inspires that dream. I shall never find in the wilds of Labrador any greater wildness than in some recess of Concord, i.e., than I import into it." The wild can be found, too, in domestic creatures other than humans; in *Walden* Thoreau revels in the thought of "the cow which kicks over the pail, leaps the cowyard fence, and runs after her calf, in milking time" (324).[37]

Thoreau ultimately links wilderness and civilization by arguing that the latter depends, literally and symbolically, on the former; wilderness is civilization's necessary complement. Great nations in the past—classical Rome and Greece, and England in the Middle Ages—were nurtured by wildness. But as their wilderness disappeared, these cultures declined. Thoreau calls for a literature of the wild, a "tawny grammar," as a way of sustaining America, at the same time expressing concern over the disappearance of wildness: "We are accustomed to say in New England that few and fewer pigeons visit us every year. Our forests furnish no mast for them. So, it would seem, few and fewer thoughts visit each growing man from year to year, for the grove in our minds is laid waste" (132). Conversely, then, there can be no wildness within unless there exists wildness without. He recognizes that the preservation of civilization and the preservation of wilderness are ultimately the same thing. Thus, "Walking" may be Thoreau's most compelling example of the pastoral as a "process of containment" that "defines itself through the forces with which it sets up its tensions."[38]

Chapter 3

My First Summer in the Sierra: John Muir

Before moving to the Bay Area of California in 1987, I had never been impressed with John Muir as a *writer*. I thought his prose florid, stiff, sentimental, lacking the introspection and metaphysical depth of Thoreau and other nature writers. Of course, I respected his work as a preservationist and as a mountaineer who had embarked on heroic journeys in the highest mountains of the Lower 48. And the more I read about him, his life and times, and the history of conservation and nature writing, the more I honored the way he effectively resolved key tensions in his life and culture: between civilization and wilderness, between religion and science, between recreation and re-creation. Moroever, after five years of hiking, skiing, and climbing in the Sierra Nevada, I also came to change my view of him as a writer. Unlike Thoreau on Katahdin, Muir, when he came face to face with the sublime, was able to articulate the movement in his thinking from Christian anthropocentrism to biocentric panentheism.

In fact, I became so inspired by Muir's writing that I spent three weeks one summer hiking the 210-mile John Muir Trail along the crest of the Sierra, from Mt. Whitney in the south (the highest peak in the continental United States) to Yosemite Valley in the north. Following in his footsteps, reading his books and journals, I came to appreciate Muir's attempt to capture in words the romantic sublime that a hiker in the Sierra must continually confront. For a four-year period, from 1869 to 1873, Muir lived the wildest life in the wildest terrain of any American nature writer. His was the "hardest" pastoral: the terrain (much of it above timberline) with the least human modification, the antithesis of landscape.

The formative events of Muir's life have been well documented, in a series of autobiographies that Muir wrote late in life as well as by recent biographers. Born in Scotland in 1838, Muir emigrated to Wisconsin with his family when he was 11 years old. In *The Story of My Boyhood and Youth* (1912) he emphasizes two themes of the Wisconsin years that came to represent a significant tension in his adult life: his father's rigid, cruel brand of Calvinism, and his own love of nature. Muir's father was a strict fundamentalist who forbade any book besides the Bible in the household and who believed in purifying the spirit by brutalizing the flesh. A single incident during the Wisconsin period symbolizes the conflict between Christianity and John Muir's developing religion of nature, for which Daniel Muir served as an unwitting catalyst: the father drove to death a favorite horse of the family's on a brutally hot and humid midwestern summer day in order to attend a religious meeting. Muir recalls:

> Of the many advantages of farm life for boys one of the greatest is the gaining of real knowledge of animals as fellow-mortals, learning to respect them and love them, and even to win some of their love. Thus godlike sympathy grows and thrives and spreads far beyond the teachings of churches and schools, where too often the mean, blinding, loveless doctrine is taught that animals have neither mind nor soul, have no rights that we are bound to respect, and were made only for man, to be petted, spoiled, slaughtered, or enslaved.[1]

Early on, then, according to Muir's autobiographical testimony, he began to feel the tensions between an anthropocentric and a biocentric view of the world. Following a two-year stint at the University of Wisconsin in Madison, where he studied botany and geology and demonstrated a talent for mechanical invention, he embarked on several lengthy walks. He tramped along the Mississippi River bluff country of Iowa and Wisconsin in 1863. The following year he sauntered across eastern Canada (perhaps to escape conscription during the Civil War). Best-known is his epic trek from Indiana to the Gulf of Mexico, his "1,000-mile walk" of 1867. The 1,000-mile walk, undertaken after a factory accident in which Muir was nearly permanently blinded, can be seen as a kind of vision quest through which he was determined to identify his proper vocation. He experienced many pleasures and picturesque scenes on this journey, but he was also forced to confront a nature that was not always benevolent. Having contracted malaria in the swamps of the southeast and having encountered many creatures that seemed downright hostile, he came to a crucial revelation, which he records in *A Thousand-Mile Walk to the Gulf* (1916):

> The world, we are told, was made especially for man—a presumption not supported by all the facts. A numerous class of men are painfully astonished whenever they find anything, living or dead, in all God's universe, which they cannot eat or render in some way what they call useful to themselves. . . .
>
> But if we should ask these profound expositors of God's intentions, How about those man-eating animals—lions, tigers, alligators—which smack their lips over raw man? Or about those myriads of noxious insects that destroy labor and drink his blood? Doubtless man was intended for food and drink for all these? Oh, no! Not at all! These are unresolveable difficulties connected with Eden's apple and the Devil. . . .
>
> Now, it never seems to occur to these far-seeing teachers that Nature's object in making animals and plants might possibly be first of all the happiness of each one of them, not the creation of all for the happiness of one. Why should man value himself as more than a small part of the one great unit of creation? And what creature of all that the Lord has taken the pains to make is not essential to the completeness of that unit—the cosmos? The universe would be incomplete without man; but it would also be incomplete without the smallest transmicroscopic creature that dwells beyond our conceitful eyes and knowledge.[2]

As is the case with all Muir's books, he wrote this account well after the experience, on the basis of journal notes, so his memory is inevitably filtered through a certain amount of hindsight and subsequent insight. Nonetheless, it is clear from reading *A Thousand-Mile Walk* that Muir, in his pastoral retreat from the cruelty of his father's Calvinism and the work ethic of 19th-century industrial America, finds nature study a source of re-creation. The walk was crucial to his eventual resolution of the conflicts between wilderness and civilization, biocentrism and anthropocentrism, and traditional Christianity and his own still-evolving religious views, which I identify as biocentric panentheism: a combination of biblical rhetoric and belief in the immanence of spirit within "inanimate" objects as well as in the transcendent presence of God.[3]

In 1868 Muir decided to visit Yosemite Valley, which was becoming the most important stop on the western equivalent of a grand tour following the gold rush of 1848–1849 and the emergence of San Francisco as a major metropolitan area. From this time until his death in 1914 occurred the confluence of a career and a place: a career as naturalist-writer-preservationist in a place called Yosemite. Though he would visit, write about, and lobby for the protection of other places in America—including the future national parks of Sequoia, Crater Lake, Mt. Rainier, and Glacier Bay—he would be forever associated primarily with Yosemite. It was in Yosemite Valley that his vocation truly blossomed into a lifelong commitment to the wilderness, and it was in this valley that he worked out the tensions in his strategy of pastoral containment.

Muir wrote many articles and several books, but for a number of reasons I have chosen *My First Summer in the Sierra* as the subject of a close reading. Although it focuses on 1869, it was not written and published until 1911, so it presents Muir's view of Yosemite at both early and late stages of his career. I also find it the most autobiographical of his writings, the work in which he provides the most revealing testimony on the interaction between the wilderness and the self. Finally, in no other text of his are key tensions more explicit: in addition to the opposition of wilderness versus civilization, there is the polarity of science and religion and the issue of how he, a bona fide field geologist, incorporates his religious views into the Darwinian paradigm of the time. Muir's discourses on Native Americans and "proper" forms of recreation provide additional insight into his character and place him in a unique, though not always flattering, light in the nature-writing canon. All in all, the resolution of these tensions justifies Muir's position as the most influential turn-of-the-century nature writer.[4]

There is a famous story about Muir's arrival in California in 1868. When he disembarked in San Francisco, he approached a stranger to ask the fastest way out of the city. The stranger asked where Muir wanted to go. "Anywhere that is wild," Muir replied. This story, perhaps apocryphal, obscures the fact that Muir knew very well where he was going—to Yosemite, which he had read about in an illustrated travel brochure back east. Once he arrived in Yosemite Valley, however, he found himself overwhelmed by it, finding it "too large, too deep, too incomprehensible for human understanding." Only after spending the fall and winter in the foothills tending sheep was he prepared for a summer of dwelling in the sublime Sierra.[5]

Along with four others—the owner of the sheep, a shepherd, a Chinese helper, and an Indian helper—Muir headed for the mountains in June 1869. With a notebook tied to his belt (a sartorial feature to which he frequently calls the reader's attention), garbed in simple outdoor clothing, Muir cut an ambivalent, if romantic, figure. His ambivalence ran deeper than apparel. He was delighted finally to be in the mountains, but he was at times guilt-stricken over the occupation by which he had gained access to this alpine country. Throughout the text he points out the deleterious effects of overgrazing on the fragile alpine environment, and more than once refers to sheep as "hoofed locusts." He would have preferred, like Thoreau, to be an inspector of snowstorms; but like Apollo he had to render service to King Admetus.

As the party wended its way to the mountain meadows, Muir made careful note of the regional biogeography and how the vegetation changed with elevation. Muir is best known for his geologic contributions, but his botanical interests should not be neglected. He dutifully catalogs blue oak trees, Digger pines, mariposa lilies, manzanita, and cedar, and then devotes a paragraph to a noxious plant—a paragraph that illustrates nicely how his writing style and philosophy of conservation merge:

Poison oak or poison ivy (*Rhus diversiloba*), both as a bush and a scrambler up trees and rocks, is common throughout the foothill region up to a height of at least three thousand feet above the sea. It is somewhat troublesome to most travelers, inflaming the skin and eyes, but blends harmoniously with its companion plants, and many a charming flower leans confidingly upon it for protection and shade. I have oftentimes found the curious twining lily (*Stropholirion Californicum*) climbing its branches, showing no fear but rather congenial companionship. Sheep eat it without apparent ill effects; so do horses to some extent, though not fond of it, and to many persons it is harmless. Like most other things not apparently useful to man, it has few friends, and the blind question, "Why was it made?" goes on and on with never a guess that first of all it might have been made for itself.[6]

This passage recalls the one cited earlier from *A Thousand-Mile Walk*, in which Muir argues for the intrinsic value of things apparently not useful to humans. Here he makes the same claim, this time resorting to the pathetic fallacy. He anthropomorphizes in order to promote the preservation of nature. Paradoxically, and effectively, he employs anthropocentrism to advance the cause of biocentrism. Muir seems willing to sacrifice scientific accuracy and objectivity and risk the charge of "nature faker"; or perhaps he wants to challenge the scientific paradigm of his time and argue for sentience in the plant world.[7]

Muir also takes note of the human presence in the land. In particular, his references to Native Americans are numerous. Yet, unlike many nature writers who saw aboriginal peoples as a model for interaction with nature, Muir for the most part is critical of the Indians he encountered around Yosemite. This sets up one of the most curious and dramatic tensions in the book: between vestiges of Muir's Protestantism, with its historic racist tendencies, and the 19th-century view of Indians as "noble savages." It reveals how much he was influenced by his father's Puritanism even as he tried to distance himself from it.[8]

As a way of beginning this discussion, consider first a statement in *The Story of My Boyhood and Youth* in which Muir criticizes the Wisconsin pioneers' typically Anglocentric idea that "it could never have been the intention of God to allow Indians to rove and hunt over so fertile a country and hold it forever in unproductive wildness, while Scotch and Irish and English farmers could put it to so much better use." Here he exposes a classic—and self-serving—misreading of the American landscape by Euramericans that occurred across the continent: the notion that

Euramericans were justified in dispossessing the Indians because they could put the land to a "better" or "higher" use than the natives. In this instance, then, Muir's sympathies apparently lie with the natives. And early in *First Summer* Muir expresses admiration for the Miwok Indians, who lived on the western slope of the Sierra. When there is a food shortage in his camp, he suggests boiling and eating edible plants as the natives do. He later marvels at the minimal impact the Miwok have made on the land in spite of their long inhabitation.[9]

Unfortunately, Muir was born too late to learn from once-vital Native American cultures in California; by the time he arrived in Yosemite the indigenous peoples had been thoroughly acculturated, even degraded. Encountering a band of Paiute Indians on the east side of the Sierra, he "tried to pass them without stopping, but they wouldn't let me; forming a dismal circle about me, I was closely besieged while they begged whiskey or tobacco, and it was hard to convince them that I hadn't any. How glad I was to get away from the gray, grim crowd and see them vanish down the trail" (219). It is clear from this passage that it is not only the nature writer's typical love of solitude that fires his passion to be free of the Paiute.[10]

Virtually every Indian Muir encounters he describes as "dirty." While camping in the Owens Valley on the east slope of the mountains, he notices some Indian women gathering wild grain. Initially he seems taken by the scene, but then he changes his mind. "Most Indians I have seen are not a whit more natural in their lives than we whites. Perhaps if I knew them better I should like them better. The worst thing about them is their uncleanliness. Nothing truly wild is unclean" (226). On one hand Muir should be congratulated for not falling prey to the romantic stereotyping of Indians as noble savages; on the other hand his puritanical attitude that "cleanliness is next to godliness" is repulsive. How can Muir, who also lives in the wilderness, remain "clean"? What does he mean exactly by "uncleanliness"? Is he making a spiritual as well as a physical insinuation? Why does he appear so unsympathetic toward the natives, of whose dispossession and degradation by Anglo-American society he must have been aware? These are troubling questions, revealing the extent to which asceticism occludes his consideration of indigenous cultures in wider contexts. Overall, with regard to

Native Americans, he is opposite in outlook from his California contemporary Mary Austin, who looked to the Indians of the region as model inhabitors.[11]

Another set of tensions in *First Summer* involves conflict between science and religion. Muir reconciles this with an emphasis on design and harmony. Geology is the key to Muir's vocation as a nature writer, in which religion and science are wedded through his belief in the grand economy of nature.

Ascending into the high country for the first time, Muir records his approach to the Merced Valley of Yosemite from a prominence above Horseshoe Bend. His response illustrates the way he melds religion and science while reading the "book of nature":

> The sculpture of the landscape is as striking in its main lines as in its lavish richness of detail; a grand congregation of massive heights with the river shining between, each carved into smooth, graceful folds without leaving a single rocky angle exposed, as if the delicate fluting and ridging fashioned out of metamorphic slates had been carefully sandpapered. The whole landscape showed design, like man's noblest sculptures. (14)

Here Muir, invoking 17th-century natural theology, employs the argument from design to confirm not only God's existence, but his geological theories. The force that sculptured the rock was a glacier, which Muir sees as God's hand on the land.[12]

At this time, there was a debate in California's scientific circles over the origins of Yosemite Valley. Josiah Whitney, one of the most eminent geologists of the day, headed a state geological survey team from 1860 to 1868 and came to the conclusion that the region's valleys were the result of cataclysmic natural events. According to Whitney, uplifting and downfaulting along a line running between the Sierra and the Owens Valley to the east caused the bottom literally to drop out of what became Yosemite Valley, lowering the canyon floor. In other words, earthquakes were responsible for the sheer verticality of such imposing features as El Capitan, the world's largest single piece of exposed granite. Whitney's theory was based on a school of thought known as "catastrophism," a biblical interpretation of Earth's history explaining the geomorphology of the planet in terms of cataclysmic events such as the Old Testament flood. When

Whitney's *Yosemite Guidebook* was published in 1869, he ridiculed the notion that glaciers had ever existed in Yosemite Valley. One of his disciples, Clarence King, went so far as to ignore evidence of glaciation in a report on the geology of the Sierra, in order to reinforce his mentor's dogmatic views.[13]

Meanwhile, Muir was making discoveries in the Sierra that would later confirm the glacial genesis of the region. He based his hypotheses on the British geologist Charles Lyell's uniformitarian view of natural processes, a scientific paradigm which had played a pivotal role in Darwin's thinking on evolution and was just starting to become influential in America at this time. Basically Lyell, and Muir, became convinced that Earth was formed by slow, steady—that is, uniform—developments over long periods of time. They did not deny the possibility that sudden upheavals might also affect the Earth's morphology, but they believed that in the long term the land as we see it now was formed by forces such as vast bodies of receding or increasing water or glaciers.[14]

There is a certain teleology in Muir's rejection of Old Testament explanations of the origins of Earth, given his desire to disengage himself from Daniel Muir's influence. This does not mean, however, that Muir abandons his father's religious rhetoric. His writing is replete with Christian metaphors. As he wrote *My First Summer in the Sierra* some 40 years after the experience—following the publication of his geologic discoveries and the general recognition that he had won the debate with Whitney—Muir, it appears, tried to come to terms with his religious upbringing and his scientific beliefs. The result is a fascinating resolution of the tension he felt between religion and science.

While making his way with the rest of the sheepherding group to the mountain meadows, Muir pauses to lie atop a granite boulder, "the most romantic spot I had yet found." Then follows a series of classic pastoral "island experiences," in which the social world with all its dysfunction and complexity becomes distant, and the only history that matters is the interaction of the self and the land. The boulder is a glacial erratic, deposited along a streambed thousands of years ago. Muir writes that "the place seemed holy, where one might hope to see God," and later refers to it as an "altar boulder" (48–49). A month later, when he climbs above Yosemite Valley, he encounters more boulders, causing him to wonder, "With what tool were they quarried and carried?" He speculates that "the region has been overswept by a glacier from the northeastward, grinding down the general mass of the mountains, scoring and polishing . . . and dropping whatever boulders it chanced to be carrying at the time it was melted at the close of the Glacial Period. A fine discovery this" (101). And finally, a few days later, arriving on one more island in time, he finds himself sketching atop North Dome, far above the valley. Having attained the best prospect yet, Muir reads the "divine manuscript" and finds himself in awe of the "delicately harmonized" rocks and streams. This last discovery is cause for one of his many ecstatic moments in the Sierra, when self and nature join in perfect unison and he experiences "terrestrial eternity. A gift of good God" (132, 134).[15]

A pictorial equivalent of this feeling was captured by one of the most famous landscape painters of the American west in the 19th century, Albert Bierstadt. The German-born Bierstadt emigrated to America and was taken by the sublimity of the American wilderness. In *Looking Up the Yosemite Valley* (1865–1867, Figure 9) he places an artist in the shadowy central

Figure 9: *Looking Up the Yosemite Valley*. Albert Bierstadt, 1830–1902. American, oil on canvas, 35 7/8 by 58 inches.
Courtesy of the Haggin Collection, 1972x.452.

foreground sketching the 4,000-foot walls of the valley. On the left is El Capitan; on the right are Bridalveil Falls and Cathedral Rocks. The Merced River flows smoothly through the middle distance, and the entire scene is suffused with an ethereal, otherworldly light. Trees form a natural frame on each side of the scene. The humans are dwarfed but not threatened by Yosemite's sublimity. Like Muir, Bierstadt succeeds in harmonizing civilization—whose emblem in the painting is the artist—and wilderness.[16]

Muir consciously crafted his account of 1869 so that it climaxes in September with an ascent of Cathedral Peak. Appropriately enough, Muir declares this "the first time I have been at church in California." It was not the highest mountain that he climbed during the summer, but the story of the experience ranks among his most rhapsodic—and most revealing. It represents another island experience of "hard" pastoralism, where the protagonist encounters "wind-swept slopes and total solitude." After making an Adamic gesture of naming all the features within sight from the summit, he focuses his attention on "the Cathedral itself, a temple displaying Nature's best masonry and sermons in stones. . . . In our best of times everything turns into religion, all the world seems a church and the mountains altars" (250). Later, camping near a mountain tarn, writing his field notes by a campfire, he observes that:

> the onlooking rocks and trees, tiny shrubs and daisies and sedges, brought forward in the fire-glow, seem full of thought as if about to speak aloud and tell all their wild stories. A marvelously impressive meeting in which every one has something worth while to tell. And beyond the firebeams out in the solemn darkness, how impressive is the music of a choir of rills singing their way down from the snow to the river! And when we call to mind that thousands of these rejoicing rills are assembled in each one of the main streams, we wonder the less that our Sierra rivers are songful all the way to the sea. (251)

This passage can be read in at least two ways: either Muir employs personification and anthropomorphism as literary devices, or he professes pantheistic beliefs. If the latter is accurate, he combines pantheism with conventional Christian imagery in an effective synthesis to create another religion: panentheism. God is in, as well as transcendent of, all things,

71

and these things of the earth can communicate with us. Moreover, God is benevolent. Like Thoreau on Katahdin, Muir mythologizes his vision. But Muir is able to establish contact with a benevolent nonhuman world and then comprehend and artic- ulate its message, unlike Thoreau, who finds the alpine wilder- ness hostile and unfathomable and is (or at least pretends to be) disoriented during his experience near the summit.[17]

It astonished and depressed Muir that so few other visitors to Yosemite were enraptured by the temple of rocks. He trans- formed mountain climbing into a form of recreation that was not merely play but also an intellectual and spiritual pursuit—that is, a vocation. But he became despondent over his failure to convert others to his creed of nature religion: "I pressed Yosemite upon [one of the shepherds] like a missionary offering the gospel, but he would have none of it" (147). Nor could he sway tourists in 1869 to turn their attention from fishing to Yosemite's geologic wonders:

> Yet respectable-looking, even wise-looking people were fixing bits of worms on bent pieces of wire to catch trout. Sport they called it. Should church-goers try to pass the time fishing in baptismal fonts while dull sermons were being preached, the so-called sport might not be so bad; but to play in the Yosemite temple, seeking pleasure in the pain of fishes struggling for their lives, while God himself is preaching his sublimest water and stone sermons! (190)

Traditional Christianity, Muir implies, is uninspirational and promotes recreation that is mundane and untranscendent. The question then becomes, when one enters the church of nature, what form of recreation is most appropriate and spiritual. Muir apparently takes issue with Thoreau here on the merits of fish- ing, in part because he sympathizes with the fish who suffer at the hands of fishermen. He extends the concept of ethics and redefines recreation in the spirit of re-creation, as an activity that will heighten one's spiritual growth and not harm other natural things. Muir thus extends the philosophy of transcendentalism further than his predecessors by not only recognizing the exis- tence of spirit in the nonhuman environment, but also arguing for its protection.[18]

Muir would of course have much more success in courting vis- itors to the wilderness in subsequent years. As president of the

Sierra Club, one of his functions (according to the organization's charter) was to help people "explore, enjoy, and render accessible the mountain regions of the Pacific Coast." Like Thoreau, he felt that "progress" ought to be redefined to include the preservation of wild lands. He wrote guidebooks such as *The Yosemite* (1912) to cultivate a "proper" landscape aesthetic among tourists and to urge them to work for wilderness preservation. In a sense Muir never totally relinquished an anthropocentric view of the nonhuman world: he envisioned one of the primary purposes of the national parks as providing recreation for people. He should hardly be criticized for this, of course, since the move toward biocentrism has been marked by evolution, not revolution.[19]

Muir wrote *The Yosemite* partly to muster opposition to a dam proposed by the city of San Francisco within the national park, in a place that Muir felt was as beautiful as Yosemite itself but far less popular, and which would be drowned by the dam's backwater. It was called Hetch Hetchy. In spite of widespread public opposition to the dam, Congress approved it, and construction began in 1914. Shortly thereafter Muir died.[20]

When I hiked the John Muir Trail for three weeks during the summer of 1991, I expected to have a series of epiphanies. And I did, but most of them came in the clarity and comfort of retrospect. On the trail the days consisted mainly of making miles— lots of them—over the most rugged up-and-down country I had ever hiked. A typical day involved hiking about 15 miles, including climbing to a pass about 12,000 to 13,000 feet above sea level, then descending to 7,000 to 8,000 feet along a major river drainage, and ascending to yet another pass the same or next day. It was all I could do—especially during the first week or so of adjusting to the high altitude, a 60-pound pack, and sore feet—to put one foot in front of the other. Gradually, I came to respect all the more Muir's aesthetic sensibilities: how he could muster so much appreciation in country that took such a heavy toll on the body, and think scientifically at the same time! As I ascended and descended through the U-shaped valleys of the Sierra, I marveled at the thought of Muir pounding stakes into glaciers and patiently measuring their movement.

As I said, it was not until the hike was over that I came to truly appreciate the significance of following in Muir's footsteps. But one day, one scene, did qualify as an on-the-spot epiphany. Hiking south to north, I came to the end of Evolution Valley just north of 11,955-foot Muir Pass. It was as barren and stark a land as I had yet seen: treeless, strewn with rocks and boulders, the valley was dominated by 13,000-foot peaks named after great thinkers (Darwin, Huxley, Emerson). It had been one more hard day, and I was anxious to find a campsite by late afternoon. Suddenly I came to a bend in the trail and overlooked the deep drainage of the South Fork of the San Joaquin River. The bottom seemed to fall out of the land. As I looked west, into the sun, the valley was filled with an ethereal light. Below, Evolution Creek, reflecting the low afternoon sunlight, formed a snaky silver ribbon. I decided right there that I would go no farther; I would camp on this overlook, at the edge of the world. It was a scene Muir could well have described, or Bierstadt painted. A paraphrase of a Wallace Stevens poem came to mind:

> The sublime comes down
> to the spirit and place.
> The empty spirit
> in vacant space.[21]

John Muir's greatest legacy, I have come to reaffirm, is not his books but the pastoral retreat he helped persuade the America of his own time and later to preserve and sanctify: the Muir Trail and the national parks and wilderness areas through which it runs. It is fitting that we remember him not only for his words but for the world he lived in, loved, and helped conserve. Muir, through his actions and writings, disproves the old cliché about mountaineers: there *are* deep thinkers at 10,000 feet.

Chapter 4

The Land of Little Rain:
Mary Austin

How unlike the landscape of *The Oxbow* is the Mojave Desert of southeastern California that Mary Austin describes in *The Land of Little Rain*! Whereas Cole portrays a river valley crowded with life—fertile agricultural fields, a thick tree cover, a humid riverscape—Austin features a xeric environment where spareness and space predominate. Through her celebration of a land often perceived as sterile and uninteresting, Austin helped create in America what had not existed before the turn of the century: a desert aesthetic.[1]

John Muir sometimes descended from the passes of the Sierra into Owens Valley in the Mojave Desert, where he encountered the desolate, stark beauty of Mono Lake. From the desert floor he could look back to the snow-rimmed mountains, to which he always returned. Mary Austin engaged in a spatial movement opposite to that of Muir: she made occasional forays into the mountains but always came back to the desert, drawn by its mysterious allure. As she writes in *The Land of Little Rain* (1903), her most famous work, it is "a land of lost rivers, with little in it to love; yet a land that once visited must be come back to inevitably."[2]

Austin's affinity for nature, and more particularly the desert, can be accounted for in a number of ways. Born in Illinois in 1868, she lived in the midwest for the first 20 years of her life. In *Earth Horizon* (1932), her autobiography (written in the third person), she discusses a number of key incidents during the Illinois years that appear to have contributed to her subsequent appreciation of the desert and her yearning for it. At age five she experienced the first of many mystical visions when "God happened to Mary under the walnut tree." Walking through an orchard near her home, she approached a giant tree whose branches seemed to reach to heaven. Earth, sky, and tree became one living thing in the luminous morning, and, in a transcendental moment of immersion in nature, Austin heard the word "God" uttered. She writes of similar moments of oneness with the desert after her family relocated to California under the terms of the Homestead Act of 1862:

> Then, and ever afterward, in the wide, dry washes and along the edge of chaparral, Mary was beset with the need for being alone with this insistent experiential pang for which the wise Greeks had the clearest name concepts . . . fauns, satyrs, the ultimate Pan. Beauty-in-the-wild, yearning to be made human. Even in the first impact, Mary gave back a kindred yearning; it was in her mind that all she needed was to be alone with it for uninterrupted occasions, in which they might come to terms.[3]

Austin was thus able to transfer the general love of the outdoors she developed as a child to the subsequent landscape of her maturity. Growing up at the turn of the century, when the "back to nature" cult flourished, she had access to a proliferation of books available as part of the "nature study" curriculum then prominent in schools. At age 12 she received a copy of a geology text, *Old Red Sandstone,* which inspired her to collect fossils. In the desert, geology is laid bare to both the amateur and the expert. Looking back at the end of her life, she wrote that "the sense of the unfolding earth never left her. There are moments still, when she is alone with the mountains of New Mexico, when the first geological pages of the past begin to open and turn, when they are illuminated by such self-generated light as first shone from the chapters of 'Old Red Sandstone'" (EH 104–5). Austin went on to study both biology and English in college, an interdisciplinary focus that would serve her well in writing *The Land of Little Rain.*[4]

Numerous biographers, and Austin herself, also point to another factor that played a key role in her development as a nature writer. "Perhaps the biggest lack in Austin's life," argues Esther Stineman, "was a rich and meaningful connection with her mother." When her father and sister died in 1878, she felt as if her mother simply cast her aside in favor of her two brothers when she sought affection and consolation. Late in life, when she attempted in her autobiography once and for all to resolve her problematic maternal relationship, Austin wrote of meeting Mary Patchen, her father's first love (Austin was convinced that she was Mary Patchen's namesake). In one of the most poignant moments of *Earth Horizon,* Patchen tells Austin, "I didn't know your mother, but I know she didn't want you." Patchen's remark so affected Austin that she described it as the most "real and moving contact I have ever known" (316–17). Perhaps, then, it was unrequited love that caused Austin to turn to the seemingly impoverished landscape of the desert as a surrogate mother. As we shall see, at times she invests this "hard pastoral" setting with endearing qualities.[5]

Austin suffered the first in a series of nervous breakdowns in 1885 while attending college in Illinois. At that time an epidemic of nervousness, affecting mainly intellectuals and other members of the cultural elite, was sweeping America, perhaps contributing to her personal stress. Her breakdown was also gender-specific, though. It could be attributed to two separate but related sources: One source was familial pressures and neglect—"The attitude of my family was crushing," she later wrote, alluding to the mother's tendency to minimize her daughter's, as opposed to her sons', needs. The other source was society's belief that women were physically incapable of sustained intellectual endeavors. At the State Normal School in Bloomington, Illinois, she felt deprived by a curriculum that left little room for creativity (she later transferred to Blackburn College, a private institution that better served her needs). Of her educational upbringing, she wrote to her younger brother in 1927 that "from my childhood on I have been accustomed to be treated as if I were morally and intellectually inferior to the rest of the family." Her mental anguish proved to be one more reason for her later attraction to the desert: nature functioned as a kind of pastoral refuge. Seeking to disengage herself from the modern world, she turned to the desert and the cultures of its aboriginal peoples after the Austins emigrated to the San Joaquin Valley of southern California in 1888.[6]

In California, Austin taught school and wrote local-color stories. It was in 1891 that she married Stanford Austin, an irrigationist. They moved to Lone Pine in Owens Valley east of the Sierra, where she began her intense study of the flora and fauna of the desert, as well as of its native inhabitants: "She began to learn how Indians live off a land upon which more sophisticated races would starve, and how the land instructed them" (EH 198). Unfortunately, the Austins were beset by troubles at this time. They could not make a successful living in the desert; their daughter Ruth was born with a severe mental disability; and their marriage floundered. In search of a pastoral "island experience," Austin took long treks in the arroyos and hills of the eastern Mojave. From her attempts to find solace and succor in the desert came *The Land of Little Rain*.[7]

Austin's version of a desert pastoral accommodates the resolution of several important tensions. First, and perhaps most significant, is the tension between two myths of 19th-century American culture: garden versus desert. Austin comes to realize, after the failed attempt to farm in the desert, that traditional Anglo-American agriculture cannot be practiced in an environment that receives only a few inches of rain annually. Yet she also recognizes, after careful study of natural history, that the perception of the desert as a lifeless environment is inaccurate, and she takes great pains to debunk this stereotype. Though most observers of the time saw the desert as unaffected by humans, Austin demonstrates through careful ethnography that aboriginal peoples had long interacted with the Mojave and adjusted to its seasons. The desert, like the bean field at Walden or the mountain meadows of the Sierra grazed by sheep, is landscape—that is, a space modified by humans, a place textured by human hands.[8]

To portray the desert favorably, Austin exploits a second form of tension, that between anthropocentrism and biocentrism. The desert was traditionally perceived as ugly and useless because it could not have utilitarian value for Anglo-American settlers; it was a place to get through or to avoid rather than a place to settle. But if Austin could show that the desert did have human value, or that it could be understood in human terms, then it might be seen in a more positive light. So, like Muir, she invokes anthropomorphism in order to advance the cause of biocentrism—even as she insists on a naturalistic view of the desert as a landscape utterly indifferent and even hostile to human needs.

A third tension has to do with her critique of Anglo-American culture in general. Austin was a self-proclaimed "Indianist" at a time in American culture when the fate of Native Americans was hotly debated, and the author of numerous articles and books on various aspects of North American Indian cultures. She finds their land-use practices not only more sustainable but also more aesthetically pleasing than those of the dominant Anglo-American culture. She is particularly enamored of Native American women, and in a double critique identifies patriarchy as the root cause of environmental degradation and women's oppression. In this respect, she anticipates the ecofeminist movement of the late 20th century, whose key principles include a belief in the intrinsic values of all things, an insistence on the interconnections between human and nonhuman life, and a strong sympathy for the lifeways of indigenous peoples.[9]

In the preface to *The Land of Little Rain* Austin makes clear her intentions. Explaining why the place names she invokes may not be familiar to her readers, she confesses to "a great liking for the Indian fashion of name-giving" and indicates that "If the Indians have been there before me, you shall have their name" (xv). Her mission, then, is to rewrite the geography of the Mojave Desert from an Indian point of view. In her spare, poetic style, she explains how one must cultivate a desert aesthetic:

> But the real heart and core of the country are not to be come at in a month's vacation. One must summer and winter with the land and wait its occasions. Pine woods that take two and three seasons to the ripening of cones, roots that lie by in the sand seven years awaiting a growing rain, firs that grow fifty years before flowering,—these do not scrape acquaintance. (xvi)

Living in a "country of lost borders," Austin comes to recognize, as she reports in the opening chapter, that "Not the Law, but the land sets the limit." The desert resists containment by arbitrary lines drawn on a map. "Lost borders" is a term of powerful resonance for Austin; she uses it as the title of one of her story collections. Just as Austin as a writer cannot be neatly labeled or categorized—she wrote social criticism, anthropological works, and philosophical essays as well as fiction, poetry, and drama—the desert defies easy classification. Anglo-Americans may refer to this liminal space as "desert," but she immediately informs her readers that the designation risks oversimplification and misleads one into thinking that it refers to lifeless land: "Void of life it never is, however dry and villainous the soil." She then goes on to provide a botanical overview of the Mojave, explaining how plants such as creosote and tree yucca (Joshua tree) manage to survive. As Vera Norwood has shown, botany was a fashionable activity for middle-class women at the turn of the century—made accessible by the publication of easy-to-read field guides—and Austin clearly benefited from this development. Her botanical summary concludes by pointing out that in Death Valley, supposedly the "very core of desolation," almost 200 species of plants have been identified (3–4). Austin's project of pointing out the oxymoronic possibilities of "desert garden" looks forward to the work of Edward Abbey, who in *Desert Solitaire* devotes an entire chapter to the rich and diverse flora of Colorado River arid lands.[10]

"Water Trails of the Ceriso" continues debunking the myth of the lifeless desert and exemplifies Austin's biocentric perspective. She opens by observing that while water trails may not be detected by human eyes, "Getting down to the eye level of rat and squirrel kind, one perceives what might easily be wide and winding roads to us if they occurred in thick plantations of trees three times the height of a man" (17). Once she moves from an ego-centered to an eco-centered view of the desert and sees it from the vantage point of a small mammal, it becomes easier to notice the procession of other creatures that visit a small spring during the day: coyotes, deer, hawks, rabbits, badgers, burrowing owls, quail, sparrows, and other birds. Animals whose lives depend on locating a permanent water source, who have long lived in the desert, have learned to adapt to desert conditions. This includes Indians, whose stone markers and pictographs confirm that they, too, knew where to find water.

Like other nature writers, Austin possessed acute powers of observation. To see what she sees—a pair of meadowlarks seeking a scant shadow at midday in the desert behind a fencepost, a trail of animals near a spring—requires a naturalist's eye. Yet, in arguing for an aesthetic of the desert, she not only calls our attention to its inhabitants but also makes us see them in a favorable light. "The Scavengers," the third chapter of the book, illustrates Austin's various rhetorical strategies. It opens with a description of 57 buzzards sitting on fenceposts on a ranch near El Tejon (where Austin was often a guest of General Edward Fitzgerald Beale, a local raconteur and a source of immense knowledge about the Mojave). Turkey vultures, of course, are normally considered ugly, even repulsive. Austin concedes this, but adds: "All their offensiveness notwithstanding, they have a stately flight. They must also have what pass for good qualities among themselves, for they are social, not to say clannish" (33). Resorting to anthropomorphism, she hopes to make her readers see the birds in human terms.[11]

She later uses a recurrent phrase in *The Land of Little Rain* to explain one of their ecological functions: "It is doubtless the *economy of nature* to have the scavengers by to clean up the carrion" (33, italics mine). In this instance she attributes to the vultures an offensive trait, referring to them as "loathsome watchers" who loom over a "squalid tragedy." Yet, though loathsome, these creatures carry out an important role. Austin's interpretation of the buzzards' niche within the larger desert ecosystem suggests that she subscribes to the scientific paradigm of her day: nature as self-regulating and in balance.[12]

She also resorts to anthropomorphism in describing the raven as a bird with "nice habits" and "likeable traits" (36). That she strikes a fine balance between accurate scientific description and pathetic fallacy is confirmed by the fact that she was not indicted as one of the "nature fakers" in the controversy at the turn of the century. Like John Muir, Austin knows that to cultivate an appreciation for wilderness one must employ a certain degree of poetic license and sentimentality. Her task is more difficult, however, because in America the desert, unlike the mountains, had not yet been appreciated as aesthetic space.[13]

Many nature writers prefer solitude to society in their version of pastoral refuge, and are thus open to the charge that they fail

to engage the larger human community in their projects of ecological reform. Austin, by contrast, promotes a more social view
of nature. The desert has been populated not only by animals
but by various human cultures. The chapter called "The Pocket
Hunter" marks a shift in focus from the nonhuman to the human
world, suggesting that by natural history Austin, like Thoreau,
means to include people and cultures who realized a sustainable
relationship with the desert environment. It is the only chapter
that features a successful adaptation to the desert by Anglo-
Americans. The "pocket hunter," or prospector, has been able,
through long habitation, to integrate himself with his nonhuman
surroundings. "He was a small, bowed man, with a face and
manner and speech of no character at all, as if he had that faculty
of small hunted things of taking on the protective color of his
surroundings" (43). The prospector is unlike the typical modern
inhabitant in an important way: he eschews much of the para-
phernalia of civilization. Austin greatly admires him because he
lives self-sufficiently: he embodies the simple life, carrying only a
cooking pot, coffeepot, and bread tin; and using no gun but only
snares and a fishing line to capture his food. Although it might
seem contradictory for a nature writer to celebrate the lifeway of
a miner, Austin exploits him for local color and appreciates the
scale of his work. "The land tolerated him as it might a gopher or
a badger" (46). In Austin's eyes he achieves a kind of oneness
with the desert: "The Pocket Hunter had gotten to that point
where he knew no bad weather, and all places were equally
happy so long as they were out of doors" (47).[14]

The prospector resolves the tension between wilderness and
civilization by straddling the border between the two. Following
a strike, he spends his earnings by embarking on a grand tour of
Europe, and then returns to the desert when his money has run
out. A deeper, more intimate relationship with the land is realized by the natives. In *The Land of Journey's Ending*, a later study
of the Colorado and Rio Grande river drainages, she concedes
that "I doubt if any white man ever completely knows an Indian.
There is perhaps no such thing as an absolutely knowable
Indian. . . ." Still, she strives to acquaint herself with desert abo-
rigines, and she comes to adopt many of their religious beliefs.
Like Muir, she rejects her fundamentalist Christian upbringing
for its sterility and harshness; but unlike Muir she embraces

Native American cultures as the source of an alternative religion. She replaces theism with "wakonda," the Shoshone term for the "effective principle of the created universe" (EH 276).[15]

There are two Native Americans in particular on whom Austin focuses in *The Land of Little Rain*. The first, Winnenap, is a Shoshone medicine man; the second, Seyavi, is a Paiute basket maker. Each embodies ideals of Native American cultures that Austin finds compelling, especially in contrast to the materialism, triviality, and shallowness of her own Anglo-American society. In celebrating these natives she at once places herself within the Indianist movement at the turn of the century and stands firmly as an antimodernist, redefining American notions of "progress" by citing the virtues of primitivism and the vices of civilization.[16]

Winnenap provides her with ethnographical information about the preassimilation era of the Shoshone. After summarizing their nomadic adjustment to the seasonality of the food supply—tracking herds of deer and bighorn sheep through the summer and winter, then following flocks of doves in the spring—Austin reports the typical death of a medicine man. She explains that when three people of the tribe die despite having come to a medicine man for a cure, the doctor must give up his life. When Euramerican diseases reached the Shoshone in the 19th century—diseases against which they had developed no immunities—Winnenap's fate was sealed. Most of his tribe is wiped out by pneumonia, and he accepts his own death stoically: he is ritually killed by a hatchet blow. Austin then projects this view of his afterlife: "It will be tawny gold underfoot, walled up with jacinth and jasper, ribbed with chalcedony, and yet no hymn-book heaven, but the free air and free spaces of Shoshone Land" (65). Her prediction of an anti-Christian, anti-"garden" resting place for Winnenap confirms her rejection of Christianity and her acceptance of Native American spirituality. The tone she strikes here is worth scrutinizing: it is neither condemnatory nor romanticized. Cultural relativism seems to be her stance in recounting a practice that Anglo-Americans of any era would find barbaric. As the subtext makes clear, it is really Euramericans who are to blame for introducing illnesses that, along with warfare, dispossession, and general neglect, wiped out more than 90 percent of the aboriginal population of the Americas.[17]

In *Earth Horizon* Austin explains how she became acquainted with Indian women:

There was a small campody [Indian encampment] up George's Creek, brown wickiups in the chaparral like wasps' nests. Mary would see the women moving across the mesa on pleasant days, digging wild hyacinth roots, seed-gathering, and, as her strength permitted , would often join them, absorbing women's lore, plants good to be eaten or for medicine, learning to make snares of long, strong hair for the quail, how with one hand to flip trout, heavy with spawn, out from under the soddy banks of summer runnels, how and when to gather willows and cedar roots for basket-making. It was in this fashion that she began to learn that to get at the meaning of work you must make all its motions, both of body and mind. (246–47)[18]

Her intimate involvement with native women is traceable to her philosophy of inhabitation, which she reiterates in *The Land of Little Rain* at the beginning of the chapter called "The Basket Maker": "To understand the fashion of any life, one must know the land it is lived in and the procession of the year" (103). The passage above from *Earth Horizon* also suggests how she learned self-integration from native women, how to balance mental and physical activities so as to achieve spiritual wholeness. This is of particular importance to a female writer who obviously suffered the alienation so common to Anglo-American intellectuals, especially women, at the time. Her quest for a pastoral refuge is deeply connected to a study of native women because she finds them models of spiritual and physical wholeness. These passages from *Earth Horizon* and "The Basket Maker" demonstrate her commitment to an environmentalist and feminist agenda. In fact, Austin is a proto-ecofeminist.[19]

Austin was determined to prove that women in all cultures could exert significant, positive influence. In the opening chapter of *Earth Horizon*, when she recounts the exploits of her ancestors, the focus falls on her great-grandmother Polly McAdams. McAdams was among the vanguard of settlers who emigrated to the frontier of Illinois in the 19th century. "Chief of the discoveries of the Polly McAdamses, as it was told to Mary, was the predominance of happenings of the hearth, as against what happens on the battlefield and in the market-place, as the determinant of events" (15). In *The Land of Little Rain*, she opens "The Basket Maker" with this statement by Seyavi, who lost her husband and never took another: "A man . . . must have a woman, but a woman who has a child will do very well." Seyavi, according to Austin, is an example par excellence of "how much more easily one can do without a man than might at first be supposed" (103). In this respect Seyavi resembles another of Austin's celebrated female characters, "The Walking Woman" (of *Lost Borders*) who "had gone about alone in a country where the number of women is as one in fifteen," perfectly happy in her itinerant life in the desert. Clearly, Austin is a feminist who seeks to reenvision both history and anthropology. Austin's beliefs were greatly influenced by a period at the turn of the century, sometimes referred to as the age of the "New Woman," when women were entering the workforce in record numbers and campaigning more strongly than ever for suffrage.[20]

Yet while she sympathized with the feminist movement of her era and later became actively involved in women's rights, Austin is also critical of Anglo-American women, who fare poorly when compared with someone like Seyavi. The basket maker's self-sufficiency and unconscious artistry are admirable in contrast to the helplessness and thoughtlessness of the Anglo-American women, whom Austin borders on caricaturing:

> In our kind of society, when a woman ceases to alter the fashion of her hair, you guess that she has passed the crisis of her experience. If she goes on crimping and uncrimping with the changing mode, it is safe to suppose she has never come up against anything too big for her. The Indian woman gets nearly the same personal note in the pattern of her baskets. (105)

Modern women, Austin observes, engage in activities that are narcissistic and ultimately useless to the culture at large; Indian women create material artifacts at once beautiful and functional. She goes on to note a physiological difference between females in the two cultures, observing that Indian women "have not the sleek look of the women whom the social organization conspires to nourish" (110). Austin insinuates that the life of women in modern society is dictated by patriarchal values, whereas Seyavi is arbiter of her own fate.

The basket maker appeals to Austin as well for her nonverbal powers of articulation. This is ironic, given Austin's vocation as writer, but Austin is taken by Seyavi's preference for expression through hands rather than mouth. "Every Indian woman is an artist," Austin writes. "Sees, feels, creates, but does not philosophize about her processes" (106). She tries to but cannot describe Seyavi's artistic process, expressing the utter futility of her attempt thusly: "If you had ever owned one of Seyavi's golden russet cooking bowls with the pattern of plumed quail, you would understand all this without saying anything" (107).

Austin pays Seyavi the ultimate compliment of giving her the status of a prophet: "In her best days Seyavi was most like Deborah, deep bosomed, broad in the hips, quick in counsel, slow of speech, esteemed of her people" (109). It is a role Austin herself assumes; she is a self-styled *chisera,* or medicine woman. In fact, one could go so far as to claim that Seyavi is Austin's alter ego.[21]

Much of the remainder of *The Land of Little Rain* focuses on "water borders," the biogeography of mountain streams: how they originate in snowfields and eventually trickle down as seasonal waterways to the desert, and how Anglo-Americans have sought to appropriate rights to this most precious desert resource. The internecine struggles of Anglos are in stark contrast to the harmony of "The Little Town of the Grape Vines," the Hispanic community that is the subject of the book's final sketch. In celebrating the food, architecture, and community of El Pueblo de Las Uvas, Austin in effect creates a desert utopia. Reading this chapter, one is reminded of the social harmony of Sara Orne Jewett's maritime communities in Maine; and in fact Jewett was a contemporary whom Austin deeply admired and by whom she was no doubt influenced. The freedoms and sense of sacred place in the village are juxtaposed against the ills of modern society: "We breed in an environment of asphalt pavements a body of people whose creeds are chiefly restrictions against other people's way of life, and have kitchens and latrines under the same roof that houses their God" (170). In sum, Austin's version of the pastoral was the most ambitious to date in its attempts at reform, promoting not only ecological but also gender and ethnic diversity.[22]

Austin moved to New York in 1910, after charging her husband with desertion (the marriage had effectively dissolved by 1904).

Before she left Owens Valley, however, she had become an active conservationist, participating in the battle to protect the region's agrarian water rights from encroachments by the city of Los Angeles. Like a number of women of her time, she became involved in conservation politics, part of a general trend of civic involvement during the progressive era. Not surprisingly, she based her vision of a desert ecotopia on the small-scale, low-impact, "primitive" settlements of the Indians and Hispanics that she had studied and mythologized for more than a decade. Although she lost the battle over Owens Valley, she went on to oppose the construction of Boulder Dam on the Colorado River after moving to Santa Fe in 1924. This time she fought the allocation of water to agribusiness interests in California, arguing that they took far more than their share from Arizona, whose residents represented a healthier, more ethnically diverse population.[23]

Austin died in 1934. During her lifetime most of her work went out of print; only *The Land of Little Rain* has had enduring success. In 1950 an abridged version was published, with photographs by Ansel Adams, whom Austin met in the 1930s and collaborated with to produce *Taos Pueblo*, a combination of photographs and essays on northern New Mexico. Interestingly, landscape photography rather than painting was largely responsible for promoting a desert aesthetic. Photographers such as William Henry Jackson, Timothy O'Sullivan, and Laura Gilpin helped popularize the drylands west of the 100th meridian. In *Alkali Flat, Alabama Hills and Sierra Nevada in Distance* (Figure 10), Adams captures the tension between the sterility and hostility of the desert and its minimalist beauty. Whether light or dark, the landforms appear to support little life. The desert here consists of a barren, poisonous, horizontal foreground and rugged, desolate maze of canyons and corrugations without trees or water—the antithesis of a pastoral environment. Yet the very absence of vegetation allows one to notice and admire the spaciousness of the flats as well as the clean lines of the landforms—the undulating swells of the hills in the middle distance, the ragged horizon formed by the peaks in the distance. In this, a visual equivalent of Austin's pastoral representation, Adams illustrates how the spareness of the desert can indeed accommodate tensions.[24]

In late autumn of 1988, when I made a pilgrimage to Death Valley—part of the Mojave Desert near where Austin lived—I was struck first of all by the place names: Badwater, Dante's

Figure 10: *The Land of Little Rain. Alkali Flat, Alabama Hills and Sierra Nevada in Distance. Photograph by Ansel Adams.*
  Courtesy of the Ansel Adams Publishing Trust.

View, Furnace Creek, Funeral Peak. They emphasize that for modern-day people the desert may well be a place not to live but only to visit, and even then at their peril. The heat and cold, even during a season known to be moderate, underscored this funda-mental lesson. Temperatures ranged from 70 degrees during the day to near zero at night, and one morning I discovered that my water bottles had frozen solid. Having enough water on hand was never far from my mind, whether I was hiking to the lowest point in the United States, Badwater (230 feet below sea level), or climbing to Wildrose Peak (more than 9,000 feet above sea level). Backpacking up Furnace Creek Wash, following no trail but the desolate arroyo, I slogged through deep sand and thus gained further firsthand knowledge of this land of extremes. At sunset the rock of Red Amphitheater caught fire, the flames gradually subsiding as darkness fell at my camp. I took out a copy of *The Land of Little Rain* and read aloud a favorite passage, the sound of my voice a lonely echo off the canyon walls:

> It is hard to escape the sense of mastery as the stars move in the wide clear heavens to risings and settings unobscured. They look large and near and palpitant; as if they moved on some stately service not needful to declare. Wheeling to their stations in the sky, they make the poor world-fret of no account. Of no account you who lie out there watching, nor the lean coyote that stands off in the scrub from you and howls and howls. (13–14)

On the drive back through Owens Valley I made another pilgrimage, this time to Austin's home in Independence. "Independence" is a fitting name for the home of an assertive, iconoclastic writer whose stylistic simplicity mirrored the minimalist beauty of the desert. At her modest home, nestled on a serene street backed up against the foothills of the Sierra, Austin, like Thoreau, lived a border life, inhabiting a liminal space between civilization and wilderness. The line she drew in the sand divided the Anglo and Indian worlds. Austin resolved the tension between the wild and the civilized by celebrating the harmonious relationship of Indians with their environment, and liberated herself through inhabitation of the vast spaces that lay to the east. A desert pastoralist, Austin found sublimity and solace in the nearly empty drylands of the American west.

Chapter 5

A Sand County Almanac:
Aldo Leopold

L ike Mary Austin, Aldo Leopold faced the challenge of inventing an aesthetic for a type of landscape that had been largely unappreciated. In Leopold's case the unappreciated landscape was the prairie. In fact, Leopold faced a greater challenge: not only to create an aesthetic but to re-create a landscape. The 120 acres of land he purchased in 1935 in southern Wisconsin, on which Part I of *A Sand County Almanac* is based, had once—prior to Anglo-American settlement—been dominated by oak savanna; but when he assumed ownership, the tract consisted mostly of worn-out farmland, a relic of the dust bowl. Published in 1949, a year after Leopold's death, *A Sand County Almanac* contains a supreme irony in our postmodern, "postnatural" era: its exhortation that wilderness can be re-created when all of nature has been tainted by human activities. That one could still disengage from society and retreat to nature in the mid-20th century testifies to the power and persistence of the pastoral tradition—and to Leopold's intelligence, vision, and lyricism. *A Sand County Almanac* is generally considered the bible of the conservation movement.[1]

Leopold's pastoral impulses originated during his childhood in Burlington, Iowa, a Mississippi River town, where he was born in 1887. Like many other conservationists—Thoreau, Muir, George Bird Grinnell, Ernest Thompson Seton, Teddy Roosevelt, Sigurd Olson, Edward Abbey—Leopold developed a love of the outdoors through hunting and fishing. His father, Carl, to whom one of his books (*Game Management,* 1933) is dedicated, possessed a "lifelong outdoorsman's ability to read the woods" and, equally important, an accompanying ethical sensibility. Leopold relates in "Red Legs Kicking," a sketch from Part II of the *Almanac,* how his father ingrained in him an environmental ethic: "My dog was good at treeing partridge, and to forgo a sure shot in the tree in favor of a hopeless one at the fleeing bird was my first exercise in ethical codes" (121). He later defines an ethic as "ecologically speaking, a limitation on freedom of action in the struggle for existence" (202). This early lesson in restraint was an important stage leading to Leopold's greatest contribution to conservation: the articulation of a land ethic.[2]

So taken was he by the outdoors that Leopold decided to attend Yale University to earn a master's degree in forestry. Founded by Gifford Pinchot, who under President Theodore Roosevelt became the first head of the United States Forest Service, the Yale School of Forestry indoctrinated its students in the utilitarian philosophy of "the greatest good for the greatest number over the long run." From 1905 to 1909, Leopold attained a technical mastery of the natural sciences by taking such courses as Mechanical Properties of Wood, Timber Management, Forest Mensuration, and Forest Insects. This kind of intensely focused scientific training distinguished him from Thoreau, Muir, and Austin, who were largely self-taught amateur natural historians.[3]

Yet Leopold did not allow his scientific training to transform him into a dispassionate scientist. Once, returning home for Christmas break during his college years, he discovered that developers, with the assistance of the Army Corps of Engineers, had diked and drained the hunting grounds he used to visit as a boy. "Perhaps no one but a hunter," he later wrote in an unpublished foreword to the *Almanac,* "can understand how intense an affection a boy can feel for a piece of marsh." From this loss he learned an important lesson about government conservation, one that he would return to in the *Almanac:* in the name of conservation, the state can actually destroy what it sets out to pre-serve.[4]

From 1909 to 1924 Leopold lived in the American southwest. He moved to the region to begin his career with the Forest Service, starting as a timber cruiser in the Apache National Forest in Arizona (some of his field experiences are described in Part II of the *Almanac*). Demonstrating scientific skill as well as leader-ship, he eventually became director of operations of the Carson National Forest in New Mexico. Leopold essentially went through several stages of intellectual development during his time in the southwest. First came the necessary fieldwork during which his romantic, greenhorn, east coast notions were read-justed to fit the realities of managing natural resources in the west. Then came a realization concerning the crucial role of the individual landowner in solving the problems of erosion due to overgrazing by livestock in the desert, an insight that proved critical in Leopold's subsequent formulation of a land ethic. He also became interested in promoting game management and predator control on public lands. Finally came his efforts, as a government official and a conservation writer, to create "primi-tive areas" in the national forests—roadless tracts of land that preserved a vignette of primeval America and on which no development could occur and only recreation would be allowed.[5]

In 1924 Leopold and his family (his wife and five children) moved to Madison, Wisconsin, returning to the upper midwest, the region of his birth. Continuing his work in game manage-ment, this time as a private consultant, he published two books and many articles on the subject, acquiring a national reputation in this newly emerging field. In 1933 he accepted an offer from the University of Wisconsin to become the country's first profes-sor of wildlife management. He would remain a professor the rest of his life.[6]

Perhaps the most important development in Leopold's career as a nature writer occurred in 1935, when he and his family pur-chased 120 acres of land in southern Wisconsin:

> In 1935 my education in land ecology was deflected by a peculiar and fortunate accident. My family and I had become enthusiastic hunters with the bow and arrow, and we needed a shack as a base-camp from which to hunt deer. To this end I purchased, for a song, an

abandoned farm on the Wisconsin River in northern Sauk County, only fifty miles from Madison.

The purpose of the property gradually assumed more import:

> Deer-hunting soon proved to be only a minor circumstance among the delights of a landed estate in a semi-wild region, accessible on week-ends. I now realized that I had always wanted to own land, and to study and enrich its fauna and flora by my own effort. My wife, my three sons, and my two daughters, each in his own individual manner, have discovered deep satisfactions of one sort or another in the husbandry of wild things on our own land. In the winter we band and feed birds and cut firewood, in spring we plant pines and watch the geese go by, in summer we hunt pheasants and (in some years) ducks, and at all seasons we record phenology. All of these ventures are family affairs; to us a landless family, relying on other people's wildlife, has become an anachronism.

The working title of what became *A Sand County Almanac* was "Great Possessions." The shack property became a place where the Leopolds could have an "island experience," where time became timeless and the dissonance of modern culture was replaced by pastoral harmony.[7]

The *Almanac* consists of three parts. Part I, "A Sand County Almanac," comprises 22 essays telling of outdoor activities and natural events on and around the family shack property during the course of a year. Part II, "Sketches Here and There," contains 15 essays recording Leopold's travels throughout the midwest, the southwest, and Canada. Part III, "The Upshot," consists of four essays espousing a philosophy of land ethics; unlike the previous pieces, these writings are not rooted in the particulars of place. Thus the book might be described as moving from the particular to the general, from ecological knowledge gained from interaction with specific locales to overarching understanding derived from a more removed perspective.[8]

My strategy here is to focus on key essays that describe Leopold's "soft" pastoral experiences in Wisconsin—several in Part I and the following three from Part II: "Marshland Elegy," "Flambeau," and "On a Monument to the Pigeon." I will relate them to important themes and principles of the rest of the *Almanac* as well as to Leopold's other works, demonstrating the intertextuality of his philosophy and his nature writing.

The tensions Leopold sought to contain and resolve in his version of the pastoral are outlined in his explanation (quoted above) of how the family came to acquire the shack property. As he states, it was his love of hunting that led him to purchase a weekend retreat. One source of tension, then, has to do with Leopold the hunter versus Leopold the preservationist: how can the two roles be reconciled? Another set of conflicts relates to the issue of conservation. Can the individual landowner as well as the government act as a steward of the land, and is economics the only or main criterion on which land-use decisions by the landowner are to be based? For the Leopolds, "a landless family, relying on other people's wildlife, had become an anachronism," and on their land they were able to fulfill the lifelong wish of studying and enriching fauna and flora through their own efforts. This desire calls attention to the most significant source of tension of the *Almanac:* conflict between the wild and the civilized, and how the Leopolds contained and resolved this conflict and redefined their notions of "progress" through the "husbandry of wild things."

Part I, "A Sand County Almanac," is based on land journals that Leopold compiled over the 14 years he and his family inhabited the shack property on weekends and vacations. These land journals consist for the most part of quantitative data: numbers and kinds of species spotted, weather observations, patterns of plant and animal behavior. He began to compose the sketches of Part I after an invitation from the publisher Alfred A. Knopf in 1941 to write "a personal book recounting adventures in the field . . . warmly, evocatively, and vividly. . . . A book for the layman . . . [with] room for the author's opinions on ecology and conservation . . . worked into a framework of actual field experience." Over the next few years Leopold engaged in a running debate with Knopf over the nature of this natural history "for the layman"; he eventually turned to Oxford University Press, which published the book in 1949. As the composition and structure of what was to become *A Sand County Almanac* evolved from 1941 to 1949, Leopold included more autobiographical pieces based on his inhabitation of the shack property, as well as previously published essays on experiences elsewhere and on conservation philosophy. Eventually the three parts emerged, along with three portraits of Leopold: as landowner, wilderness traveler, and prophet of conservation. These three figures coalesce in Part I.[9]

A typical farmer's almanac includes seasonal observations and predictions. What the Leopolds practice, phenology, is more sophisticated. *Phenology*, the study of the seasonality of natural phenomena, is one of the primary activities of the family on the shack property, and it becomes the organizing device of Part I. It also distinguishes the author from the typical hunter; he is more interested in reading the book of nature than in bagging a bird or landing a fish. But Leopold learns that attaining ecological literacy is by necessity an incremental education. One of the April sketches begins with Leopold's admission that "I owned my farm for two years before learning that the sky dance is to be seen over my woods every evening in April and May" (30). As a hunter of woodcock he is a student of the habits of game birds, but it is only after patient observation as a landowner and phenologist that he is able to witness the bird's aesthetic mating ritual.

In an essay in Part III, "Conservation Esthetic," he articulates a distinction between different forms of recreation—hunting and nature observation—and his rationale for nature study as a "higher" activity: "The outstanding characteristic of perception is that it entails no consumption and no dilution of any resource" (173). Like Muir, Leopold comes to believe that there is recreation on one hand and there is re-creation on the other. Re-creation occurs in "Skydance" only when he has witnessed the woodcock spiral skyward and then tumble "like a crumbled plane, giving voice in a soft liquid warble that a March bluebird might envy" (32). Re-creation is more ethical because it has less impact on nature and (Leopold alleges) greater impact on the perceiver; it results in spiritual renewal.[10]

In the tension between the sportsman and the preservationist, the latter wins out in part because of Leopold's scientific interests. As an examination of his land journals reveals, he meticulously correlated sunlight and birdsong, and he notes in "Skydance" that "The show begins on the first warm evening in April at exactly 6:50 P.M. The curtain goes up one minute later each day until 1 June, when the time is 7:50." But notice the scientist's anthropomorphic observation that follows: "This sliding scale is dictated by vanity, the dancer demanding a romantic light intensity of exactly 0.05 foot-candles" (30). By attributing human qualities to the bird, Leopold, like Muir and Austin, advances the cause of biocentrism through the use of anthropomorphism.[11]

Describing the male woodcock's extravagant courtship flight, Leopold reveals aesthetic as well as scientific interests. Yet he readily acknowledges that in spite of his intensive study of the bird, some questions about the mating ritual remain unanswered. Where is the female woodcock? What is her role in the mating ritual? Is the twittering of the male while performing the dance vocal or mechanical? In this sense Leopold's quest continues, and the trophy is elusive. He will return for another "hunt."

His appreciation of the aesthetic value of a game bird was part of his ongoing self-education. *A Sand County Almanac* is actually a series of well-constructed myths idealizing this process. "Thinking Like a Mountain," perhaps the most famous essay in the book, is a classic example of how Leopold reconstructs facts to serve his literary purposes. The sketch (in Part II) tells how Leopold encountered a wolf while working for the Forest Service in the southwest. As Leopold explains, "In those days we had never heard of passing up a chance to kill a wolf." So he and his crew shoot it, in the name of predator control—according to the conventional wisdom of the day, fewer wolves would mean more deer. Only years later, after witnessing the denuding of the land by too many deer, does he recognize that wolves perform a valuable function in the mountain ecosystem by controlling the deer population. In "The Land Ethic" he explains the ecological concept of the biotic pyramid: successive "layers" of species with soil on the bottom, and then plants, insects, and mammalian predators in successive order, with each layer containing a smaller number. The extermination of wolves is an example of what he describes as "the larger predators . . . lopped off the apex of the pyramid" with the result that "food chains, for the first time in history, become shorter rather than longer" (217). To think like a mountain, then, means to think ecologically, to protect the role of all organisms in an ecosystem. The sketch effectively traces the movement in Leopold's thinking over several decades from an ego-centered to an eco-centered perspective.[12]

Yet Leopold's education was not as neat as the sketch implies. A study of the correspondence between him and a former student reveals that he was not ready to confess his "sin" (as he describes it in the 1947 foreword) until he was prodded into recognizing that it might be good for readers to know about his errors. This is not a criticism of Leopold so much as a revelation that he was a writer as well as a scientist, and like all writers was willing to sacrifice facts—though not scientific accuracy—to further his literary aims.[13]

A similar reconstruction occurs in Leopold's thinking regarding game animals. In *Game Management*, published in 1933, he defines the field as the "art of making land produce sustained annual crops of wild game for recreational use." The "art" of producing "crops" is an interesting oxymoron, especially in a textbook that makes it clear that "recreational use" means wild game on the table or the den wall. Leopold also writes in *Round River*, a posthumous publication of selected journal entries edited by one of his sons, that "the love of hunting is almost a physiological characteristic."[14]

By the time he wrote *A Sand County Almanac*, however, he had refined his philosophy of hunting, and thus resolved the tension between the hunter and the preservationist, as revealed in the conclusion of "Skydance":

> The woodcock is a living refutation of the theory that the utility of a game bird is to serve as a target, or to pose gracefully on a slice of toast. No one would rather hunt woodcock in October than I, but since learning of the sky dance I find myself calling one or two birds enough. I must be sure that, come April, there be no dearth of dancers in the sunset sky. (34)

By concluding with this characteristic burst of alliteration, Leopold ends on a sentimental note, perhaps with the intention of mitigating the cultural criticism implicit in the sketch.[15]

The attack is directed not only at hunters; he also takes to task his fellow landowners, of whom he makes at least two criticisms. Noting that the male woodcock seems to insist on dancing on and above a bare patch of earth, Leopold boasts "I have more woodcocks than most farmers because I have more mossy sand, too poor to support grass" (30). The soil is poor in part because of the exploitative farm-and-run tactics of the previous landowner, and Leopold intends to keep a portion of his land in "marginal" condition in order to re-create a game habitat. The implication is that other farmers prefer to plant their crops from fencerow to fencerow, allowing no room for game, in order to maximize their economic profits. They seem oblivious to the fact that their land can be "harvested" in other ways to produce game "crops." This is a failure of perception and a lapse of ethics.[16]

The second criticism Leopold makes of the typical landowner also relates to perception—the perception of life in rural areas in an age when progress appears to exclude or devalue life on the farm. "The drama of the sky is enacted nightly on hundreds of farms, the owners of which sigh for entertainment, but harbor the illusion that it is to be sought in theaters. They live on the land, but not by the land" (34). Here Leopold audaciously maintains that someone who lives on a farm only on weekends and vacations can actually live "closer" to the land—be more observant of and in tune with its nonhuman processes and activities— than someone who lives on it year-round.

In focusing on the landowner, Leopold's work represents a significant advance in the pastoral and conservation traditions. While Muir lobbied the federal government to set aside huge tracts of public land to preserve wilderness and encouraged people to visit these areas, Leopold concentrated on the "back 40" where there had previously been no conservation efforts. Leopold also favored the preservation of wilderness areas on public lands; he helped create "primitive areas" within the national forests, and as a founding member of the Wilderness Society he actively campaigned for a national wilderness system. But he detected at least two problems with government conservation: it did not treat the issue of conservation closer to home, that is, on one's own (private) land; and it often retarded rather than advanced conservation on the whole. One of his major contributions is his call for a land ethic in which the private landowner would recognize that in the long run it is better—aesthetically, morally, and economically—to act as steward of one's property.[17]

Stewardship, and awareness of a landscape's history, are the themes of "Good Oak," the February sketch for Part I. Again, the tension Leopold contains and resolves is between traditional agricultural land use and his own practices. "Good Oak" begins with a self-portrait of a landowner warming his shins by a fireplace while a February blizzard blows outside. Thoreauvian self-sufficiency is one of the subtexts: "If one has cut, split, hauled, and piled his own good oak, and let his mind work the while, he will remember much about where the heat comes from" (6). As he recalls the felling of the oak, he also takes a wider view, using dendrochronology (the study of tree rings) as a narrative device to recount the natural history of not only the oak but the state of Wisconsin as a whole. The point is to historicize the individual's role (that of human and nonhuman species) within the larger bioregional community. The sketch is an example of what Leopold calls for in "The Land Ethic" of Part III: an "ecological interpretation of history" (205). He thus anticipates by some 30 years the emergence of a new discipline: environmental history.[18]

The tree has 80 growth rings. While cutting it, Leopold observes (in one of many "book of nature" metaphors) that "fragrant little chips of history spewed from the saw cut. . . . We sensed that these two piles of sawdust were something more than wood: that they were the integrated transect of a century; that our saw was biting its way, stroke by stroke, decade by decade, into the chronology of a lifetime" (9). He sets an example here of a landowner who is mindful of the land's past, who does not take for granted the natural resources bestowed on him through land ownership. The oak is a gift, and he regards it as such. It is also a historical document. He reads it to provide a biotic chronicle of nonhuman species and their unfortunate fate during the period of frontier expansion in the upper midwest. Reading like an elegy to the state's wildlife, the sketch records the death of the last marten killed in Wisconsin, in 1925; the last cougar, 1908; the last passenger pigeon, 1899; and the last elk, 1866—one year before the tree sprouted from an acorn.[19]

Yet, in the classic inverse relationship between declines in wildlife and increases in conservation Leopold also cites landmarks in the history of Wisconsin conservation legislation: the prohibition of spring shooting in 1915; protection of does in 1912; appointment of the first game warden in 1887; and in 1865, "the birth-year of mercy for things natural, wild, and free" (16), John Muir's offer to buy farmland from his brother-in-law in order to reserve it as a sanctuary for wildflowers. In "The Land Ethic" he traces an evolution in the course of ethics, from recognizing the rights of individuals to protecting the rights of society as a whole. But there was yet "no ethic dealing with man's relation to land and to the animals and plants which grow upon it" (203). The conservation measures passed by the state of Wisconsin, however, were a first, albeit piecemeal, step. As Leopold declares in "On a Monument to the Passenger Pigeon" (in Part II), "for one species to mourn the death of another is a new thing under the sun" (110). What he seeks to do in an essay like "Good Oak" is make readers recognize that "All ethics so far evolved rest upon a single premise: that the individual is a member of a community of interdependent parts"; that "The land ethic simply enlarges the boundaries of the community to include soils, waters, plants, and animals, or collectively: the land"; and that, finally, "a land ethic changes the role of *Homo sapiens* from conqueror of the land-community to plain member and citizen of it" (203–4). "Good Oak" amounts to a call for recognition of the rights of nature.[20]

This essay is also a critique of wrongful, ill-conceived government-sponsored conservation, in which tension between government and private conservation is highlighted. In Part III, in an essay called "Wilderness," Leopold calls for creation of large tracts of wildlands by the federal government for historical, scientific, and recreational reasons; in "Good Oak," however, he is highly critical of the efforts of certain government agencies. He mocks the "alphabetical conservation" of the dust bowl years—a reference to the New Deal and the CCC (Civilian Conservation Corps)—when wetlands were burned to create more farmland, at the expense of wildlife that depended on the marshes. As Leopold says in "The Land Ethic," "There is a clear tendency in American conservation to relegate to government all necessary jobs that private landowners fail to perform" (213). The failure of individual landowners to practice sustainable agriculture had resulted in the demise of wetland species. As members of the ecological community, farmers had not lived up to their responsibilities, and government intervention in this case only made the situation worse.

In "Good Oak" Leopold refers scathingly to the "Babbittian decade" of the 1920s when "everything grew bigger and better in heedlessness and arrogance" (10). Like Thoreau, Muir, and Austin, he questions and redefines our notions of progress. "Marshland Elegy," the opening sketch in Part II, stands for this strain of cultural criticism. It also exemplifies Leopold's point about governmental destruction of wetlands, supposedly for conservation purposes. While on a fishing trip in central Wisconsin in 1934, Leopold spotted a pair of sandhill cranes in an undrained marsh. His interest piqued, he sought the birds out on subsequent excursions, and then wrote an essay in which he compressed his numerous encounters into a single experience. Its style, marked by metaphor, personification, and alliteration, is as poetic as any in the entire *Almanac:*

> A dawn wind stirs on the great marsh. With almost imperceptible slowness it rolls a bank of fog across the wide morass. Like the white ghost of a glacier the mists advance, riding over phalanxes of tamarack, sliding across bog-meadows heavy with dew. A single silence hangs from horizon to horizon. (95)[21]

The cranes appear, announced by their clangorous cries. Why ought one to value them? Certainly the sandhill crane has historic and scientific value. It evolved during an ice age—the Eocene period, 12,000 years ago. "When we hear his call we hear no mere bird. We hear the trumpet in the orchestra of evolution. . . . Amid the endless mediocrity of the commonplace, a crane marsh holds a paleontological patent of nobility . . ." (97–98). The crane also has cultural importance: it is a symbol of wildness, so to preserve its habitat is to preserve a remnant of wildness and wilderness. This truth went unrecognized by the CCC, which transformed the marshes into farmland—"What good is an undrained marsh anyhow?" (100)—and built a maze of roads "that inevitably follow governmental conservation. To build a road is so much simpler than to think of what the country really needs" (101). As Leopold says in "Conservation Esthetic" in Part III, "To promote perception is the only truly creative part of recreational engineering" (173). The CCC was guilty of a failure of perception.

It is true that Leopold evaluates government conservation harshly. But when it comes to preserving large parcels of relatively undisturbed land, i.e., wilderness, he feels that public as opposed to private management is more effective. This is made clear in "Flambeau," a sketch describing a canoe trip in northern Wisconsin. Again the government is criticized, this time for acting tardily to preserve a stretch of free-flowing river and the forest along its shore. Encountering two young men on the river on one last adventure before their induction into the army, Leopold assigns another value to wilderness: "This trip was their first and last taste of freedom, an interlude between two regimentations: the campus and the barracks." The two men, as well as Leopold, participate in the classic pastoralist pattern of disengagement from society in order to seek a simpler, more harmonious life, closer to nature. Though "as a wilderness [the Flambeau] was on its last legs"—with cottages, resorts, and bridges materializing— the men are able to realize an "island experience" during which they enjoy much wildlife and a unique mixture of hardwood and coniferous forests, as well as the tranquillity and serenity of floating the river.

But a power dam is proposed for the Flambeau, and the thought of this intrusion disrupts the idyllic mood like the whistle of the locomotive in *Walden*. The state has failed to preserve the river's wildness. Rather than muster Muir-like outrage over the damnation of a river, however, Leopold resorts to elegiac understatement: "Perhaps our grandsons, having never seen a wild river, will never miss the chance to set a canoe in singing waters" (115–16). With one arm of the government opposing the building of the dam, and another—in support of the dairy industry, which stands to benefit from the dam—promoting it, Leopold gently criticizes the state of Wisconsin for working at cross-purposes. The restraint exhibited here is typical of the tone of the *Almanac* as a whole, another reason that the book has been so well received; unlike, say, the polemical style of Thoreau or the vitriolic prose of Edward Abbey, Leopold's writing rarely provokes harsh reactions.[22]

I close my discussion of *A Sand County Almanac* by returning to a sketch from Part I. While "Marshland Elegy" and "Flambeau" record the experiences of a pastoral visitor, "Axe in Hand" details the activities of a pastoral inhabitant at work on the shack property. As Leopold reflects one November day on which trees to cut, the elements of "The Land Ethic" are exemplified. The individual landowner must

> quit thinking about decent land-use as solely an economic problem. Examine each question in terms of what is ethically and esthetically right, as well as what is economically expedient. A thing is right

when it tends to preserve the integrity, stability, and beauty of the biotic community. (224–25)

In this, the most famous passage of the book, Leopold identifies the essential ingredients of health for the land over the long term.[23]

The author is aware, however, that the land ethic contains certain paradoxes and tensions. Leopold is mindful of the irony of the conservationist with ax in hand. He explains that "A conservationist is one who is humbly aware that with each stroke he is writing his signature on the face of his land" (68). But he has come to recognize, as Thoreau did in "Walking," that landscape and wildness are not antithetical but complementary; and that wildness, like civilization, must be cultivated. In *Game Management* he makes the bold claim that "environmental manipulation can be accomplished only by the landowner." Here he carries out his belief, showing that a "hands-off" policy of "letting nature be" simply will not do. He preserves the pine and cuts the birch for a variety of reasons: he himself planted the pine, which is scarce and longer-lived, and it produces more valuable wood and promotes greater ecological diversity. By carrying out the "husbandry of wild things," by successfully resolving the tension between wilderness and civilization, the wild and the cultivated, he stands, ax in hand, as a pastoral exemplar.[24]

Leopold's writings and the substantial critical attention he has received since the 1987 centennial celebration of his birth are not his only legacy; another takes a more material form. The shack property is now part of a foundation to promote sustainable land use. Expanded to some 1,500 acres, it is a model for prairie and forest restoration and an educational resource for students, businesses, and landowners.[25]

I visited the shack for several days in August 1994 as a guest of Nina Leopold and Charles Bradley, who run the foundation. Walking the trails, canoeing the sloughs of the nearby Wisconsin River, I came to understand and appreciate how much work the Leopold family invested in the property as they tried over 15 years to restore prairie and forest on worn-out farmland. The work continues, with apparent success; during the three days I was there I saw much evidence of a healthy ecosystem. Wood ducks filled the slough, beavers on the ponds slapped their tails at my approach, bald eagles cruised the waterways—and yes, one evening in the marsh I heard the bugling of sandhill cranes. When Nina gave me a guided tour of the property, she pointed to the flourishing prairie near the shack and said proudly, "That used to be worn-out farmland!"

It is one thing to re-create a prairie, but it is another to cultivate its aesthetic appreciation by the general public. When I show slides of the Leopold property to audiences, I sense that images of wetlands, pine forests, and meadows do not hold the same appeal as, say, sublime, snowcapped mountains or even the vast, austere desert. There may be too much of the landscape of the familiar in the Leopold property. Quite simply, until recently there has been no widespread or influential school of prairie appreciation. Perceived as flat, with no visual center, prairies (and wetlands) require a different aesthetic and perhaps a more careful, discriminating eye in order to be appreciated.

Figure 11: *Leopold and His Dog in Wisconsin Farm Country.*
Bradley Study Center Files, Aldo Leopold Shack Foundation.

A photograph of Leopold near the shack property (Figure 11) bears this out. No single feature stands out to center one's perspective; details of the landscape are lost in an apparent sameness of composition. There is, or course, the sublime sense of space that one feels while out in the open fields, but, surprisingly, Leopold does not exploit this element in *A Sand County Almanac*. What the photograph does suggest, however, is Leopold's involvement in the perception and restoration of landscape. His stance of "lord and master of all I survey" is belied by the humility and grace of his prose, and the Leopolds' efforts to live with the land stand as their commitment to the simple life. Unlike many preservationists of his time, Leopold envisioned a place for humans in the wilderness—not merely as visitors or tourists, but as inhabitants. Through reinhabiting the land and re-creating a wilderness landscape, he crafted a new version of the pastoral.

Chapter 6

Desert Solitaire:
Edward Abbey

During spring break of 1978 some friends and I made a pilgrimage from Oregon to the Four Corners region of the southwest. Our destination: Arches and Canyonlands national parks in Utah. Having read Edward Abbey's *Desert Solitaire* and *The Monkey Wrench Gang*, we all wanted to see for ourselves the exotic desert Abbey so appealingly evoked. Like Muir on his first visit to Yosemite, though, I was initially overwhelmed. A Pennsylvania native who had moved to the lush, rainy, temperate Pacific northwest, I simply lacked the proper aesthetic to immediately appreciate slickrock country. I still recall vividly one early evening at camp, near the confluence of the Green and Colorado rivers. After dinner I climbed to the top of a red sandstone dome overlooking the confluence and the redrock labyrinth known as the Land of Standing Rocks. And gawked. My journal entry for that evening remained blank, reflecting my state of mind. In addition to the sense of vast space—the vistas unfolded for what seemed hundreds of miles—I was struck by the peculiarity of the landforms. The rock assumed the weirdest configurations—spires, domes, pinnacles, and contorted appendages. There was no vegetation, "only" hundreds of square miles of stone and space. The geological sublime.

Only after returning from the pilgrimage, in the clarity of retrospect, could I come to terms with Abbey country. I wouldn't know until years afterward that I had then taken the first tentative steps in the direction of a career and vocation: the study of nature writing.

"Much as I admire the work of Thoreau, Muir, [and] Leopold . . . ," Edward Abbey writes in the introduction to one of his works, "I have not tried to write in their tradition." Abbey's self-assessment recalls D. H. Lawrence's statement in *Studies in Classic American Literature:* "Never trust the artist. Trust the tale. The proper function of a critic is to save the tale from the artist who created it." The truth of the matter is that Abbey, for all his disclaimers to the contrary, *is* a "nature writer." Like his predecessors (among them Mary Austin, for whose *The Land of Little Rain* he wrote an introduction), he desires to transcend mere description of nature. "The few such writers whom I wholly admire," he reveals in a new introduction to *Desert Solitaire,* "are those, like Thoreau, who went far beyond simple nature writing to become critics of society, of the state, of our modern industrial culture. . . . It is not enough to understand nature; the point is to save it."[1]

In fact, it is as a cultural critic that Abbey gained wide recognition. The chief distinguishing characteristics of his nature writing are its radical, iconoclastic tone and theme. The cultural-historical context of Abbey's work is important in understanding his rhetoric of rage: he wrote in the wake of *Silent Spring,* during the flowering of modern environmentalism and the peak of the counterculture movement, amid emerging evidence of the significant harm human cultures—especially first-world countries like the United States—had caused our natural resources. Thus Abbey is more strident than many others of the generally genteel nature writing tradition. The tensions of his life and times may well have been so great that they could be resolved only in a version of the pastoral based on radical environmentalism as a viable solution.[2]

By the time of his death in March 1989, Edward Abbey had written 19 works of fiction and nonfiction. The setting of most of his writing is the American west, particularly the desert south-west. Though raised in the Allegheny Mountains of Pennsylvania, Abbey was in effect "born again" as a westerner after hitchhiking and riding the rails cross-country in 1944, a year before he joined the army at age 18. In the opening essay of *The Journey Home*, "Hallelujah on the Bum," he tells of his initial encounter with the desert of Arizona:

> . . . a land that filled me with strange excitement: crags and pinnacles of naked rock, the dark cores of ancient volcanoes, a vast and silent emptiness smoldering with heat, color, and indecipherable signifi-cance, above which floated a small number of pure, clear, hard-edged clouds. For the first time I felt I was getting close to the West of my deepest imaginings—the place where the tangible and the mythi-cal become the same.[3]

After completing his army service, Abbey moved to the south-west in 1947. He enrolled at the University of New Mexico under the GI Bill, taking 10 years to earn an M.A. in philosophy. His thesis, "Anarchism and the Morality of Violence," prefigured the radical environmentalism he would later advocate. In college, as editor of the student newspaper, he provoked some controversy by publishing an article entitled "Some Implications of Anarchy"; a cover quotation, "Man will never be free until the last king is strangled with the entrails of the last priest," ironically attributed to Louisa May Alcott, caused university officials to seize copies of the issue and end Abbey's editorship. By this time, as he was later to learn, he had become the subject of a covert FBI investi-gation owing to his apparently "un-American" activities. In 1952 Abbey published a letter in the student newspaper stating his opposition to the cold war and expressing dismay over the indi-vidual's lack of power to halt it. The FBI would continue to investigate Abbey for the rest of his life.[4]

To support the needs of his growing families over the years (he was married five times and fathered five children), and to satisfy his urge to spend as much time as possible outdoors, he began a long career as a seasonal employee with the U.S. Park and Forest services. He also continued his career as a writer, pub-lishing his first book, *Jonathan Troy*, a bildungsroman based on his Pennsylvania boyhood, in 1954. In 1956 and 1957, and again several years later, he served as a ranger at Arches National

Monument in Utah. This experience became the basis of *Desert Solitaire,* his best-known book.[5]

Arches National Monument in the late 1950s was a seldom-visited, primitive unit of the national park system, and Abbey preferred it that way. As a ranger he maintained hiking trails, collected campground fees, and provided information to the public. His self-declared role was as "sole inhabitant, usufructuary, observer, and custodian" (5) of 33,000 acres of slickrock wilderness. He lived in a house trailer provided by the Park Service but, finding the living quarters claustrophobic, ate and slept outdoors under a ramada he built himself. During his seasonal stints at Arches he accumulated four volumes of notes and sketches. Since his first three works, all novels, were commercial failures, he finally took the advice of a New York publisher to "write about something you know" and typed up an account of "those [first] two seamless perfect seasons" at Arches and sent it to his agent. Thus (according to Abbey) was *Desert Solitaire* born.[6]

The book describes a "hard" pastoral experience in a land of rock and sand and cactus. Aside from a few mining claims, some Anasazi ruins, and canyons grazed by cattle of nearby ranchers, the terrain Abbey inhabited was mostly unmodified by humans, thus qualifying as bona fide wilderness. In the tradition of his pastoral predecessors, Abbey sought refuge in the nonhuman world in order to resolve key conflicts between himself and society. In all of his works a recurrent theme is "the efforts of individuals, families, and communities to preserve their freedom and integrity against the overwhelming power of the modern techno-industrial military superstate." One source of tension, then, is conflict between the idyllic life of the individual in the wilderness and the dissonant, sometimes intrusive life of civilization. Another source has to do with his preference—along with Thoreau, Muir, Austin, and Leopold—for a biocentric over an anthropocentric philosophy. And more than any other nature writer, he takes the stance of an extremist, creating a new tension within the environmental movement itself: eschewing traditional environmental strategies in favor of radical, sometimes illegal, political activism. Abbey once issued this warning to readers:

> If certain ideas and emotions are expressed in these pages with what seems an extreme intransigence, it is not merely because I love an

argument and wish to provoke (though I do), but because I am—really am—an extremist, one who lives and loves by choice far out on the very verge of things, on the edge of the abyss, where this world falls off into the depths of another.

Desert Solitaire represents the correspondence of man and environment, a kind of literary environmental determinism. As one commentator has observed, "An extreme and intractable landscape might . . . appeal to a more extreme and intractable man."[7]

Near the end of the opening chapter of *Desert Solitaire*, "The First Morning," Abbey describes a walk he takes near his trailer on the first day on the job. Noticing a huge 50-foot boulder balanced on a pedestal of the same size, he compares it to "a head from Easter Island, a stone god or a petrified ogre." Then he makes this self-criticism:

> Like a god, like an ogre? The personification of the natural is exactly the tendency I wish to suppress in myself, to eliminate for good. I am here not only to evade for a while the clamor and filth and confusion of the cultural apparatus but also to confront, immediately and directly if it's possible, the bare bones of existence, the elemental and fundamental, the bedrock which sustains us. I want to be able to look at and into a juniper tree, a piece of quartz, a vulture, a spider, and see it as it is in itself, devoid of all humanly ascribed qualities, anti-Kantian, even the categories of scientific description. To meet God or Medusa face to face, even if it means risking everything human in myself. I dream of a hard and brutal mysticism in which the naked self merges with a non-human world and yet somehow survives still intact, individual, separate. Paradox and bedrock. (6)

The passage reveals Abbey's passionate desire for sanctuary from civilization, for an "island experience" in which time and the forces of history float by, leaving him undisturbed during an idyllic retreat. Yet at the same time he wants to maintain his individualism, his own identity, in the predominantly nonhuman environment.

This tension between wildness and the civilized becomes a recurrent theme. Another instance occurs when he is out on one of his nocturnal saunters and considers using a flashlight. He chooses not to, explaining that "like many other mechanical gadgets it tends to separate a man from the world around him" (13). With a flashlight, he tends to concentrate only on the spot of light in front of him; without it, he remains a part of the environment by using wider nocturnal vision. A similar lesson ensues when he returns to the trailer intending to write in his journal and cranks up a generator to power the lights. Once the noisy machine kicks in, he is deaf and blind to the outside world: "I have cut myself off completely from the greater world which surrounds the man-made shell. The desert and the night are pushed back—I can no longer participate in them or observe; I have exchanged a great and unbounded world for a small, comparatively meager one" (13). It is as Leopold argued in Part III of *A Sand County Almanac:* too many gadgets detract from rather than enhance the wilderness experience. As soon as Abbey finishes writing, he shuts off the machine and returns outside, where he revels in the isolation and silence.[8]

The quest for oneness with the nonhuman world continues in "The Serpents of Paradise." Like *Walden* and *A Sand County Almanac, Desert Solitaire* is organized by the seasons, and this chapter marks the movement from winter to spring. Drinking coffee one morning on the steps of the trailer, he looks down between his feet and discovers a rattlesnake. What should he do? On the one hand the snake obviously represents a physical threat. But as a ranger, it is his job to protect all living creatures within the park. Moreover, by predilection he cannot kill the reptile. Paraphrasing a line from a poem by Robinson Jeffers, he claims "I prefer not to kill animals. I'm a humanist; I'd rather kill a man than a snake" (7). So he opts for an ecological alternative, capturing a gopher snake, a species that is known to drive off rattlers, to keep as a pet in the trailer.[9]

Other encounters with animals, however, suggest that the line between anthropocentrism and biocentrism is not always to be drawn so easily. Abbey encounters a pair of gopher snakes performing (he speculates) a mating ritual on the desert sands. Playing the part of voyeur, Abbey approaches the snakes at ground level and is mesmerized by their caduceus-like glide. But when the snakes approach too closely he backs off, "stung by a fear too ancient and powerful to overcome." He seems unable to make the leap across the chasm between wilderness and civilization. Were it not for this atavistic fear, he "might have learned something new or some truth so very old we have all forgotten it" (21). As he follows the reptiles, he engages in a debate with himself over the validity of likening animals to humans: "How can I descend to such anthropomorphism?" he asks, as he speculates on the lovemaking habits of the snakes. On the other hand he thinks that "it's a foolish, simple-minded rationalism which denies any form of emotion to all animals but man and his dog. . . . We are obliged, therefore, to spread the news, painful and bitter though it may be for some to bear, that all living things on earth are kindred" (21). The moment recalls similar sea changes in attitude among other nature writers from an ego-centered to an eco-centered perspective.

In spite of this declaration, shortly thereafter Abbey gratuitously kills a rabbit with a rock to demonstrate his primitive hunting capabilities. When I teach *Desert Solitaire,* many students are upset by this episode—so upset that some judge and reject the book and author on the basis of this one incident. Part of their reaction has to do with Abbey's lack of contrition: "I try but cannot feel any sense of guilt. I examine my soul: white as snow. Check my hands: not a trace of blood." He defends his action, saying:

> No longer do I feel so isolated from the sparse and furtive life around me, a stranger from another world. I have entered into this one. We are kindred all of us, killer and victim, predator and prey, me and the sly coyote, the soaring buzzard, the elegant gopher snake, the trembling cottontail, the foul worms that feed on our entrails, all of them, all of us. Long live diversity, long live the earth! (34)

The cat sometimes plays with rather than eats the mouse it kills; birds peck at but do not always devour the worms they unearth. Perhaps Abbey reverts too far back to our wild ancestry here, offending more civilized types. He thus extends the pastoral into new, unexplored territories of temperament. The implication for some readers may be that biocentrism can be taken only so far, if in the process we lose our distinctly human traits of compassion, mercy, and justice.[10]

Abbey himself confronts these feelings after a hunt for a tourist who has disappeared in the region. When the search party discovers the body, Abbey vacillates between thinking "we are well rid of him. His departure makes room for the living," and thinking that the life of the individual "is significant and unique and supreme beyond all limits of reason and nature" (214–15). Later, back at the trailer, Abbey spots a vulture and imagines the dead man from the scavenger's point of view, as carrion. Taking a wider view, he then arrives at an ecological vision in an amoral universe:

> I feel myself sinking into the landscape, fixed in place like a stone, a small motionless shape of vague outline, desert-colored, and with the wings of imagination look down at myself through the eyes of the bird, watching a human figure that becomes smaller, smaller, smaller in the receding landscape as the bird rises into the evening—a man at a table near a twinkling campfire, surrounded by a rolling waste-land of stone and dune and sandstone monuments, the wasteland surrounded by dark canyons and the course of rivers and mountain ranges on a vast plateau stretching across Colorado, Utah, New Mexico and Arizona, and beyond this plateau more deserts and greater mountains, the Rockies in dusk, the Sierra Nevadas shining in their late afternoon, and farther and farther yet, the darkened East, the gleaming Pacific, the curving margins of the great earth itself, and beyond earth that ultimate world of sun and stars whose bounds we cannot discover. (216)

In this, one of the most remarkable passages of *Desert Solitaire*, Abbey moves, in an ever-widening gyre, from the microscopic to the macroscopic, from anthropocentrism to biocentrism. He discovers a sense of place by thinking both locally and cosmically. Taking a more expansive view of the universe, he comes to realize his own insignificance. The lococentrism of pastoralism results not in provincialism but in true cosmopolitanism, a realization that from *here* one can view all the world.

The tension between wilderness and civilization, between biocentrism and anthropocentrism, is strongest in "Down the River," the longest chapter of the book. An account of a 10-day raft trip down the Colorado River through Glen Canyon, it is also an elegy to a formerly undam(n)ed stretch of the river. Abbey and his companion achieve "intersubjectivity," taking on the mahogany color of the water and canyon walls, smelling like the catfish they catch and eat, accumulating grains of sand in their hair and clothing. They fulfill a "dream of childhood and one as powerful as the erotic dreams of adolescence—*floating down the river*. Mark Twain, Major Powell, every man that has ever put forth on flowing water knows what I mean" (154). Fishing, exploring side canyons, traveling at their leisure, they experience a pastoral reverie that recalls Huck and Jim, Nick Adams, and Ike McCaslin—protagonists of classic American literature who also discover sacred space.[11]

But even as Abbey and his friend float through Glen Canyon, they know it is a last voyage. The Bureau of Reclamation intends to dam the river and flood the canyon, selling power to southwestern cities. Abbey explains all this in the opening paragraph. Once again (as with Leopold), the government, supposedly the preserver of wilderness, is its destroyer. A further irony is that at the time, environmental organizations such as the Sierra Club supported—or at least did not oppose—flooding Glen Canyon in exchange for preventing the construction of a dam in Dinosaur National Monument in Colorado. The desecration of Abbey's desert paradise results from political compromise by traditional environmentalists.[12]

"Syphilization," then, comes to include those environmentalists who would sell out the wilderness. To assuage his anger and anguish, he imagines that "some unknown hero with a rucksack full of dynamite strapped to his back will descend into the bowels of the dam" (165) and blow it up. This fantasy becomes the ultimate goal of a fictional group of eco-raiders—the Monkey Wrench Gang—in a later work. In preparation for their mission, these raiders uproot survey stakes, destroy road-building equipment, and generally wreak havoc with developers across the Four Corners region.[13]

Pulling up survey stakes is an activity Abbey himself performs in "Polemic: Industrial Tourism and the National Parks," a chapter in *Desert Solitaire* that he describes (in a later edition) as an "enflamed member, in the midst of an otherwise simple pastorale." As a ranger who is supposed to abide by and enforce the laws of the federal government within the park, his actions are a blatant violation of his charge. But when Abbey encounters surveyors who are reconnoitering a route for a new paved road into the park to encourage more visitors, he feels he has no choice but to break the law. "The survey crew had done their job; I would do mine. For about five miles I followed the course of their survey back toward headquarters, and as I went I pulled up each little wooden stake and threw it away and cut all the bright ribbons from the bushes and hid them under a rock" (59). This action represents a historic moment in nature writing: it is the first time a pastoral writer knowingly and willingly breaks the law in order to preserve the rights of nature. Like Thoreau in "Resistance to Civil Government," Abbey resolves to "let your life be a counter friction to stop the machine."[14]

Such prose inspired the creation of Earth First!—a group formed in 1980 and now including more than 15,000 members. On numerous occasions members of Earth First! have spiked trees to prevent the logging of old-growth forest in the Pacific northwest and sabotaged machinery to prevent the building of roads in potential wilderness areas. Their activities, which go beyond the nonviolent resistance Thoreau called for in opposing slavery in the 19th century, have outraged traditional environmental groups.[15]

Why was Abbey's reaction so extreme? He recites the usual arguments for the preservation of wilderness—its cultural, historical, and aesthetic values—but also advances a new rationale. Wilderness ought to be preserved for political reasons "as a refuge from authoritarian government" because "history demonstrates that personal liberty is a rare and precious thing" (130). Citing contemporary examples such as Vietnam, Cuba, and Algeria, he points to wilderness as a haven for revolutionaries, a base for mounting effective resistance to totalitarian regimes. Readers familiar with Abbey's oeuvre know well his obsession with an Orwellian scenario. A later novel, *Good News*, portrays the southwest of the 21st century as horrific, with a military dictatorship in control of Phoenix and at war with renegades who remain at large in the wilderness. As Abbey sees it, in wilderness lies hope for the preservation of political freedom in the world. In the political sense of the pastoral Abbey's tone is more urgent than that of his predecessors in representing nature as a refuge. He envisions the wilderness as a permanent "island" or sanctuary for political dissidents.[16]

In "Down the River," the safe slack water formed by Glen Canyon Dam and the wild water of the rapids are transformed into contrasting symbols of civilization and wilderness. The signs along the reservoir shore that order recreationists to "PLAY SAFE, SKI ONLY IN CLOCKWISE DIRECTION" (152) are evidence of Leopold's dictum that "too much safety seems to yield only danger in the long run." In "Polemic: Industrial Tourism and the National Parks," Abbey criticizes the Park Service for promoting automobile tourism instead of slower-paced recreation, and in "Down the River" he continues his critique of the government's failure to encourage leisurely, meditative enjoyment of the wilderness—just as Muir advocated re-creation over recreation in Yosemite. Hiking the six-mile trail to Rainbow Bridge, Abbey contemplates what will happen when the floodwaters transform the trek to the site into an effortless cruise for motorboaters. "All things excellent are as difficult as they are rare," he believes. "If so, what happens to excellence when we eliminate the difficulty and the rarity?" (192) But he finds solace in the ultimate biocentric realization: "Men come and go, cities rise and fall, whole civilizations appear and disappear—the earth remains, slightly modified. The earth remains, and the heartbreaking beauty where there are no hearts to break" (194).[17]

Surprisingly, however, for all his tributes to the wild, Abbey chose not to remain permanently in the wilderness. Leo Marx, in his study of classic pastoral literature, claims that "American writers seldom, if ever, have designed satisfactory resolutions for their pastoral fables," and it would appear that Abbey's quest for sanctuary is also a failure. But Marx's assessment does not really hold true in Abbey's case. At the conclusion of his seasonal stint at Arches he decides to return to civilization. He trades the redrock canyons of Utah for the concrete canyons of New York City, where he becomes a welfare caseworker. "Moderate extremism" is how Abbey describes his peripatetic lifestyle and his strategy for reconciling the tension between wilderness and civilization:

> After twenty-six weeks of sunlight and stars, wind and sky and golden sand, I want to hear once more the crackle of clamshells on the floor of the bar in the Clam Broth House in Hoboken. I long for a view of the jolly, rosy faces on 42nd Street and the cheerful throngs on the sidewalks of Atlantic Avenue. Enough of Land's End, Dead Horse Point, Tukuhnikivats and other high resolves; I want to see somebody jump out of a window or off a roof. I grow weary of nobody's company but my own—let me hear the wit and wisdom of the subway crowds again, the cabdriver's shrewd aphorisms, the genial chuckle of a Jersey City cop, the happy laughter of Greater New York's one million illegitimate children. (265–66)[18]

As he contemplates leaving there is time for one last indulgence in anthropocentrism. "How difficult to imagine this place without a human presence; how necessary. I am almost prepared to believe that this sweet virginal primitive land will be grateful for my departure and the absence of tourists. . . ." But he catches himself:

> Grateful for our departure? One more expression of human vanity. The finest quality of this stone, these plants and animals, this desert landscape is the indifference manifest to our presence, our absence, our coming, our staying or our going. Whether we live or die is a matter of absolutely no concern whatsoever to the desert. (267)

Like Austin, Abbey is drawn to the desert because of its stark indifference to human fate. This appreciation could come only from confidence in one's own beliefs and an understanding of one's place in the larger scheme of things.

Abbey was a man of many contradictions, and he reveled in them. He was fond of quoting Whitman's statement, "Resist much. Obey little," and one could also quote another of Whitman's utterances here to good effect: "Do I contradict myself? / Very well then I contradict myself. / (I am large I contain multitudes.)" In trying to convert the public to the cause of wilderness preservation Abbey collaborated on a number of occasions with landscape photographers to produce "coffee-table" nature books, though he often boasted that he never took a camera into the wild, claiming that one word was worth a thousand pictures. In 1971 Sierra Club Books published *Slickrock,* a joint effort by Abbey and the photographer Philip Hyde that portrays in words and color images the canyon country of the Four Corners region. One purpose of this book, like *Desert Solitaire,* was to cultivate appreciation of the desert. Abbey writes of a view from one particular vantage point:

> I hesitate, even now, to call that scene beautiful. To most Americans, to most Europeans, natural beauty means the sylvan—pastoral and green, something productive and pleasant and fruitful—pastures with tame cows, a flowing stream with trout, a cottage or cabin, a field of corn, a bit of forest, in the background a nice snow-capped mountain range. At a comfortable distance. But from Comb Ridge you don't see anything like that. What you see from Comb Ridge is mostly red rock, warped and folded and corroded and eroded in var-

ious ways, all eccentric, with a number of maroon buttes, purple mesas, blue plateaus and gray dome-shaped mountains in the far-off west. Except for the thin track of the road . . . we could see no sign of human life. Nor any sign of any kind of life, except a few acid-green cottonwoods in the canyon below. In the silence and the heat and the glare we gazed upon a seared wasteland, a sinister and savage desolation. And found it infinitely fascinating.[19]

Abbey and Hyde, like artists before them who tried to capture and express the desert's beauty—the writers Powell, Austin, and Van Dyke; the photographers Timothy O'Sullivan, William Henry Jackson, and Laura Gilpin—focus on the unique qualities of dry lands, what distinguishes them from the eastern landscape: aridity, clarity of air, apparent lifelessness, their general antipastoral appearance.[20]

In *Early Morning in Chesler Park* (Figure 12), a scene in Canyonlands National Park, Hyde exploits some of these antitheses. The

Figure 12: *Early Morning in Chesler Park.*
© *Philip Hyde from* Slickrock, *by E. Abbey and P. Hyde. Reprinted courtesy of Philip Hyde.*

118

green, parklike foreground, mostly in the shadows, contrasts with the bald domes lit up by the morning sun. The jeep track suggests the presence of humans, but there are no people in this wild landscape; the desert is emphasized as a place to escape if one desires solitude. Hyde effectively juxtaposes the green pastoral, symbolized by the parklike foreground, and the lifeless desert, represented by the naked rocks in the rear. Like Abbey in *Desert Solitaire*, he depicts a dessicated Eden, a pastoral desert paradise.

By the time Abbey died in March 1989, he had become the most popular nature writer in the country, the leading figure in radical environmentalism, and a focus for criticism of the movement. Before his death (caused by pancreatic cancer), he instructed his family and close friends to inter his body in the wilderness; he wanted none of the trappings of a normal wake or funeral. So he was buried in a sleeping bag under some rocks at an undisclosed location somewhere in the desert outside Tucson, Arizona. Just as he inspired illegal acts in life, so did he in death.[21]

Chapter 7

Pilgrim at Tinker Creek: Annie Dillard

awrence Buell argues that the ideology of pastoralism
defies easy categorization as "conservative" or "liberal."
Pilgrim at Tinker Creek testifies to the truth of this claim. On
one hand it is "conservative" in that it represents a throwback to
the 17th century, when natural theologians such as John Ray
wrote primarily to prove the existence of God. On the other
hand it is "liberal" in its postmodern view of nature as a verbal
and psychological construct. Similarly, classifying Annie Dillard
as a "nature writer" does her a disservice. She herself once said,
"There's usually a bit of nature in what I write, but I don't consider myself a nature writer." All of her work, including *Pilgrim,*
reveals her desire to use the pastoral retreat to explore spiritual
issues. Investigating the nonhuman world is for Dillard a religious experience, a way to communicate with God.[1]

I first read *Pilgrim at Tinker Creek* in the late 1970s, at a time
when I was thoroughly taken by the work of Edward Abbey. In
the introduction to *Abbey's Road* he surveys the field of contemporary nature writing and recommends, among other writers,
Annie Dillard. So I read her work. But I remember telling friends

how boringly microscopic and theological I found her writing. I could not get into *Pilgrim*—in part because, as an eastern expatriate, I had fallen for the mountains and big skies of the west and was interested in rooting myself in its literature as well as its geography. I rejected Dillard on religious grounds, too; a staunchly disenfranchised Catholic, I could have no truck with an apparently conventional Christian such as the author of *Pilgrim at Tinker Creek*. It was only years later, following the publication of *The Living* in 1992, that I came back to her writing and realized how much I had missed. Experiencing a spiritual crisis of sorts, I found solace in reading of Dillard's own struggles over religious faith. I came to appreciate as well her powerful habit of attention, of noticing.[2]

Born Meta Ann Doak in 1945, Dillard was the oldest of three children. Some of the formative events of her first 16 years are related in *An American Childhood*, a memoir published in 1987. She was the daughter of an oil company executive, and her family lived among well-heeled neighbors in Pittsburgh. Both her parents were rather eccentric and nurtured their children's creativity. The father was so taken by Mark Twain's *Life on the Mississippi* that when Dillard was 10 he quit his job, bought a 24-foot cabin cruiser, and decided to float down the Ohio and Mississippi rivers. Though the pilgrimage lasted only six weeks (he got bored and lonely), it testified to the importance of literature in the Doak household. If her father favored *On the Road*, her mother pressed all kinds of books on her children; so as an adolescent Dillard read *Mad* magazine, *Native Son*, *Walden*, Augustine's *Confessions*, *The Little Shepherd of Kingdom Come*.[3]

One of her favorite books was *The Field Book of Ponds and Streams*, a work on how to study and collect flora and fauna. In a statement that anticipates a pattern in *Pilgrim at Tinker Creek*, Dillard recalls in *An American Childhood* that "The visible world turned me curious to books; the books propelled me reeling back to the world" (160). She acquired a microscope and for the first time saw an amoeba; confirming its existence caused her to declare, "I had a life" (149). Another important event related to her interest in science occurred after she enrolled in private school. Her biology teacher released a freshly hatched Polyphemus moth from a mason jar and let it escape outside. Dillard grew horrified as it emerged from the container; the jar had been too small, preventing the moth from spreading its wings:

I knew that this particular moth . . . could not travel more than a few more yards before a bird or a cat began to eat it, or a car ran over it. Nevertheless, it was crawling with what seemed wonderful vigor, as if . . . it was still excited from being born. I watched it go till the bell rang and I had to go in. I have told this story before and may yet tell it again, to lay the moth's ghost, for I still see it crawl down the broad black driveway, and I still see its gold wing clumps heave. (161)

Perhaps she sympathized with the moth for another reason: conscious of her privileged upbringing, she felt like an outcast, a moral defective in a society in which amorality was the norm. She grew to hate what she perceived as the hypocrisy of her fellow Presbyterians, and at age 16 she quit the church over the issue of Job, writing in one of her schoolgirl papers, "If the all-powerful creator directs the world, then why all this suffering?" (228) Her parents were aghast; her minister, to whom she wrote a letter of resignation, loaned her several works by C. S. Lewis and offered the hope that she would soon return to the flock.

She was something of a rebel in high school, but she also demonstrated such creativity that the headmistress advised her to go to Hollins College, where she sent all her brilliant "problem students." There Dillard enrolled in creative writing courses and also took a number of classes in theology. At the end of her sophomore year she married her creative writing teacher (whose surname she has retained). She received a B.A., and then went on for her M.A., in English, writing a master's thesis entitled "Walden Pond and Thoreau." After finishing her formal education in 1968, she continued to live near the Blue Ridge Mountains of Virginia for the next seven years. In 1970 she began to keep a journal, recording her impressions of daily excursions around Tinker Creek. A near-fatal bout with pneumonia in 1971 made her determined to live life more fully and to increase her sensitivity to the world outside the mind. The result was *Pilgrim at Tinker Creek,* published in 1974.[4]

If the issue of theodicy in Job caused her to leave the church, it also forced her to return. The tension between religious doubt and faith, between the senseless prodigality of the world and her need to believe in a benevolent creator, is a major theme of *Pilgrim.* Another conflict has to do with epistemology: how we acquire trustworthy knowledge about our physical surroundings. Dillard vacillates between nature as empirical truth and nature as a social construct; in this sense she is a product of 20th-century uncertainty over the nature of knowing. A third conflict has to do with her desire to realize oneness ("at-one-ment," atonement) with nature and God versus her desire to write of nature, to articulate her vision of it. This third conflict manifests itself in a struggle between unconsciousness, which she projects onto animals; and self-consciousness, a state she always reverts to after achieving momentary "oneness" with nature. Last, there is a conflict between the wild and the civilized. Like all nature writers, especially those of the 20th century, she seeks in the nonhuman world a refuge or escape from the discord and anomie of human society. At Tinker Creek Dillard learns that nature can be an effective basis for self-culture, and that immersion in nature can lead to the physical, intellectual, and spiritual rejuvenation of the pastoralist.

Dillard calls herself an "anchorite," one who seeks seclusion for religious reasons. Quoting Thoreau, she expresses her intention to keep a "meteorological journal of the mind," or a record of impressions the events of the creek make on her consciousness. She is concerned with phenomena but perhaps even more with phenomenology, the study of the world the mind constructs from sensory data. And like many other nature writers, she prefers the simple life: "If you cultivate a healthy poverty and simplicity, so that finding a penny will literally make your day, then, since the world is in fact planted in pennies, you have with your poverty bought a lifetime of days" (16). At a critical juncture in *Pilgrim*, when she must confront the rampant profligacy of the world—its seemingly meaningless death and strife and tragedy—she agonizes over returning to the library or the creek. She opts for the creek, because she brings "human values to the creek, and so [I] save myself from being brutalized" (182).[5]

Although she prefers the wild to the civilized, her terrain, like that of Thoreau's Walden, can hardly be classified as wilderness; topographically and aesthetically, the Blue Ridge Mountains, with their modest elevations and undulating valleys and ridges, qualify as "soft" pastoral. Yet an important contribution of Dillard's is her demonstration that one need not venture to an exotic desert or a sublime alpine wilderness in order to have a pastoral experience. She comes to the creek "to forget about life for a while," and it is a triumph of her imagination to create a sanctuary in a place she elsewhere describes as "suburban." Moreover, her retreat to nature is not accompanied by the environmental pleas or polemics characteristic of much 20th-century nature writing; she does not write to criticize the national park system or to preserve an endangered species. What she writes about primarily is modern humanity's crisis of faith and separation from nature. Her encounters with animals do not take her away from herself so much as cause her to wonder how and why she is different from other creatures.[6]

Like the transcendentalists Emerson and Thoreau, whose lifelong aim was to confirm a correspondence between the physical and metaphysical, nature as fact and nature as spirit, Dillard immerses herself in the "not-me" (Emerson's term) for religious reasons—to become one with God. Yet paradoxically, achieving oneness sometimes leads to alienation from nature. A compelling example of this paradox occurs as she drives back to her retreat on an interstate highway and stops at a gas station, where she drinks coffee and plays with a puppy:

> This is it, I think, this is it, right now, the present, this empty gas station, here, this western wind, this tang of coffee on the tongue, and I am patting the puppy. I am watching the mountain. And the second I verbalize this awareness in my brain, I cease to see the mountain or feel the puppy. I am opaque, so much black asphalt. But at the same second, the second I know I've lost it, I also realize that the puppy is still squirming on his back under my hand. Nothing has changed for him.

She goes on to recognize that "It is ironic that the one thing that all religions recognize as separating us from our creator—our very self-consciousness—is also the one thing that divides us from our fellow creature. It was a bitter birthday present from evolution, cutting us off at both ends" (80). She confronts a dilemma unnoticed by many nature writers. How does a person become one with nature, that is, lose one's self-consciousness, and at the same time retain a sense of self or otherness in order to record and re-create the experience? How can one truly become, as well as write, nature?[7]

She has a similar experience with a muskrat, described in a later chapter entitled "Stalking." While smoking a cigarette along

124

the creek one summer day, she is joined by a muskrat who climbs out of the stream and feeds within an arm's length of her. She watches the rodent for 40 minutes.

> I never knew I was there, either. For that forty minutes last night I was as purely sensitive and mute as a photographic plate; I received impressions, but I did not print out captions. My own self-awareness had disappeared; it seems now almost as though, had I been wired with electrodes, my EEG would have been flat. I have done this sort of thing so often that I have lost self-consciousness about moving slowly and halting suddenly; it is second nature to me now. And I have often noticed that even a few minutes of this self-forgetfulness is tremendously invigorating. (201)

The last statement testifies to the power of the pastoral as therapy in the modern world. But Dillard adds that others she has talked with about the experience are not capable of losing themselves in nature: "The other people invariably suffer from a self-consciousness that prevents their stalking well" (202). She is so in tune with the nonhuman world that she is capable of losing herself in it, yet she is so acutely self-conscious that she cannot long remain immersed in nature. Edward Abbey revels in his biocentric epiphanies; Annie Dillard implies that it is impossible to avoid anthropocentrism. Apparently she cannot fully make the move from an ego-centered to an eco-centered perspective. Dillard sets for her readers an example of watchfulness, but she does not preach environmental sermons. She may denigrate contemporary fiction for its solipsism and excessive self-referentiality (see *Living by Fiction*), but her writing is certainly characteristic in key respects of the postmodern era. She is a postmodern nature writer.[8]

The irony is that in writing the book, Dillard—a nature writer, someone who is supposed to devote herself to fieldwork—secluded herself from the outside world as much as possible. She wrote the first half at home in early 1973, and the remainder at a study carrel in the Hollins College library later that year. "Appealing workplaces are to be avoided," she explains in *The Writing Life*. "One wants a room with no view, so imagination can meet memory in the dark." After a while she shut the blinds of her carrel for good and proceeded to craft a narrative about life at Tinker Creek and her prodigious reading. The narrative was based on her journals; these consisted of 20 volumes, and she transferred the significant contents to 1,100 index cards. One night as she wrote in the carrel, she was distracted by the sound of frequent thumps outside her window. Thinking it was a persistent June bug, she opened the blinds to witness the flashing and explosion of fireworks. "It was the Fourth of July, and I had forgotten all of wide space and all of historical time." Here is proof that the pastoral sense of timelessness can occur almost anywhere.[9]

Dillard immerses herself in the "book of nature," in both the primary and the secondary senses of the term. She stalks authors of natural history as well as the phenomena of nature, reading and quoting naturalists from Pliny to Edwin Way Teale. In describing the horrifying mating ritual of the praying mantis, for example, she relies heavily on the entomologist J. Henri Fabre. *Pilgrim at Tinker Creek* is a veritable tome of natural history statistics: she tells us that monarch butterflies fly over Lake Superior without resting, walking sticks are able to feign death, and barnacle larvae survive by attaching themselves to gobs of tar in the Atlantic Ocean. Dillard seems to depend more heavily on her predecessors than other contemporary nature writers do (or perhaps she is just more honest about citing authorities). At any rate, there is a "meta–nature writing" quality to her work, further evidence of postmodern self-reflexiveness.[10]

For all the facts she cites, however, she is also skeptical about their ultimate value. Shortly after describing her stalking of the muskrat, Dillard brings up Werner Heisenberg's principle of indeterminacy—that one cannot know both a particle's velocity and its position (1927)—from which it has been extrapolated that the universe and all its phenomena cannot be known. This famous principle, according to Dillard, transformed scientists into mystics. . "We know now for sure that there is no knowing. . . . Physicists are saying that they cannot study nature per se, but only their own investigation of nature. . . . Heisenberg himself says, 'method and object can no longer be separated. *The scientific world-view has ceased to be a scientific view in the true sense of the word'*" (207). If this is true of physics, how can it be less true of nature writers recording and articulating their observations, sometimes secondhand through other authorities? By accepting the principle of indeterminacy, she provides a new slant on nature writing, traditionally defined as a nonfiction narrative based on an appreciative aesthetic response to a scientific view of nature. If science cannot be science—that is, if it cannot be "objective" reporting of natural phenomena—nature writing becomes one more "fiction" in a relativistic world.[11]

Dillard seemingly adopts the most anthropocentric and most antienvironmental stance of all: since everything we perceive is a construct created by each individual observer, there is no single "reality" out there; things exist only in the mind. This is empiricism and scientific positivism turned on their heads. And if the world does not exist, then we can do with it as we wish—environmentalists be damned. If this is indeed her view, then it is more than a little ironic that she is regularly cited and praised in environmental magazines, journals, and books.[12]

Even more significant than her crisis over epistemology is her spiritual conflict over religious faith and doubt. In the opening chapter of *Pilgrim,* she recalls an incident that occurred a few years earlier while she was walking along the creek. Practicing "stalking" animals had made her good enough at it to sneak up on frogs. One day, however, she approached a frog that

> didn't jump. I crept closer. At last I knelt on the island's winterkilled grass, lost, dumbstruck, staring at the frog in the creek just four feet away. He was a very small frog with wide, dull eyes. And just as I looked at him, he slowly crumpled and began to sag. The spirit vanished from his eyes as if snuffed. His skin emptied and drooped; his very skull seemed to collapse and settle like a kicked tent. He was shrinking before my eyes like a deflating football. I watched the taut, glistening skin on his shoulders ruck, and rumple, and fall. Soon, part of his skin, formless as a pricked balloon, lay in floating folds like bright scum on top of the water: it was a monstrous and terrifying thing. I gaped bewildered, appalled. An oval shadow hung in the water behind the drained frog; then the shadow glided away. The frog skin bag started to sink. (6)[13]

The "oval shadow" is a giant water bug that paralyzes and then sucks dry its prey. Dillard transforms this natural drama into a metaphysical issue:

> That it's rough and chancy out there is no surprise. Every living thing is a survivor on a kind of extended emergency bivouac. But at

the same time we are also created. In the Koran, Allah asks, "The heaven and the earth and all in between, thinkest thou I made them *in jest?*" It's a good question. What do we think of the created universe, spanning an unthinkable void with an unthinkable profusion of forms? . . . If the giant water bug was not made in jest, was it then made in earnest? (7)

The issue she addresses is theodicy: how to reconcile the existence of a brutal and seemingly horrid mortality with a belief in an all-powerful and benevolent creator. Whereas Thoreau revels in nature's profligacy—"We are cheered when we observe the vulture feeding on the carrion which disgusts and disheartens us and deriving health from the repast"—Dillard is appalled when she sees nature's own limits transgressed. The remainder of the book describes a pilgrimage through the seasons at Tinker Creek in search of a humanistic interpretation of God's ways.[14]

Dillard's view of nature seems much less affirmative than that of the 19th-century transcendentalists. While she interprets natural facts in terms of their spiritual significance, she envisions a macabre, tragedy-ridden universe. Observing a pregnant praying mantis slobbering over its egg case, she recalls the horror of the mating ritual as the female devours the male part by part. In the colloquial style she uses occasionally, she observes that "insects gotta do one horrible thing after another." The entire insect world, she decides, is a "horrible nature movie" (65–66). Reading accounts of Thor Heyerdahl's Atlantic expedition, she is fascinated by the report of barnacle larvae that manage to survive and grow by clinging to gobs of tar floating in the ocean. "How many gooseneck barnacle larvae must be dying out there in the middle of the oceans for every one that finds a glob of tar to fasten to?" (177). Her obsession with death calls to mind a statement from *On the Origin of Species:* "With all beings there must be much fortuitous destruction." Dillard takes a decidedly Darwinian view (in the popular sense of Darwinism) when she concludes: "Evolution loves death more than it loves you or me" (179).[15]

At this point, about midway through her account, she reaches an impasse. She wants to return to nature, but she finds it repugnant because of its apparent amorality. "Are my values then so diametrically opposed to those that nature preserves? . . . Must I then part ways with the only world I know? I had thought to live by the side of the creek in order to shape my life to its free flow. But I seem to have reached a point where I must draw the line. It looks as though the creek is not buoying me up but dragging me down" (179). The conclusion she arrives at is this: "We [human cultures] value the individual supremely, and nature values him not a whit. . . . We are moral creatures, then, in an amoral world. The universe that suckled us is a monster that does not care if we live or die . . ." (180). Humans are freaks, she decides. But they are helpful freaks in that they bring morality to nature. Death is "spinning the globe" (183), and the small consolation we have as a species is that we can recognize and value moral issues.[16]

She ultimately falls back on her Judeo-Christian heritage and into panentheistic beliefs. Panentheism: the belief that God not only is contained in the natural world but extends beyond it as well; God is both immanent and transcendent. Dillard's position is like Muir's in this sense, but hers is a much darker view of God and the dynamics of the natural world. As a Christian mystic, she believes she can experience direct, unmediated contact with God through nature. She may not always fully fathom the nature of this contact; nonetheless, the contact itself is proof of the existence of a supreme being. However, it is not proof of this being's design or intentions. For God is inscrutable. We are back to the lesson of Job.[17]

In "Northing," the chapter that advances the narrative into autumn, Dillard describes a literal fall as well as a figurative rise toward further revelations. Through a cabin window she watches a goldfinch land on the head of a purple thistle and proceed to empty its case of down, sowing seeds for new life. This ordinary event becomes the basis for another epiphany, and reminds one of Emerson's dictum that the invariable mark of wisdom is to transform the common into the miraculous. In transcendental fashion Dillard creates a fable of renewal. The deflowering of the thistle through the agency of the finch will lead to rebirth. Beauty coexists with death. Death is the mother of beauty. This is a key moment in her pilgrimage, her spiritual confirmation.[18]

The penultimate chapter returns to the "tree with lights in it," an image that figures in the opening chapter. The vision of the incandescent tree occurs one day in the woods when, thinking of nothing at all, she suddenly sees a cedar tree in her backyard explode into flame. "I had been my whole life a bell, and never knew it until at that moment I was lifted and struck" (34). It is a vision of God, a way to reconcile science and theology by capturing, for a moment, the shimmering force of the transcendent. Now, as she speculates once more about widespread "imperfections" in nature, this time rampant parasitism, she remembers the tree with lights in it. Were the twigs of the cedar bloated with galls? Is the tree with lights in it one more flawed work of creation? It doesn't matter. "Corruption is one of beauty's deep-blue speckles" (247).

In the tradition of Augustine's spiritual autobiography, the narrative has moved toward a grand conversion experience. Without death, Dillard realizes, there can be no beauty. A falling maple key is a final confirmation of just this message. Dillard seizes it and hurls it into the wind. "Bristling with animate purpose, not like a thing dropped or windblown . . . but like a creature muscled and vigorous" (275), the maple key carries out its function. It does what it has been designed through evolution to do: spread its seed and procreate. There is beauty and design after all.[19]

A postmodern pastoralist who invokes the 17th-century concept of the argument from design to confirm her Christian mysticism, Annie Dillard synthesizes new and old traditions. Her life at Tinker Creek also rebuts the argument that we are living in a "postnatural" world where, because of human impacts (such as global warming and ozone depletion), there is no longer a wild nature in which to take refuge. Like Thoreau, she reminds us that wildness can exist anywhere, even in a suburban setting like her former haunt at the creek. Tinker Creek may not become a world-famous site of nature pilgrimage like Walden Pond, however, perhaps because Dillard celebrates a mental terrain more than a physical terrain, the invisible over the visible landscape.[20]

In concluding with Dillard, I have come full circle, back to the landscape of my youth. I grew up in the Appalachian Mountains of Pennsylvania, a chain of ranges running from Maine to Georgia, of which Dillard's Blue Ridge is a part. I left Pennsylvania after college because the forests were destroyed by stripmining and the creeks polluted by acid mine drainage. On occasion, though, I return, if only temporarily, to the mountains of memory, the deep woods of my boyhood. And when I do, I always make a pilgrimage to Hawk Mountain, a world-famous bird sanctuary on the Appalachian Trail.

Each time the ritual is the same. I walk out along the Escarpment Trail, descend into the River of Rocks, and loop back to the ridgetop for a final view from South Lookout (Figure 13). The mountains, billions of years old, represent the landscape of endurance as well as the landscape of loss. The modest prospects and elevations of the Appalachians still seem dramatic to me, despite my many years of climbing the far higher peaks of the American west. The forested slopes of the valley, logged and re-logged over the years, contain and absorb the human artifacts— the meadows, farmland, roads, and houses. I am in a wild landscape. Human and nonhuman elements, the wild and the civilized, merge in a picturesque late-20th-century version of the pastoral.

Figure 13: *South Lookout, Hawk Mountain.*
© *1990 Jim Battles. Reprinted courtesy of Jim Battles.*

Near the end of the hike, on a rocky island above the trees overlooking a U-shaped valley once carved by glaciers and now filled with forest and farms, I recite aloud a poem by Wendell Berry, "A Homecoming":

> One faith is bondage. Two
> are free. In the trust
> of old love, cultivation shows
> a dark graceful wilderness
> at its heart. Wild
> in that wilderness, we roam
> the distances of our faith,
> safe beyond the bounds
> of what we know. O love,
> open. Show me
> my country. Take me home.[21]

Chapter 8

Conclusion

One of my favorite writers of the 20th century is the poet Robinson Jeffers. Jeffers, a Californian, built a stone retreat—Tor House—from which he could contemplate the Pacific Ocean and its metaphysical implications. Through long walks in the rugged Coast Range, Jeffers became intimate with his surroundings and transformed the land's edge into a metaphor for the end of American civilization. Because manifest destiny had reached its continental termination at the California shore, Jeffers prophesied that American culture had climaxed and was thus doomed to collapse like all the great civilizations of the past.[1]

Jeffers earned a reputation for misanthropy by taking the pastoral desire for disengagement from human society to its furthest limits. "The Place for No Story" is a paradigm of what some critics have identified as his "inhumanism":

> The coast hills at Sovranes Creek;
> No trees, but dark scant pasture drawn thin
> Over rock shaped like flame;
> The old ocean at the land's foot, the vast
> Gray extension beyond the long white violence;

> A herd of cows and the bull
> Far distant, hardly apparent up the dark slope;
> And the gray air haunted with hawks:
> This place is the noblest thing I have ever seen.
>   No imagi-
> nable
> Human presence here could do anything
> But dilute the lonely self-watchful passion.[2]

Nature writers celebrate place, the locale that becomes the locus of their affections. "Celebrate" is derived from the Latin *celebrar*, which means to frequent, to visit often, to come to know well. Nature writing, the pastoral tradition, is typically about the confluence of a place and a writer, the physical and the meta-physical, where—in the solitude of retreat from modernity—imagination and fact, the word and the world, merge. But in "The Place for No Story" Jeffers takes the quest for solitude to its ultimate epistemological and ontological extensions by imagining a place with no human presence. What species, then, is the "I" of the poem? It isn't clear—"lonely self-watchful passion" may imply that another species besides humanity is capable of self-consciousness (*contra* Dillard). Or perhaps the speaker, through practice, has been able to rid himself of his humanity in order to merge with the nonhuman surroundings.[3]

As much as I admire and respect Jeffers's poetry and passion, I think he got it wrong in this case. Instead, I agree with the writer Wallace Stegner, another Californian, who in his last book, *Where the Bluebird Sings to the Lemonade Springs*, writes:

> The deep ecologists warn us not to be anthropocentric, but I know no way to look at the world, settled or wild, except through my own human eyes. I know that it wasn't created especially for my use, and I share the guilt for what members of my species, especially the migratory ones, have done to it. But I am the only instrument that I have access to by which I can enjoy the world and try to understand it. So I must believe that, at least to human perception, a place is not a place until people have been born in it, have grown up in it, lived in it, known it, died in it—have both experienced and shaped it, as indi-viduals, families, neighborhoods, and communities, over more than one generation. Some are born in their place, some find it, some real-ize after long searching that the place they left is the one they have

been searching for. But whatever their relation to it, it is made a place only by slow accrual, like a coral reef.[4]

Throughout this book I have argued that nature writers generally participate in a mental movement from an ego-centered to an eco-centered perspective. But Stegner reminds us—and Annie Dillard confirms—that we can never wholly escape ourselves. Nor should we try. We inhabit space, as do other species; and what's more, we pass on information about that space, creating place. "Man—let me offer you a definition—is the story-telling animal. Wherever he goes he wants to leave behind not a chaotic wake, not an empty space, but the comforting marker-buoys and trail-signs of stories. He has to keep on making them up. As long as there's a story, it's all right. Even in his last moments, it's said, in the split second of a fatal fall—or when he's about to drown—he sees, passing rapidly before him, the story of his whole life."[5]

Some contemporary observers believe we have managed to create a "geography of nowhere"—a culture in which place, the relationship between the human species and the nonhuman physical environment, seems not to matter. A culture in which there are no stories about places. I think otherwise. I think stories can and still do affect us, connect us with "nature," the other, and result in the creation of place. The continuing popularity of nature writing belies the assertion that we now inhabit a geography of nowhere. Countless writers and readers have reaffirmed the power of place.[6]

I dwell on these matters, especially when I walk the local countryside, which is often. Many people require some form of pastoral refuge, and every place deserves its *genius loci*, its resident guardian spirit. And so it happened the other day, as I strolled along a nearby river and watched the floodplain meadow turn golden in the certain slant of a late autumn light, that I noticed, for the first time, the bright reddish-purple branches of shrubs. After years of neglect, I *saw* these bushes. This formerly inconspicuous plant connected me with, made me more aware of, this *place*.

Why? Why then, now? It had to do with the light; it had to do with my mood that particular day; it had to do with the writing

of this book; and—most important—it had to do with the fundamental fact of the land's presence. Later, when I returned to my
study, I did some research and learned that I had "discovered"
bebb willows, which grow mainly in northern latitudes. I then
recalled that Thoreau occasionally remarked in his Journal about
a shrub with a conspicuous red bark, referring to it as an "osier."
After some searching, I turned to this passage, which epitomizes
the attempt by nature writers to represent both word and world
and provides, I think, an appropriate close to this study: "Notice
the brightness of a row of osiers this morning. This phenomenon, whether referable to a change in the condition of the twig
or to the spring air and light, or even to our imaginations, is not
less a real phenomenon affecting us annually at this season."[7]

Bibliographic Essay

I t is no longer accurate to invoke the once-standard lament over the critical neglect of nature writing. Since 1960, in fact, the study of the literature of the environment has increased at a rate so prolific it might well terrify Annie Dillard. In this bibliographic essay, I have found it useful to organize the pre–1960 literature by periods; however, the scholarship since the 1960s becomes more amenable to classification by disciplines.

My focus here is on general literary, historical, and philosophical studies of nature writing and its various manifestations. In addition to my own reading, I have used the following works to track down important secondary sources: Thomas J. Lyon, "Bibliography: Secondary Studies," *This Incomperable Lande: A Book of American Nature Writing* (Boston: Houghton Mifflin, 1989); Frederick Waage, ed., *Teaching Environmental Literature: Materials, Methods, Resources* (New York: Modern Language Association, 1985); and *Association for the Study of Literature and Environment: Bibliography 1990–1993*, eds. Zita Ingham and Ron Steffens (Jonesboro, AR: ASLE, 1994).

To update this listing, consult subsequent bibliographies compiled by the Association for the Study of Literature and the Environment (ASLE), the annual volumes of *PMLA International Bibliography* (under the appropriate subject and author headings), Dissertations Abstract International (DAI), and *Environmental Periodicals Bibliography*.

Turn of the Century

It is not coincidental that when nature writing first became widely popular, as part of a general "back to nature" cult around 1900, critical commentary on the nature of nature writing began to appear. The term "nature writer" was in currency as early as 1902; Francis W. Halsey in "The Rise of the Nature Writers," *American Monthly Review of Reviews* 26.5 (Nov. 1902): 567–71, comments on "the increase in the production of Nature-books, both in numbers and in sales" (567). Halsey cites Gilbert White and John James Audubon as early English and American progenitors, and John Burroughs, John Muir, Mabel Osgood Wright, and Ernest Seton as major contemporary figures. Burroughs himself, in a series of essays later reprinted in his books, makes the case for Thoreau as the nature writer par excellence: "Thoreau was not a great philosopher, he was not a great naturalist, he was not a great poet, but as a nature-writer and an original character he is unique in our literature" ("Another Word on Thoreau," *The Last Harvest* [Boston: Houghton Mifflin, 1922], 120). In an earlier essay, "Thoreau's Wildness," Burroughs distinguishes between the natural historian and the nature writer by using Thoreau as an example of the latter: "What Thoreau was finally after in nature was something ulterior to science, something ulterior to poetry, something ulterior to philosophy; it was that vague something which he calls 'the higher law,' and which eludes all direct statement" (*Literary Values and Other Papers* [Freeport, NY: Books for Libraries Press, 1902], 201). One of the most useful early discussions of the elements of nature writing is by Dallas Lore Sharp, another turn-of-the-century nature writer. In "The Nature Writer," *New Outlook* (16 April 1910): 994–1000, Sharp argues that attachment to a particular place, personal interpretation of natural facts, and fidelity to scientific truths are critical to the success of the genre.

The "nature faker" controversy also produced a spate of commentary about the nature of nature writing at this time. A typical piece is "Real and Sham Natural History" by Burroughs, which appeared in *Atlantic Monthly* (March 1903): 298–309. Burroughs chastises Ernest T. Seton and Rev. William J. Long for their sins of anthropomorphism, arguing that to maintain credibility (especially in the eyes of knowledgeable scientists) nature writers must adhere to strict standards of accuracy in their field reporting.

These articles represent a multiplicity of essays about the genre at the turn of the century.

1920–1960

During the period 1920–1960, a debate took place over nomenclature—whether "nature writer," "natural historian," or "naturist" was the most appropriate term to apply to writers in the Thoreauvian vein. Other developments relating to the critical study of nature writing included the emergence of an American literary canon based on the (perceived) dominant theme of the white male escaping to the wilderness, and a cognate development, the emergence of western American literary studies, often featuring the same major motif.

D. H. Lawrence in *Studies in Classic American Literature* (London, 1921) broke new ground in criticism by interpreting works such as *The Leatherstocking Tales* and *Moby-Dick* as paradigmatic examples of the American white male protagonist fleeing civilization; the same argument could be (and was) applied to nature writers, the vast majority of whom were male. F. O. Matthiessen's *American Renaissance: Art and Expression in the Age of Emerson and Whitman* (London: Oxford, 1941) is now recognized as a landmark study in American literary criticism for its argument that a second flowering of American literature occurred during the transcendental period; Matthiessen places heavy emphasis on the "man in the open air" theme in the literature of Emerson, Thoreau, Melville, Whitman, and Hawthorne. Although Henry Nash Smith focuses on popular literature of the west in the 19th century in *Virgin Land: The American West as Symbol and Myth* (Cambridge: Harvard UP, 1950; rev. ed. 1970), other "myth-symbol" critics from American Studies such as R. W. B. Lewis in *The American Adam: Innocence, Tragedy, and Tradition in the Nineteenth Century* (Chicago: U of Chicago P, 1955) and Leslie Fiedler in *Love and Death in the American Novel* (New York: Dell, 1960) focus on such canonical figures as Hawthorne, Melville, and Twain to make the case that many important figures in American literary culture sought a pastoral refuge in the wilderness.

In a kind of self-reinforcing dynamics, works of criticism focusing on emerging canonical works, authors, and protagonists became "mainstream" secondary studies. A concomitant school of literary critics treated authors who, aside from Thoreau, were fading from an emergent literary canon. Norman Foerster's *Nature in American Literature: Studies in the Modern View* (New York: Macmillan, 1923) is actually a transitional work in this regard, because in addition to examining the writing of standard figures such as Emerson, Thoreau, and Whitman, it presents John Muir and John Burroughs as equally significant and influential. In my opinion, the best early study of the nonfiction natural history essay is by Philip Marshall Hicks, *The Development of the Natural History Essay in American Literature* (Philadelphia: U of Pennsylvania P, 1924). In surveying the tradition from colonial explorers and naturalists to Burroughs, Hicks formulates a compelling definition of the genre, including elements still cited today: "scientific observation, aesthetic appreciation of nature, the belief in the immanence of the creative principle in nature, and the feeling of compassion for the suffering of the lower orders" (28). Hicks may celebrate a few writers whose reputations were not enduring and neglect to discuss some crucial figures (such as Muir), but overall his evaluations still ring true today.

A series of studies followed, some employing the term "natural historian," others "naturist," and still others "nature writer"; their common denominator is their focus on (mostly) noncanonical male literary natural historians who wrote mainly nonfiction prose, from Alexander Wilson in the 18th century to John James Audubon in the 19th to Burroughs and Muir in the 20th. Henry Tracy in *American Naturists* (New York: Dutton, 1930) is among the earliest critics to place Mary Austin in this tradition and emphasize the importance of place to the genre; Herbert West's annotated bibliography, *The Nature Writers: A Guide to Richer Reading* (Brattleboro, VT: Stephen Daye, 1939), includes descriptions of what he considers the best 250 works, an indication of the genre's popularity even at this early stage. Donald Culross Peattie (*Green Laurels: The Lives and Achievements of the Great Naturalists* [New York: Simon & Schuster, 1936]), William and Mabel Smallwood (*Natural History and the American Mind* [New York: Columbia UP, 1941]), and William Beebe (*The Book of Nat-*

uralists: An Anthology of the Best Natural History [New York: Knopf, 1941]) all take similar approaches, placing the genre of the nonfiction natural history essay in the larger context of historical and cultural developments, the difference being that Peattie and Beebe use wider spatial and temporal lenses in their analyses. All agree on the demise of the field naturalist and generalist in the 19th century as the sciences became increasingly specialized and professional. This is also the theme—and lament—of *The Nature of Natural History* (New York: Scribner's, 1950) by Marston Bates, who observes that the word "naturalist" has "got rather into academic disrepute in recent years," is often confused with the term "nature lover," and suffers because science has a reputation for dispassionate, objective study (255–56).

Bates himself was a practicing natural historian, as were Aldo Leopold and Joseph Wood Krutch, who also wrote about the genre as well as within it. In *Round River: From the Journals of Aldo Leopold*, ed. Luna B. Leopold (New York: Oxford UP, 1953), Leopold argues for natural history as a hobby, defining the term as "a defiance of the contemporary" and a hobbyist as a "radical" member of a minority ("A Man's Leisure Time," 4). In "Natural History: The Forgotten Science" he equates modern natural history with ecology and criticizes the scientific profession for its narrow focus and specialization, ignoring interrelationships among organisms in the larger ecosystem. Krutch wrote what may still be the most succinct and compelling history of natural history in the "Prologue" to *Great American Nature Writing* (New York: Sloane, 1950), which he also edited. Pointing to the age-old pastoral impulse of preferring the country to the city, Krutch argues that a significant element in writers from Thoreau onward was an expressed desire for kinship with nonhuman creatures.

Another intellectual history of sweeping scope (though terminating in the 18th century) is Marjorie Hope Nicolson's *Mountain Gloom and Mountain Glory: The Development of the Aesthetics of the Infinite* (Ithaca: Cornell UP, 1959), a study of how and why attitudes toward mountains changed from fear and loathing to appreciation and worship. Her thesis debunks to some degree the myth that America was exceptional by showing that an intellectual revolution in attitudes toward wilderness first occurred in Europe.

Hans Huth in *Nature and the American: Three Centuries of Changing Attitudes* (Berkeley: U of California P, 1957) argues the contrary, drawing not only on literature but also on the visual arts to make the case that America was where the preservationist movement was first *legally* established. Much of his evidence was drawn from the American west, the subject of Earl Pomeroy's study *In Search of the Golden West: The Tourist in Western America* (New York: Knopf, 1957). Linking tourists' appreciation of the scenic splendors of the west with its eventual preservation through national parks and monuments, Pomeroy demonstrates how landscape aesthetics connect the tourist and the nature writer, and how even someone like John Muir, who denigrated tourists, recognized the need to court them in order to succeed at preserving wilderness.

Finally, of the many fine Ph.D. dissertations done both before and after 1960 on this subject, I will cite just one: Robert Bradford's "Journey into Nature: American Nature Writing, 1783–1860" (Syracuse University, 1957). I find this thesis invaluable for its taxonomy of the genre; Bradford identifies and discusses four common patterns—journey account, diary, calendar of the seasons, and analysis.

1960–1994

With the flowering of the environmental movement in the 1960s, studies of nature from a variety of disciplinary perspectives increased geometrically. For the sake of convenience, I classify them by discipline, citing interdisciplinary overlap where it occurs.

Anthologies

As more works of nature writing began to appear after 1960, it is no surprise that anthologies of nature writing were published with increasing frequency. Among the earliest were *The Wilderness Sampler*, edited by Jean Vermes (Harrisburg, PA: Stackpole, 1968); and *Voices for the Wilderness*, edited by William Schwartz (New York: Ballantine, 1969). For its interdisciplinary depth and wide coverage of genres (including fiction, poetry, and landscape art), John Conron's *The American Landscape: A Critical Anthology of Prose and Poetry* (New York: Oxford UP, 1974) is excellent, as is its editorial commentary. Selections are arranged in this way: "The first of thirteen sections focuses on contemporary landscapes of ruin; the last, on contemporary landscapes of harmony. The sections in between sketch the complex perspectives that have led to both" (xx). Another of the valuable earlier anthologies is *The Wilderness Reader*, edited by Frank Bergon (New York: New American Library, 1980). I find Bergon's selections of nonfiction prose from William Byrd through David Roberts compelling, and his introduction a succinct overview of the tradition. He defines nature writing as "literature of the American wilderness that blends feeling with informed observation" (2).

Several more anthologies appeared between 1987 and 1990. *Of Discovery and Destiny: An Anthology of American Writers and the American Land*, edited by Robert C. Baron and Elizabeth Darby Junkin (Golden, CO: Fulcrum, 1986), includes excerpts from fiction and nonfiction as well as poetry (though the collection suffers from arbitrary and vague classification labels). I find Ann Ronald's *Words for the Wild: The Sierra Club Trailside Reader* (San Francisco: Sierra Club, 1987) valuable for its introductory remarks to each selection and the first-person narratives of her own wilderness excursions; like Bergon's, her selections work well in the classroom. Stephen Trimble provides a useful survey of contemporary nature writing and insightful commentary by each author whose writings are excerpted, based on interviews with the editor in *Words from the Land: Encounters with Natural History Writing* (Salt Lake City: Peregrine Smith, 1988). Interviews with contemporary authors are also collected in Edward Lueders's *Writing Natural History: Dialogues with Authors* (Salt Lake City: U of Utah P, 1989); among the authors interviewed are Barry Lopez, Robert Finch, Terry Tempest Williams, and Gary Paul Nabhan.

The two largest anthologies to appear since Conron's in 1978 are Thomas J. Lyon's *This Incomperable Lande: A Book of American Nature Writing* (Boston: Houghton Mifflin, 1989) and Robert Finch and John Elder's *The Norton Book of Nature Writing* (New York: Norton, 1990). These use different strategies for anthologizing. Whereas Finch and Elder aim for inclusiveness, seeking to cover as many figures as possible with short excerpts, Lyon aims for greater depth by selecting longer pieces (all of Thoreau's "Walking" is included, for example, as well as excerpts from *Walden* and the Journal). Lyon's editorial apparatus—taxonomy, chronology, and 75-page historical overview—is superb, some of the wisest commentary yet written on the tradition.

Two anthologies that focus strictly on the literature of rivers are *River Reflections: A Collection of River Writings,* edited by Verne Huser (Chester, CT: Globe Pequot, 1985); and the more narrowly focused *A Republic of Rivers: Three Centuries of Nature Writing from Alaska and the Yukon* (New York: Oxford UP, 1990), edited by John A. Murray.

Murray is also editor of *American Nature Writing 1994* (San Francisco: Sierra Club, 1994), which is part of an annual series. Another collection of contemporary nature writing is *On Nature's Terms: Contemporary Voices,* edited by Thomas Lyon and Peter Stine (College Station: Texas A&M UP, 1992).

There are at least four anthologies devoted solely to nature poetry; the last three include contemporary poets only. Cort Conley edited *Gathered Waters: An Anthology of River Poems* (Cambridge, ID: Backeddy Books, 1985); Brian Swann and Peter Borrelli, *Poetry from the Amicus Journal* (Palo Alto: Tioga, 1990); Christopher Merrill, *The Forgotten Language: Contemporary Poets and Nature* (Salt Lake City: Peregrine Smith, 1991); and Robert Pack and Jay Parini, *Poems for a Small Planet: Contemporary American Nature Poetry* (Middlebury, VT: UP of New England, 1993).

Several anthologies with nature writing as the unifying focus have appeared as texts for teaching composition. These include *Being in the World: An Environmental Reader for Writers* (New York: Macmillan, 1993), edited by Scott Slovic and Terrell F. Dixon; *The Literature of Nature: The British and American Traditions,* edited by Robert Begiebing and Owen Grumbling (Medford, NJ: Plexus, 1993); *Reading the Environment* (New York: Norton, 1994), edited by Melissa Walker; *Writing Nature,* edited by Carolyn Ross (New York: St. Martin's, 1994); and *A Forest of Voices: Reading and Writing the Environment* (Mountain View, CA: Mayfield, 1995), edited by Chris Anderson and Lex Runciman.

The growing popularity of nature writing has been accompanied by a renascence of regionalism. Among anthologies that use nature writing to focus on a particular region are *A Place Apart: A Cape Cod Reader,* edited by Robert Finch (New York: Norton,

1990); *The Desert Reader,* edited by Peter Wild (Salt Lake City: Peregrine Smith, 1991); *From the Country: Writings About Rural Canada,* edited by Wayne Grady (Ontario: Camden House, 1991); *North Writers: A Strong Woods Collection,* edited by John Henricksson (Minneapolis: U of Minnesota P, 1991); *Late Harvest: Rural American Writing,* edited by David Pichaske (New York: Paragon House, 1991); *Inheriting the Land: Contemporary Voices from the Midwest,* edited by Mark Vinz and Thom Tammaro (Minneapolis: U of Minnesota P, 1993); and *Named in Stone and Sky: An Arizona Anthology,* edited by Gregory McNamee (Tucson: U of Arizona P, 1993).

I am aware of at least two anthologies that focus on specific animals: *The Great Bear: Contemporary Writings on the Grizzly,* edited by John Murray (Anchorage: Alaska Northwest Books, 1992); and *Counting Sheep: 20 Ways of Seeing Desert Bighorn,* edited by Gary Paul Nabhan (Tucson: U of Arizona P, 1993).

A number of journals have devoted entire issues to nature writing. Perhaps best known is the Autumn 1986 issue of *Antaeus,* edited by Daniel Halpern, which includes articles by many famous writers as well as editorial commentary by Thomas Lyon. (It was later republished as *On Nature: Nature, Landscape, and Natural History* [Berkeley: North Point Press, 1986].) The Spring 1991 issue (59.2) of *North Dakota Quarterly,* "Nature Writers/Writing," edited by Sherman Paul and Don Scheese, is unique in that it includes essays both of and about the genre. John Murray edited a special issue on nature writing of *Manoa: A Pacific Journal of International Writing* for Fall 1992. Both *The Ohio Review* (#49, 1993) and *The Georgia Review* (Spring 1993) have assembled special issues that include commentary on nature writing as well as original examples of the genre.

Some periodicals that regularly feature nature writing are *Orion Nature Quarterly, Sierra, Wilderness, Audubon, Backpacker,* and *Canoe & Kayak.*

Literary Criticism: 1960 to the Present

Here I concentrate on scholarship (mostly in book-length form) that approaches nature literature mainly from the perspective of the literary critic, as opposed to that of the historian, although the distinctions are not always clear-cut.

145

Let us begin with literary pastoralism, because some of the most ground-breaking scholarship has come from this approach. A seminal study is *The Machine in the Garden: Technology and the Pastoral Ideal in America* by Leo Marx (New York: Oxford UP, 1964). Considering "classic" works of American literature—by Thoreau, Hawthorne, Twain, Fitzgerald, Faulkner—Marx points to a pattern involving a confrontation between the protagonist and the "machine in the garden," i.e., some form of technology that disrupts the pastoral idyll. Marx continues his application of the pastoral theory in *The Pilot and the Passenger: Essays on Literature, Technology, and Culture in the United States* (New York: Oxford UP, 1988). He revises his theories somewhat in "Pastoralism in America," included in a collection of essays edited by Sacvan Bercovitch with Myra Jehlen, *Ideology and Classic American Literature* (Cambridge: Cambridge UP, 1986), offering the hope that "pastoralism might yet provide the basis for an effective political ideology" (66). In "American Pastoral Ideology Reappraised," *American Literary History* 1.1 (Spring 1989): 1–29, Lawrence Buell extends theories of pastoralism to include nonfiction nature writing by Mary Austin, Susan Cooper, and Aldo Leopold, as well as works by international writers such as Chinua Achebe. Buell argues that it is difficult to classify pastoral ideology as either conservative or liberal without locating texts within their historical frame. Glen Love also extends pastoral theories to works of nature writing not generally included in the canon of classic American literature with two articles in *Western American Literature:* "*Et in Arcadia Ego:* Pastoral Theory Meets Ecocriticism" (27.3 [Nov. 1992]: 195–207), and "Revaluing Nature: Toward an Ecological Criticism" (25.3 [Nov. 1990]: 201–15). The latter is a particularly important piece because many younger scholars have responded to his charge that the English profession has failed to acknowledge the contemporary "greening" of American culture. One response has been the formation of a new scholarly society, Association for the Study of Literature and the Environment (ASLE); founded in 1992, it now has more than 800 members.

Marx, following in the tradition of Henry Nash Smith and R. W. B. Lewis, represents an American studies approach to the subject of nature and American culture. Another "myth-symbol" study is Richard Slotkin's *Regeneration through Violence: The*

Mythology of the American Frontier, 1600–1860 (Middletown, CT: Wesleyan UP, 1973), which finds in the "classic" literature of the period a tendency for the protagonist to resolve tension between civilization and wilderness on the frontier through violent actions. Other important American studies works concerning literature and the environment include Wayne Franklin's *Discoverers, Explorers, Settlers: The Diligent Writers of Early America* (Chicago: U of Chicago P, 1977) and David Wilson's *In the Presence of Nature* (Amherst: U of Massachusetts P, 1978). Both focus on natural historians such as John and William Bartram as major contributors to American culture and the history of literature and the environment.

Natural history as a literary genre has received significant attention from nonliterary scholars and writers interested in the broader cultural implications of nature study. Alexander Adams surveys the entire tradition from Aristotle to the 20th century in *Eternal Quest: The Story of the Great Naturalists* (New York: Putnam, 1969), including the American natural historians Alexander Wilson and John James Audubon. Wayne Hanley's *Natural History in America: From Mark Catesby to Rachel Carson* (New York: Quadrangle/New York Times, 1977) is more an anthology than a critical study, containing long passages from various writers' works. I find most readable and thorough Joseph Kastner's *A Species of Eternity* (New York: Knopf, 1977), which discusses natural historians in America from Cadwallader Colden to Audubon; included are handsome color plates of natural history illustrations over the years. Kastner's focus is narrower, but his historical coverage is broader, in *A World of Watchers* (New York: Knopf, 1986): he provides an informal history of bird-watching from precontact Native American times to the present; again, color illustrations serve the textual treatment well. Also useful is Robert Elman's *First in the Field: America's Pioneering Naturalists* (New York: Mason/Charter, 1977) for its focus on the scientific contributions of Mark Catesby, the Bartrams, Wilson, Audubon, etc. Two works that consider natural history and its relation to the rise of cultural nationalism in America in the 19th century are Barbara Maria Stafford's *Voyage into Substance: Art, Science, Nature, and the Illustrated Travel Account, 1760–1840* (Cambridge: MIT P, 1984) and Charlotte Porter's *The Eagle's Nest: Natural History and American Ideas,*

1812–1842 (University: U of Alabama P, 1986). Good definitions of natural history and its role in the nature writing tradition are provided by John Hildebidle in *Thoreau: A Naturalist's Liberty* (Cambridge: Harvard UP, 1980) and by Robert Sattlemeyer's introduction to Henry David Thoreau's *The Natural History Essays* (Salt Lake City: Peregrine Smith, 1980). Thomas Dunlap charts the evolution of the genre in response to changing paradigms in the natural sciences in "Nature Literature and Modern Science," *Environmental History Review* 14.1–2 (Spring/Summer 1990): 33–44. In *Describing Early America: Bartram, Jefferson, Crèvecoeur, and the Rhetoric of Natural History* (DeKalb: Northern Illinois UP, 1992), Pamela Regis argues that these influential natural historians included humans as a natural species by resorting to the "manners and customs" account, but at times they also regressed to racism, placing blacks and Indians below "*Homo sapiens europaeus*" in the great chain of being.

Nature writing and literature of the frontier overlap in significant ways—both focus on a place where humans are generally absent or ignored, and both present a significant encounter with the wilderness. A number of important scholarly studies pursue these and other themes. *The Necessary Earth: Nature and Solitude in American Literature* (Austin: U of Texas P, 1964), by Wilson Clough, proposes that literature of the frontier, by relying on autobiographical experience, has a unique freshness and vitality. Edwin Fussell in *Frontier: American Literature and the American West* (Princeton: Princeton UP, 1965) makes a similar case for mainly "classic" literature. Lee Clark Mitchell's *Witnesses to a Vanishing America: The Nineteenth-Century Response* (Princeton: Princeton UP, 1981) records the widespread lament among American writers and artists on the frontier over the disappearance of "virgin" nature and American Indians. Paul Bryant's essay, "Nature Writing and the American Frontier," in *The Frontier Experience and the American Dream*, edited by David Mogen, Mark Busby, and Paul Bryant (College Station: Texas A & M UP, 1989), is vital for its point that the concept of the romantic sublime has persisted in nature writing of the west from the 19th into the 20th century. *Desert, Garden, Margin, Range: Literature on the American Frontier*, edited by Eric Heyne (New York: Twayne, 1992), includes essays on regional frontiers in the southwest and Canada. Critical essays on individual western nature writers as well as good overviews can be found in *A Literary History of the American West,* edited by Thomas J. Lyon (Fort Worth: Texas Christian UP, 1987).

The "greening" of literary studies and "ecocriticism" originated in the late 1970s. Sherman Paul's *Repossessing and Renewing: Essays in the Green American Tradition* (Baton Rouge: Louisiana State UP, 1976) studies an organic tradition that began with Emerson, flowered in Thoreau, and continued to bloom in 20th-century writers such as William Carlos Williams, Gary Snyder, and Alfred Kazin. Paul focuses on nature essayists— Thoreau, Leopold, Muir, Henry Beston, Loren Eiseley, Richard Nelson, and Barry Lopez—in his last work, *For Love of the World: Essays on Nature Writers* (Iowa City: U of Iowa P, 1992). William Rueckert's groundbreaking essay, "Literature and Ecology: An Experiment in Ecocriticism" (*Iowa Review* 9.1 [Winter 1970]: 71–85), calls for professors of literature to "resolve the fundamental paradox of this profession and get out of our heads" (85) and criticizes the academy for its overly refined literary theories and failure to deal with the larger biospheric community. Joseph Meeker in *The Comedy of Survival* (New York: Scribner's 1974) similarly urges critics to study literature from an ecological standpoint, using as case studies examples of classic literature. Cecilia Tichi points to early examples of an environmental reformist impulse in her study *New World, New Earth: Environmental Reform in American Literature from the Puritans through Whitman* (New Haven: Yale UP, 1979).

Since 1980 a number of excellent studies have appeared on nature writing, most on nonfiction. In *Speaking for Nature: How Literary Naturalists from Henry Thoreau to Rachel Carson Have Shaped America* (San Francisco: Sierra Club Books, 1980), Paul Brooks argues that the genre has been marked by authors seeking an "intimate acquaintance with one cherished spot on earth" (141) and fighting "against the heedless destruction of the landscape" (284). Combining studies of nature poets, an analysis of the philosophy of Alfred North Whitehead, and his own experiences in nature, John Elder sees Robinson Jeffers, A. R. Ammons, Gary Snyder, and others as continuing the Wordsworthian tradition of reinhabiting the land, in *Imagining the Earth: Poetry and the Vision of Nature* (Urbana: U of Illinois P, 1985). Alfred Kazin's *A Writer's America: Landscape in Literature* (New York: Knopf, 1988) begins with Jefferson's Monticello, concludes with Norman Mailer's *Of a Fire on the Moon,* and includes images of many famous landscape paintings and photographs. Frederick Turner also takes a place-centered approach in *Spirit of Place: The Making of an American Literary Landscape* (San Francisco: Sierra Club Books, 1989), going so far as to make literary pilgrimages to places made famous by American writers from Thoreau to Leslie Marmon Silko; Turner himself is living proof that these authors "allow people to participate emotionally in their place of living" (x). In *Nature Writing and America: Essays upon a Cultural Type* (Ames: Iowa State UP, 1990), Peter Fritzell offers extended close readings of *Walden, A Sand County Almanac,* and *Pilgrim at Tinker Creek* as well as a thorough history and taxonomy of nature writing. Scott Slovic in *Seeking Awareness in American Nature Writing: Henry Thoreau, Annie Dillard, Edward Abbey, Wendell Berry, Barry Lopez* (Salt Lake City: U of Utah P, 1992) makes a compelling case for these figures as "not merely, or even primarily, analysts of nature or appreciators of nature—rather, they are students of the human mind, literary psychologists" (3). *Pilgrims to the Wild: Everett Ruess, Henry David Thoreau, John Muir, Clarence King, Mary Austin* (Salt Lake City: U of Utah P, 1993) by John O'Grady interprets the subjects' secular pilgrimages into nature as forays into erotic space and as further examples of American spiritual autobiography. James McClintock in *Nature's Kindred Spirits: Aldo Leopold, Joseph Wood Krutch, Edward Abbey, Annie Dillard, and Gary Snyder* (Madison: U of Wisconsin P, 1994) argues that these writers have "integrated Thoreauvian Romanticism and twentieth-century ecological biology," and, through dramatic conversion experiences, their outlooks have been transformed "from modernist alienation characteristic of mainstream American literary intellectuals to affirmations based upon experiences in nature" (3, 17). Frank Stewart in *A Natural History of Nature Writing* (Washington, D.C.: Island Press, 1994) also sheds new light on the genre. He claims that "nature writers interpret and vivify their observations through aesthetic language. More important, they are mindful of the role that storytelling and dramatic narration play in our psychic and cultural well-being" (xix). Stewart also argues that nature writing reminds us that "nature is separate from us [humans] neither biologically nor culturally" (229). The book includes chapters on Gilbert White, Thoreau, Burroughs, Muir, Leopold, Carson, and Abbey. Finally, published too late to be fully absorbed into this study, Lawrence Buell's *The Environmental Imagination: Thoreau, Nature Writing, and the Formation of American Culture* (Cambridge: Harvard UP, 1995) should prove to be a landmark, not only in ecocriticism but in literary criticism in general, for its magisterial command of both the primary and the secondary literature. Buell may well gain the attention of mainstream contemporary theoreticians, a goal as yet unrealized by ecocriticism since its founding (or at least the coining of the term) in the 1970s.

The New York Times Book Review has from time to time offered good overviews of various aspects of nature writing. David Rains Wallace's "The Nature of Nature Writing" defines the genre as an "appreciative aesthetic responses to a scientific view of nature" (22 July 1984: 1). Paul Schullery surveys the evolution of the subgenre of nature writing produced by outdoor sportsmen in "Hope for the Hook and Bullet Press" (22 Sept. 1985: 1, 34–35). Frederick Turner traces the emergence of a literature of place back to Thoreau in "Literature Lost in the Thickets" (15 Feb. 1987: 1, 34–35). And Diane Ackerman offers a sampling of nature writers from Gilbert White to E. B. White in "Nature Writers: A Species unto Themselves" (13 May 1990: 1, 42).

Three anthologies of critical articles on nature writing— in addition to the issues of *Antaeus, North Dakota Quarterly,* and *Manoa* cited above under "Anthologies"—are *Teaching Environmental Literature: Materials, Methods, Resources,* edited by Frederick O. Waage (New York: Modern Language Association, 1985); "The Literature of Nature," a special issue of *The CEA Critic* 54.1 (Fall 1991); and *Earthly Words: Essays on Contemporary American Nature and Environmental Writers* (Ann Arbor: U of Michigan P, 1994), edited by John Cooley. Forthcoming in 1996 is *The Ecocriticism Reader: Landmarks in Literary Ecology,* edited by Harold Fromm and Cheryll Glotfelty (Athens: U of Georgia P).

A concise overview of the history of nature writing in America is Don Scheese's "Nature Writing: A Wilderness of Books," *Forest & Conservation History* 34.4 (Oct. 1990): 204–8. SueEllen Campbell connects ecocriticism and contemporary literary theory in "The Land and Language of Desire: Where Deep Ecology and Post-Structuralism Meet," *Western American Literature* 24.3 (Nov. 1989): 199–211. Michael Branch provides an informative treatment in "Ecocriticism: The Nature of Nature Writing in Literary Studies,"

Weber Studies 11.1 (Winter 1994): 41–55. Michael Kowalewski relates nature writing to the contemporary social phenomenon of bioregionalism in "Writing in Place: The New American Regionalism," *American Literary History* 6.1 (1994): 171–83.

The poststructuralist argument that everything, including the material world of the nonhuman environment, is a verbal and social construct is discussed in Neil Evernden's *The Social Creation of Nature* (Baltimore: Johns Hopkins UP, 1992) and in the collection *Reinventing Nature: Responses to Postmodern Deconstruction* (Washington, D.C.: Island Press, 1995), edited by Michael E. Soulé and Gary Lease. Bill McKibben in *The End of Nature* (New York: Random House, 1989) makes the compelling argument that we are now living in a "postnatural" world because of the harms resulting from greenhouse gases and ozone depletion; in changing the weather, he claims, we have altered nature in fundamental and irrevocable ways. Ronald Bailey disputes the claims of McKibben and other environmentalists in *Eco-Scam: The False Prophets of Ecological Apocalypse* (New York: St. Martin's, 1993).

Scribner's is coming out in 1996 with a two-volume reference work entitled *American Nature Writers*, edited by John Elder. It will contain more than 70 essays on individual nature writers and related topics. Other forthcoming reference works that will include essays on themes and figures in nature writing are *American Environmentalists: A Selective Biographical Encyclopedia, 1850–1990*, edited by Richard Harmond and George Cevasco (New York: Scarecrow), and the *Garland Encyclopedia on Literature and the Environment*, edited by Patrick Murphy.

Two journals that regularly feature critical articles on nature writing are *Western American Literature* and *ISLE* (*Interdisciplinary Studies in Literature and the Environment*). A new journal that will "explore how environmental issues are at the focus of general cultural debate" invites "essays, reportage on environmental disasters and solutions, fiction, poetry, art, and all forms of reflection on the human relationship to nature": *Terra Nova*, edited by David Rothenberg and published by the Press of the Massachusetts Institute of Technology.

Environmental History

Ecocritics and environmental historians both operate under two basic assumptions: that humans are part of, not separate from, the nonhuman world; and that humans are only a part, albeit an important part, of the much larger story of Earth's history. The following are important discussions of the meaning and practice of environmental history, a field which recently developed out of the environmental crises of the 1970s and which is an outgrowth of another field, historical geography: Roderick Nash, "American Environmental History: A New Teaching Frontier," *Pacific Historical Review* 41.3 (August 1972): 362–72; Richard White, "American Environmental History: The Development of a New Historical Field," *Pacific Historical Review* 54.3 (August 1985): 297–335; "A Round Table: Environmental History," special issue of *Journal of American History* 76.4 (March 1990); William Cronon, "A Place for Stories: Nature, History, and Narrative," *Journal of American History* 78.4 (March 1992): 1347–76; and William Cronon, "The Uses of Environmental History," *Environmental History Review* 17.3 (Fall 1993): 1–22.

I restrict my discussion of environmental history to works in which nature writers figure. For purposes of discussion I divide environmental history into exploration history, intellectual history, conservation history, and period studies.

William Goetzmann in *Exploration and Empire: The Explorer and the Scientist in the Winning of the West* (New York: Norton, 1962) includes such writers as John Wesley Powell in his argument that government-sponsored explorers were important cultural heroes in the 19th century. Howard Mumford Jones in *O Strange New World* (New York: Viking, 1964) makes the point that explorers in the colonial period fashioned important myths in American culture—e.g., the myth of the "new world"—which have been of lasting influence. Peter Matthiessen's *Wildlife in America* (New York: Viking, 1959; rev. ed., 1987) is a classic study of how early nature writers such as Audubon and Catlin left us an invaluable catalog of animal species, significant numbers of which have become extinct. Frederick Turner offers a compelling explanation of the alienation of Euramerican civilization from nature on its "discovery" of the New World in *Beyond Geography: The Western Spirit against the Wilderness* (New York: Viking, 1980). *Desert Passages: Encounters with the American Deserts* by Patricia Limerick (Albuquerque: U of New Mexico P, 1985) analyzes the writings of more genteel explorers in the 19th and 20th centuries to demonstrate the significance of deserts in American history.

Intellectual historians have traced the evolution of such concepts as nature and the wilderness by examining nature writing.
Arthur Ekirch, Jr., in *Man and Nature in America* (New York:
Columbia UP, 1963) charts an America increasingly at odds with
the wilderness as it moves away from Jeffersonian and transcendental ideals into the 20th century. Two seminal studies
appeared in 1967: Paul Shepard's *Man in the Landscape: A Historic
View of the Esthetics of Nature* (New York: Knopf, 1967; rev. ed.,
1991, Texas A & M UP), and Roderick Nash's *Wilderness and the
American Mind* (New Haven: Yale UP, 1967; 3d rev. ed., 1982).
Shepard goes back to classic Greece and Rome to show how such
images as the garden and virgin nature have evolved and been
reenvisioned to apply to the American west. Nash focuses on key
figures (including Thoreau, Muir, and Leopold) to argue convincingly that wilderness has long been a key force in defining
America as a nation; his work remains a landmark. Nash has followed up with *The Rights of Nature: A History of Environmental
Ethics* (New Haven: Yale UP, 1989), in which he claims, "If the
abolition of slavery marked the limits of American liberalism in
the nineteenth century, perhaps biocentrism and environmental
ethics are at the cutting edge of liberal thought in the late twenti-
eth" (200). To provide another perspective on the intellectual history of the environment, Nash has edited a collection entitled
American Environmentalism: Readings in Conservation History (New
York: McGraw-Hill, 1990), which includes some nature writing.

Another important study is *Nature's Economy: A History of
Ecological Ideas* (San Francisco: Sierra Club Books, 1977) by
Donald Worster, who sees ecology as having separated into two
contrasting strains: an "arcadian" vision, represented by Gilbert
White, emphasizing harmony and benevolence in nature; and an
"imperial" vision, represented by Francis Bacon, with nature as a
machine to be dominated by humans. Worster provides analyses
of White, Thoreau, Darwin, and Leopold, and argues that their
arcadian views lost out to the Baconian concept by the 20th century. Worster turns his attention to the American west in two
more recent books, both collections of essays: *Under Western
Skies: Nature and History in the American West* (New York: Oxford
UP, 1992) and *The Wealth of Nature: Environmental History and the
Ecological Imagination* (New York: Oxford UP, 1993). David Shi in
The Simple Life: Plain Living and High Thinking in American Culture

(New York: Oxford UP, 1985) relates the title concept to certain nature writers like Thoreau, Muir, and Leopold, showing how important voluntary simplicity has been to many intellectuals in this country. Max Oelschlaeger extends Roderick Nash's analysis to the paleolithic, medieval, and modern periods to demonstrate the diverse heritage of wilderness in *The Idea of Wilderness: From Prehistory to the Age of Ecology* (New Haven: Yale UP, 1991). Finally, potentially revolutionary nomenclature was popularized by *Deep Ecology: Living As If Nature Mattered* (Salt Lake City: Peregrine Smith, 1985) by Bill Devall and George Sessions. "Deep," as opposed to "shallow," ecology calls for "cultivating an ecological consciousness" (8); a key example is Muir, who lived out a nonanthropocentric philosophy. Devall and Sessions praise Gary Snyder as a 20th-century "dweller" in the tradition of the German philosopher Martin Heidegger, "taking care of and creating that space within which something comes into its own and flourishes" (98). Sessions also provides a good overview in "The Deep Ecology Movement: A Review," *Environmental Ethics* 8.2 (Summer 1987): 105–25.

By "conservation history" I mean studies that focus on some aspect of public lands: our national parks, forests, and wilderness areas. Nature writers have played important roles in shaping conservation history, as many scholars have demonstrated. John Muir, as president of the Sierra Club, was influential in shaping preservation politics at the turn of the century, and his role is analyzed in *National Parks: The American Experience* (Lincoln: U of Nebraska P, 2d ed., 1987) and *Yosemite: The Embattled Wilderness* (Lincoln: U of Nebraska P, 1990), both by Alfred Runte, as well as in *Westward in Eden: The Public Lands and the Conservation Movement* by William K. Wyant (Berkeley: U of California P, 1982). Several works devote chapters to various nature writers who the authors feel contributed substantially to the movement: *Pioneer Conservationists of Western America* (Missoula, MT: Mountain Press, 1979) and *Pioneer Conservationists of Eastern America* (Missoula, MT: Mountain Press, 1987), both by Peter Wild; *Wilderness Visionaries* (Merrilville, IN: ICS Books, 1985) by Jim Dale Vickery; and *Dreamers and Defenders: American Conservationists* (Lincoln: U of Nebraska P, 1988) by Douglas H. Strong. In *Endangered Rivers and the Conservation Movement* (Berkeley: U of California P, 1986), Tim Palmer argues that Leopold's concept of a land ethic was instrumental in securing protection of American rivers. John F. Reiger in *American Sportsmen and the Origins of Conservation* (Norman: U of Oklahoma P, 1985) argues that it was outdoor sportsmen such as George Bird Grinnell who were most instrumental in the genesis of the conservation movement at the turn of the century, and that it was concern over animals rather than forests that led to conservation legislation. I reserve for last my favorite work in this category: *Mountains without Handrails: Reflections on the National Parks* by Joseph L. Sax (Ann Arbor: U of Michigan P, 1980), in which the author articulates a vision of the national parks by frequently drawing on the writings of nature writers such as Thoreau and Muir.

The late 1800s and early 1900s and the post–1960s era were important periods in environmental history. Peter J. Schmitt in *Back to Nature: The Arcadian Myth in Urban America* (1969; Baltimore: John Hopkins UP, 1990) analyzes the "back to nature" cult at the turn of the century as it manifested itself in the proliferation of nature writing (for both adults and children), the growth of nature study in educational curricula, the emergence of the suburbs, and the appearance of numerous outdoor and conservation organizations. Stephen Fox focuses on Muir in *The American Conservation Movement: John Muir and His Legacy* (Madison: U of Wisconsin P, 1981) and traces his influence to contemporary America. Lisa Mighetto in "Science, Sentiment, and Anxiety: American Nature Writing at the Turn of the Century," *Pacific Historical Review* 54.1 (Feb. 1985): 33–50, claims that Muir, Ernest T. Seton, and John Burroughs, among others, offered a benevolent view of nature to counter the Darwinian and mechanical views held by scientists. Sometimes writers like Seton exaggerated the benevolence of nature to such a degree that they were derided by their own colleagues, as Ralph Lutts shows in *The Nature Fakers: Wildlife, Science, and Sentiment* (Golden, CO: Fulcrum, 1990). Both positive and negative assessments of the post–1960s environmental movement are offered in a number of recent works: Christopher Manes's *Green Rage: Radical Environmentalism and the Unmaking of Civilization* (Boston: Little, Brown, 1990); Kirkpatrick Sale's *The Green Revolution: The American Environmental Movement* (New York: Hill and Wang, 1993); and Martin W. Lewis's *Green Delusions: An Environmental*

Critique of Radical Environmentalism (Durham, NC: Duke UP, 1992).

Two journals that regularly feature articles on nature writers' roles in the history of the environment include *Environmental History Review* and *Forest & Conservation History;* an excellent essay on the problem of defining such terms as "natural" can be found in a recent issue of the latter: Kristin S. Shrader-Frechette and Earl D. McCoy, "Natural Landscapes, Natural Communities, and Natural Ecosystems" 39.3 (July 1995): 138–42.

Ecofeminism

"Ecofeminism," according to Irene Diamond and Gloria Femen Orenstein in their introduction to *Reweaving the World: The Emergence of Ecofeminism* (San Francisco: Sierra Club Books, 1990), "is a term that some use to describe both the diverse range of women's efforts to save the Earth and the transformations of feminism in the West that have resulted from the new view of women and nature" (ix). "Ecofeminism's basic premise," according to Greta Gaard in the opening essay of the collection she edited entitled *Ecofeminism: Women, Animals, Nature* (Philadelphia: Temple UP, 1993), "is that the ideology which authorizes oppressions such as those based on race, class, gender, sexuality, physical abilities, and species is the same ideology which sanctions the oppression of nature" (1). I have found these two anthologies the most helpful in coming to an understanding of this philosophy and movement, which dates from the 1970s and is a result of the dovetailing of the environmental and feminist movements.

Annette Kolodny has written two significant works in this field: *The Lay of the Land: Metaphor as Experience and History in American Life and Letters* (Chapel Hill: U of North Carolina P, 1975) and *The Land Before Her: Fantasy and Experience of the American Frontiers, 1630–1860* (Chapel Hill: U of North Carolina P, 1984). In the first, Kolodny examines the writings of classic male American authors to show how deeply the myth of "the land as woman" has become embedded in our culture, and its harmful environmental consequences. In the second work she analyzes pioneer women's writings and concludes: "Massive exploitation and alteration of the continent do not seem to have been part of women's fantasies. They dreamed, more modestly, of locating a home and a familial human community within a cultivated garden" (xiii).

Another important early work of ecofeminism is Susan Griffin's *Woman and Nature: The Roaring Inside Her* (New York: Harper & Row, 1978). Griffin contrasts the "unnatural" patriarchal view of nature as abstract, egotistical, reductionist, and ultimately alienating with the "natural" view (held by women) of nature as nurturing, holistic, and biocentric. Carolyn Merchant in *The Death of Nature: Women, Ecology, and the Scientific Revolution* (San Francisco: Harper & Row, 1980) examines the scientific revolution of the 1700s and finds that it replaced the view of nature as woman with the metaphor of nature as machine. The nature writer Anne LaBastille provides sketches of women who have been pioneers in outdoor recreation and education in *Women and Wilderness* (San Francisco: Sierra Club Books, 1980). And with the excellent recent study *Made from This Earth: American Women and Nature* (Chapel Hill: U of North Carolina P, 1993), Vera Norwood has written the ecofeminist counterpart to Roderick Nash's *Wilderness and the American Mind.* Relying on various kinds of evidence, Norwood ably demonstrates that women contributed to American culture in significant ways as scientific illustrators, nature writers, gardeners, landscape designers, field scientists, and philosophers.

Not surprisingly, with the emergence of ecofeminism as a movement and a philosophy came anthologies devoted to women and nature. Three that provide wide coverage are *Sisters of the Earth: Women's Prose and Poetry about Nature* (New York: Vintage, 1991), edited by Lorraine Anderson; *Women in the Field: America's Pioneering Women Naturalists* (College Station: Texas A & M UP, 1991), edited by Marcia Bonta; and *Celebrating the Land: Women's Nature Writings, 1850–1991* (Flagstaff, AZ: Northland Publishing, 1992), edited by Karen Knowles. A special issue of *Environmental History Review* (8.1 [Spring 1984]) is devoted to "Women and Environmental History."

Ethnohistory and Ethnocriticism

Traditionally, nature writing has been an activity of white middle- and upper-class Anglo-Americans. Only relatively recently have scholars begun to consider writing by nonwhites. Ethnohistorians have illustrated the way Native Americans have been depicted by Euramericans and the roles they have played in environmental history. Two seminal studies are by Roy Harvey Pearce, *Savagism and Civilization: A Study of the Indian and the American Mind* (Berkeley: U of California P, rev. ed., 1988); and Robert Berkhofer, *The White Man's Indian: Images of the American Indian from Columbus to the Present* (New York: Knopf, 1978). William Cronon lucidly demonstrates how Indians in the northeast manipulated natural environments to their benefit in *Changes in the Land: Indians, Colonists, and the Ecology of New England* (New York: Hill & Wang, 1983). A good overview of this interaction is Richard White's "Native Americans and the Environment," in *Scholars and the Indian Experience: Reviews of Recent Writing in the Social Sciences,* edited by W. R. Swagerty (Bloomington: Indiana UP, 1984). White maintains that because of deliberate land-use practices by aboriginal peoples, the term "wilderness" is meaningless for much of North America. Calvin Martin has stimulated much debate by questioning the degree to which Indians were practicing ecologists; see "The American Indian as Miscast Ecologist," *The History Teacher* 14 (Feb. 1981), and *Keepers of the Game: Indian-Animal Relationships and the Fur Trade* (Berkeley: U of California P, 1978). More positive assessments are those by Rennard Strickland, "The Idea of Environment and the Ideal of the Indian," *Journal of American Indian Education* 10 (Oct. 1970); and by J. Donald Hughes, whose *American Indian Ecology* (El Paso: Texas Western UP, 1983) is a good survey of various tribes' environmental ethics. A special issue of *Environmental History Review* (9.2 [Summer 1985]) is devoted to "American Indian Environmental History." See also two essays by J. Baird Callicott in his collection *In Defense of the Land Ethic: Essays in Environmental Philosophy* (Albany: SUNY P, 1989): "Traditional American Indian and Western European Attitudes toward Nature: An Overview" (177–201) and "American Indian Land Wisdom? Sorting Out the Issues" (203–19). A concise summary of American Indians' land-use practices and history of the myth of the Indian as "noble ecologist" is Samuel M. Wilson's "'That Unmanned Wild Countrey,' " *Natural History* (May 1992): 16–17.

Arnold Krupat has done a fine job of seeing Native American writing from the Indian point of view in a series of books; see, for example, *Ethnocriticism* (Berkeley: U of California P, 1988). Robert Sayre studies Thoreau in the context of 19th-century Anglo-American savagism in *Thoreau and the American Indians* (Princeton: Princeton UP, 1977). But we are only on the threshold of interpreting Native American literature as nature writing. A good start has come in Lee Schweninger, "Writing Nature: Silko and Native Americans as Nature Writers," *MELUS* 18.2 (Summer 1993): 47–60. An important essay by a Native American writer is Leslie Silko's "Landscape, History, and the Pueblo Imagination," *Antaeus* 57 (Autumn 1986): 83–94. The anthropologist Keith Basso provides insight into a specific southwestern tribe's relationship with nature in "'Stalking with Stories': Names, Places, and Moral Narratives among the Western Apache," *Antaeus* 57 (Autumn 1986): 95–116. And for an illuminating view of a subarctic tribe, see the anthropologist and nature writer Richard Nelson's *Make Prayers to the Raven: A Koyukon View of the Northern Forest* (Chicago: U of Chicago P, 1983).

Anthologies of Native American writing with an emphasis on environmental themes include *Mother Earth Spirituality: Native American Paths to Healing Ourselves and Our World*, Ed Eagle Man McGaa (New York: HarperCollins, 1990); *Sacred Earth: The Spiritual Landscape of Native America*, Arthur Versluis (Rochester, VT: Inner Traditions International, 1991); *Profiles in Wisdom: Native Elders Speak about the Earth*, Steven McFadden (Sante Fe: Bear and Co., 1991); *Wisdom of the Elders: Honoring Sacred Native Visions of Nature*, David Knudson and Peter Suzuki (New York: Bantam, 1992); and *Story Earth: Native Voices on the Environment* (San Francisco: Mercury House, 1993).

Little scholarship exists on the relationship between other minority groups and the natural environment. See Melvin Dixon, *Ride Out the Wilderness: Geography and Identity in Afro-American Literature* (Urbana: U of Illinois P, 1987), for an analysis of the role of nature in the writings of, among others, Zora Neale Hurston, Alice Walker, and Toni Morrison. The presence of the nonhuman world is powerful in the Chicano author Rudolfo Anaya's *Bless Me, Ultima*, a source of much commentary by critics; see, for example, the author's own reflection, "An American Chicano in King Arthur's Court," in *The Frontier Experience and the American Dream: Essays on American Literature*, edited by David

Mogen, Mark Busby, and Paul Bryant (College Station: Texas A & M UP, 1989), 180–85. A wide-ranging, integrative approach to the nonhuman realm in the literature of American ethnic groups is desperately needed.

Art History

As I have tried to show in the present study, nature writers and visual artists have emerged from the same cultural matrix over the years. Some studies by art historians that I have found helpful in my analysis include James Thomas Flexner's *History of American Painting, Vol. 3: That Wilder Image* (Toronto: General Publishing, 1962), the first book-length work to make the case for a vital landscape painting tradition in America that began in the 19th century; *America as Art* by Joshua Taylor (New York: Harper & Row, 1976), who makes a similar case in several chapters and extends his analysis to frontier painting of the west; and the seminal study *Nature and Culture: American Landscape and Painting, 1825–1875* by Barbara Novak (New York: Oxford UP, 1980), which links Emersonian transcendentalism and the Hudson River school in a search for God in nature. The exhibition catalog *American Paradise: The World of the Hudson River School* (New York: The Metropolitan Museum of Art, 1988) is the finest collection of images and articles on this famous movement in American landscape painting.

The conventional wisdom that Cole and his descendants painted mainly for artistic and religious reasons has been questioned in recent studies. New perspectives on the connections between verbal and visual arts include David Miller's argument that American artists turned to previously neglected landscapes for spiritual renewal, in *Dark Eden: The Swamp in Nineteenth-Century American Culture* (Cambridge: Cambridge UP, 1989). John Sears uses both paintings and photographs to track the emergence of American tourist attractions in *Sacred Places: American Tourist Attractions in the Nineteenth Century* (New York: Oxford UP, 1989). Elizabeth McKinsey considers writers and artists who celebrate the grandest of American sacred places in *Niagara Falls: Icon of the American Sublime* (Cambridge: Cambridge UP, 1985). In a study that applies as well to nature writers who climbed mountains, Albert Boime in *The Magisterial Gaze:*

Manifest Destiny and American Landscape Painting, c. 1830–1865 (Washington, D.C.: Smithsonian Institution Press, 1991) demonstrates that landscape painters with their topographical perspectives were sometimes unwitting champions of the westward movement and the conquest of nature. Angela Miller links landscape art and a program of cultural nationalism in *The Empire of the Eye: Landscape Representation and American Cultural Politics, 1825–1875* (Ithaca: Cornell UP, 1993). And in "Everywhere and Nowhere: The Making of the National Landscape," *American Literary History* 4 (Summer 1992): 207–29, Miller contends that landscape art was "invented" in the pre–Civil War period to serve the ideology of a unified America.

Geography

To my knowledge, more than a few geographers have contributed to the study of nature writing. I consider George Perkins Marsh's 19th-century classic *Man and Nature* (1864; New York: Scribner's, 1965) to be a work of historical geography that considers the worldwide impact of humans on their environments over thousands of years. A 20th-century follow-up to Marsh's work is the collection edited by William Thomas, *Man's Role in Changing the Face of the Earth* (Chicago: U of Chicago P, 1956). Among the contributors is Carol O. Sauer, author of *Sixteenth Century North America: The Land and Its Peoples As Seen by the Europeans* (Berkeley: U of California P, 1971), who complicates the notion of Indians as nomadic hunters by demonstrating that many tribes in the southwest were intensive agriculturalists. A monumental study by Clarence Glacken, *Traces on the Rhodian Shore: Nature and Culture in Western Thought from Ancient Times to the End of the Eighteenth Century* (Berkeley: U of California P, 1967), seeks to answer three questions in discussing the interaction between western cultures and nature from ancient Greece to the 18th century: Is Earth a purposeful creation? How has the natural environment influenced human culture? How has human culture changed the nonhuman environment?

More recently, J. B. Jackson has demonstrated how interesting the "common" landscape can be, in *Discovering the Vernacular Landscape* (New Haven: Yale UP, 1984). I have found his definition of landscape—"not a natural feature of the environment but a *synthetic* space, a man-made system of spaces superimposed on the face of the land" (8)—essential in revising my own notions of "wilderness" over the years. See also his *A Sense of Place, a Sense of Time* (New Haven: Yale UP, 1994) for more recent essays in this tradition. And Yi-Fu Tuan's *Topophilia: A Study of Environmental Perception, Attitudes, and Values* (Englewood, NJ: Prentice Hall, 1974) ties in well with the study of nature writing; one definition of "topophilia" is "the feeling one has toward a place because it is home, the locus of memories, and the means of gaining a livelihood" (93).

Religious Studies and Philosophy

A good bridge between geography and religion is provided by Linda Graber, who in *Wilderness as Sacred Space* (Washington, D.C.: Association of American Geographers, 1976) maintains that the wilderness preservationist movement has been motivated largely by religious impulses. The seminal essay on the much-debated relationship between western Christian culture and the nonhuman world is by Lynn White, "The Historical Roots of Our Ecologic Crisis," *Science* 155 (1967): 1203–7.

A number of works in the field of religious studies have been helpful to me in linking nature writing to such religious concepts as "pilgrimage" and "sacred place." An early study is George H. William's *Wilderness and Paradise in Christian Thought* (New York: Harper, 1962). Belden Lane in *Landscapes of the Sacred: Geography and Narrative in American Spirituality* (New York: Paulist Press, 1988) combines first-person narratives of pilgrimages to sacred natural places with studies of the Puritans, Edward Abbey, and the Shakers, among others; one of his most compelling points is that "Landscape is first of all an effort of the imagination. . . . Landscape is never simply something 'out there.' . . . The very choice and framing of the scene is itself a construction of the imagination. Landscape is always an expectation which is brought to the environment, an interpretive lens placed over an otherwise dull, placeless void" (103). Thomas Berry integrates the Judeo-Christian tradition, the religions of Native Americans, and "new age" spirituality in a cogent analysis of the environmental crisis in *The Dream of the Earth* (San Francisco: Sierra Club Books, 1988). Catherine Albanese furnishes a historical overview in

Nature Religion in America: From the Algonkian Indians to the New Age (Chicago: U of Chicago P, 1990), discussing nature writers such as Thoreau, Muir, and Dillard. Douglas Burton-Christie surveys contemporary nature writing from a religious studies perspective in "'A Feeling for the Natural World': Spirituality and Contemporary Nature Writing," *Continuum* 2.1 (Feb. 1992): 229–52; he argues that nature writers both seek and promote a feeling for the natural world in order to witness the "shimmering presence of the transcendent" (230). A worldwide survey of religious views is offered in *Spirit and Nature: Why the Earth Is a Religious Issue,* edited by Steven C. Rockefeller and John Elder (Boston: Beacon, 1992); and *Ecotheology: Voices from North and South,* edited by David G. Hallman (New York: Orbis Books, 1994).

A related field is environmental ethics. Some often-cited book-length studies are Christopher Stone, *Should Trees Have Standing? Toward Legal Rights for Natural Objects* (Los Altos: William Kaufmann, 1974); John Passmore, *Man's Responsibility for Nature: Ecological Problems and Western Traditions* (New York: Scribner's, 1974); Peter Singer, *Animal Liberation: A New Ethics for Our Treatment of Animals* (New York: NY Review, 1975); Tom Regan, *The Case for Animal Rights* (Berkeley: U of California P, 1985); J. Baird Callicott, *In Defense of the Land Ethic: Essays in Environmental Philosophy* (Albany: SUNY P, 1989); Paul W. Taylor, *Respect for Nature: A Theory of Environmental Ethics* (Princeton: Princeton UP, 1986); and David Rothenberg, *Hand's End: Technology and the Limits of Nature* (Berkeley: U of California P, 1993). The journal *Environmental Ethics* has excellent articles on this topic.

Psychology

I divide psychologists' treatment of the relationship between humans and the nonhuman world into the study of perceptions of place and the study of nature as psychological refuge. In the first category, some of the more important treatments are T. R. Herzog, "A Cognitive Analysis of Preference for Natural Environments: Mountains, Canyons, and Deserts," *Landscape Journal* 6 (1987): 140–52; R. Kaplan and S. Kaplan, *The Experience of Nature: A Psychological Perspective* (New York: Cambridge UP, 1989); and Tony Hiss, *The Experience of Place* (New York: Knopf,

1990). A seminal argument on landscape preferences is the chapter "The Right Place," in E. O. Wilson's *Biophilia* (Cambridge: Harvard UP, 1984). The second category has spawned a new field, "ecopsychology." See Theodore Roszak, *The Voice of the Earth* (New York: Simon & Schuster, 1992); and *Ecopsychology: Restoring the Earth, Healing the Mind,* edited by Theodore Roszak, Mary E. Gomes, and Alan D. Kanner (San Francisco: Sierra Club Books, 1995). For a first-person perspective on this emergent form of therapy, see *"See My Name Is Chellis and I'm in Recovery from Western Civilization"* (Boston: Shambhala, 1995).

British Studies

Although this study is shamelessly American-centered, I would like to mention a few works by and about British writers that have helped me to comprehend transatlantic influences in the history of nature writing. I owe a large debt to William Empson's *Some Versions of the Pastoral* (London: Chatto & Windus, 1935) for the theory that the pastoral is a process of simplifying the complex. Frank Kermode provides a good introduction in *English Pastoral Poetry: From the Beginnings to Marvell* (1952; New York: Norton, 1972). Raymond Williams traces (mostly) English attitudes toward nature from the time of Virgil to the 20th century in his seminal work *The Country and the City* (New York: Oxford UP, 1973). Keith Thomas's *Man and the Natural World: A History of the Modern Sensibility* (New York: Pantheon, 1983) is a readable and insightful survey from 1500 to 1800. Another study in this same mode is Simon Schama's *Landscape and Memory* (New York: Knopf, 1995), which includes a discussion of non-English-speaking peoples' attitudes (including those of the French and the Germans) toward mountains, forests, and waters; the book is wonderfully illustrated, with images ranging from medieval woodcuts to 19th-century landscape paintings to contemporary photography. A recent work focusing on the British romantic poets that provides insight into the practice of ecocriticism and offers a sharp critique of contemporary literary theory for its exclusion of nature is Karl Kroeber's *Ecological Literary Criticism: Romantic Imagining and the Biology of Mind* (New York: Columbia UP, 1994). Finally, I find Jonathan Bate's *Romantic Ecology:*

Wordsworth and the Environmental Tradition (London: Routledge, 1991) immensely helpful in formulating a theory of and justification for ecocriticism. In response to poststructuralists and deconstructionists, he states: "It is profoundly unhelpful to say *'There is no nature'* at a time when our most urgent need is to address and redress the consequences of human civilization's insatiable desire to consume the products of the earth. We are confronted for the first time in history with the possibility of there being no part of the earth left untouched by man. . . . There is a difference not merely in degree but in kind between local changes to the surface configuration of the land and the profound transformations of the economy of nature that take place when the land is rendered radioactive or the ozone layer is depleted. When there have been a few more accidents at nuclear power stations, when there are no more rainforests, and when every wilderness has been ravaged for its mineral resources, then let us say *'There is no nature'*" (56). Although Bate is in error when he claims that nature will no longer exist after a catastrophically self-destructive action by humans—it is hubris to think that the nonhuman world will not continue without a human presence—I praise his work and find it a cogent counterresponse to the anthropocentric excesses of poststructuralist literary theory.

This bibliographical essay would be incomplete without mention of a work that sharply criticizes the failure of academics to carry ecological thinking beyond the walls of the classroom. See *Ecological Literacy: Education and the Transition to a Postmodern World* by David Orr (Albany: SUNY P, 1992), particularly for its call for interdisciplinary study of the environment, its syllabus for ecological literacy, and its emphasis on the necessity of fieldwork and experiential outdoor education.

Recommended Titles

I have read the following works over a period of about 20 years, from 1976 to 1995. The list I have compiled is certainly not exhaustive, although I have tried to include every "classic" work as well as some undeservedly neglected or obscure works. The list includes fiction and poetry but consists mainly of nonfiction. Annotations are provided for key works, neglected works, and works whose titles do not reveal the author's territory or purpose.

I must acknowledge a great debt to Tom Lyon, who blazed a long and careful trail with his annotated bibliography in *This Incomperable Lande: A Book of American Nature Writing* (Boston: Houghton Mifflin, 1989). *The Norton Anthology of Nature Writing,* edited by Robert Finch and John Elder (New York: Norton, 1990), is useful for its wide range of mostly nonfiction selections. Other good bibliographies of primary works can be found in Frederick Waage, ed., *Teaching Environmental Literature* (New York: Modern Language Association, 1985); and Daniel Halpern, ed., *On Nature: Nature, Landscape, and Natural History* (Berkeley: North Point Press, 1986).

Abbey, Edward. *Abbey's Road.* New York: Dutton, 1979.

———. *Appalachian Wilderness.* New York: Dutton, 1970.

———. *Beyond the Wall: Essays from the Outside.* New York: Holt, Rhinehart and Winston, 1984.

————. *Black Sun.* New York: Harold Matson Co., 1971. A novel about the romance of a fire lookout.

————. *The Brave Cowboy.* New York: Harold Matson Co., 1956. A novel about a 20th-century cowboy who flees the law.

————. *Cactus Country.* New York: Time-Life, 1973.

————. *Confessions of a Barbarian: Selections from the Journals of Edward Abbey, 1951–1989.* Boston: Little, Brown, and Company, 1994.

————. *Desert Solitaire.* New York: McGraw-Hill, 1968. The nonfiction work that launched radical environmentalism.

————. *Down the River.* New York: Dutton, 1982

————. *Fire on the Mountain.* New York: Harold Matson Co. 1962. A novel about a rancher trying to save his property from being taken over by the federal government.

————. *The Fool's Progress.* New York: Henry Holt, 1988. Autobiographical fiction tracing the protagonist's cross-country journey by pickup back to his home in Pennsylvania.

————. *Good News.* New York: Dutton, 1980. Orwellian eco-fiction depicting a struggle between a military dictatorship in the desert and eco-raiders who fight for democracy and wilderness.

————. *Hayduke Lives!* Boston: Little, Brown, 1990. Sequel to *The Monkey Wrench Gang.*

————. *The Hidden Canyon.* New York: Penguin, 1977.

————. *The Journey Home.* New York: Dutton, 1977.

————. *The Monkey Wrench Gang.* Philadelphia: Lippincott, 1975. The novel that further popularized radical environmentalism.

————. *One Life at a Time, Please.* New York: Henry Holt, 1988.

————. *Slickrock.* San Francisco: Sierra Club, 1971.

————. *Slumgullion Stew.* New York: Dutton, 1984.

Anderson, Chris. *Edge Effects: Notes from an Oregon Forest.* Iowa City: U of Iowa P, 1993.

Audubon, John James. *Audubon Reader: The Best Writings of John James Audubon.* Ed. Scott Russell Sanders. Bloomington: Indiana UP, 1986.

Austin, Mary. *Earth Horizon: Autobiography.* Boston: Houghton Mifflin, 1932.

————. *The Land of Journey's Ending.* New York: Century, 1924. Natural and cultural history of New Mexico and Arizona.

————. *The Land of Little Rain.* Boston: Houghton Mifflin, 1903. A celebration of the Mojave Desert.

Bartram, William. *Travels through North and South Carolina, Georgia, East and West Florida, the Cherokee Country, the Extensive Territories of the Muscogulges, or Creek Confederacy, and the Country of the Choctaws.* Philadelphia: James & Johnson, 1791. The most important colonial work of natural history, and one of the earliest works to express an appreciation for wilderness.

Bass, Rick. *The Ninemile Wolves.* New York: Ballantine, 1992. Essays on a wolf pack in northwestern Montana.

Bates, Marston. *The Forest and the Sea.* New York: Random House, 1960.

Bedicheck, Roy. *Adventures with a Texas Naturalist.* Garden City, NY: Doubleday, 1947.

Berry, Wendell. *A Continuous Harmony: Essays Cultural and Agricultural.* New York: Harcourt Brace Jovanovich, 1972. The work that established Berry as a major figure in the sustainable agriculture movement.

———. *Farming: A Hand Book.* New York: Harcourt Brace Jovanovich, 1970. Poems celebrating farm life.

———. *The Gift of Good Land.* Berkeley: North Point Press, 1981.

———. *Home Economics.* San Francisco: North Point Press, 1987.

———. *The Long-Legged House.* New York: Harcourt, Brace & World, 1969. Essays on the Berry farm in Kentucky.

———. *The Memory of Old Jack.* San Diego: Harcourt Brace Jovanovich, 1974.

———. *Sex, Economy, Freedom & Community.* New York: Pantheon, 1992.

———. *The Unsettling of America: Culture & Agriculture.* San Francisco: Sierra Club Books, 1977.

———. *What Are People For?* San Francisco: North Point Press, 1990.

Beston, Henry. *The Outermost House.* Garden City, NY: Doubleday, 1928. A classic work of nature writing celebrating a year on Cape Cod.

Bird, Isabella. *A Lady's Life in the Rocky Mountains.* New York: Putnam's, 1879–1880. An English tourist traveling in what is now Rocky Mountain National Park.

Black Elk. *Black Elk Speaks: Being the Life Story of a Holy Man of the Oglala Sioux.* Lincoln: U of Nebraska P, 1962. Told through the poet John Neihardt, the most famous Native American autobiography relates Great Plains Indian life in the 19th century.

Bolz, Arnold J. *Portage into the Past.* Minneapolis: U of Minnesota P, 1960. Retracing the voyageur route through the Quetico-Superior country.

Boyle, Robert. *The Hudson River: A Natural and Unnatural History.* New York: Norton, 1969.

Bradbury, John. *Travels in the Interior of America in the Years 1809, 1810, and 1811.* London: Sherwood, Neely, and Jones, 1819.

Brewer, William. *Up and Down California in 1860–1864.* New Haven: Yale UP, 1930.

Broome, Harvey. *Faces of the Wilderness.* Missoula, MT: Mountain Press, 1972. An influential member of the Wilderness Society recounts journeys to wild lands across America.

Broun, Maurice. *Hawks Aloft: The Story of Hawk Mountain.* New York: Dodd, Mead, 1948.

Brown, Bruce. *Mountain in the Clouds: A Search for the Wild Salmon.* New York: Simon & Schuster, 1982.

Browning, Peter. *The Last Wilderness: 600 Miles by Canoe and Portage in the Northwest Territories.* Lafayette, CA: Great West Books, 2d ed., 1989.

Burroughs, John. *A Sharp Lookout: Selected Nature Essays of John Burroughs.* Ed. Frank Bergon. Washington: Smithsonian Institution Press, 1987. An excellent sampling of works by the turn-of-the-century's most popular nature writer.

Byrd, William. *William Byrd's Histories of the Dividing Line Betwixt Virginia and North Carolina.* Ed. William K. Boyd. Raleigh: North Carolina Historical Commission, 1929.

Callenback, Ernest. *Ecotopia: The Notebooks and Reports of William Weston.* New York: Bantam, 1975. Futuristic fiction focusing on the Pacific northwest, which has seceded from the United States for ecological reasons.

Carey, Ken. *Flat Rock Journal: A Day in the Ozark Mountains.* San Francisco: Harper, 1994.

Carrighar, Sally. *One Day on Beetle Rock.* New York: Knopf, 1944. Focuses on animals in the Sierra Nevada.

Carson, Rachel. *The Edge of the Sea.* Boston: Houghton Mifflin, 1955.

———. *The Sea Around Us.* New York: Oxford UP, 1951.

———. *Silent Spring.* New York: Houghton Mifflin, 1962. Exposing the dangers of DDT, this work launched the modern environmental movement.

———. *Under the Sea-Wind: A Naturalist's Picture of Ocean Life.* New York: Oxford UP, 1941.

Catesby, Mark. *The Natural History of Carolina, Florida and the Bahama Islands.* 2 vols. London: published by author, 1731–1743.

Cather, Willa. *My Antonía.* Boston: Houghton Mifflin, 1920. A celebration of the Nebraska prairie; the title character's story is told by a male narrator.

Catlin, George. *Letters and Notes on the Manners, Customs, and Conditions of the North American Indians, Written during Eight Years' Travel amongst the Wildest Tribes of Indians in North America.* New York: Wiley and Putnam, 1841. Includes the first call for a national park to protect the Plains Indian tribes and the bison on which they depended.

Clemens, Samuel (Mark Twain). *The Adventures of Huckleberry Finn.* 1883. The classic pastoral escape: floating down the Mississippi River on a raft.

Colvin, Verplanck. *Report on the Topographical Survey of the Adirondack Wilderness of New York, for the Year 1873.* Albany: Weed, Parsons, 1874.

Cooper, James Fenimore. *The Pioneers*. Philadelphia: 1823. One of the five Leatherstocking novels celebrating the career of Natty Bumppo, mythical wilderness guide.

Cooper, Susan Fenimore. *Rural Hours*. New York: G. P. Putnam, 1850. Nonfiction account of the change of seasons in upstate New York.

Crèvecoeur, Hector St. John de. *Letters from an American Farmer*. London: T. Davies, 1782. One of the earliest Anglo-American works of nature writing, based on observations of farm life in New York state.

Daniel, John. *The Trail Home*. New York: Pantheon, 1992. Essays on the Pacific northwest.

Darwin, Charles. *On the Origin of Species*. London: John Murray, 1859.

————. *The Voyage of the Beagle*. London: 1839. An account of the author's world travels from 1831 to 1836, during which the seeds of his theory of natural selection were planted.

Dickinson, Emily. *The Complete Poems of Emily Dickinson*. New Haven: Yale UP, 1955.

Dillard, Annie. *Holy the Firm*. New York: Harper & Row, 1977. Meditations on God during three days on an island off the Washington coast.

————. *The Living*. New York: HarperCollins, 1992. A novel tracing the fate of 19th-century emigrants to the Washington coast.

————. *Pilgrim at Tinker Creek*. New York: Harper & Row, 1974. A work that won the Pulitzer Prize for nonfiction.

————. *Teaching a Stone to Talk: Expeditions and Encounters*. New York: Harper & Row, 1982.

Douglas, Marjorie Stoneman. *The Everglades: River of Grass*. New York: Rinehart, 1947.

Douglas, William O. *My Wilderness: East to Katahdin*. Garden City, NY: Doubleday, 1961.

————. *My Wilderness: The Pacific West*. Garden City, NY: Doubleday, 1960.

Duncan, David James. *The River Why*. San Francisco: Sierra Club Books, 1983. A novel about tracing a river to its source on the Oregon coast.

Dutton, Clarence. *Tertiary History of the Grand Canyon District*. Washington: U.S. Government, 1882.

Dwight, Timothy. *Travels in New England and New York*. New Haven: T. Dwight, 1821–1822.

Ehrlich, Gretel. *The Solace of Open Spaces*. New York: Viking, 1985. Essays by an eastern woman who ranches in the west.

Eiseley, Loren. *All the Strange Hours: The Excavation of a Life*. New York: Charles Scribner's Sons, 1975. Autobiography of the famous anthropologist-naturalist.

————. *The Firmament of Time.* New York: Atheneum, 1960.

————. *The Immense Journey.* New York: Random House, 1957.

————. *The Invisible Pyramid.* New York: Scribner's, 1970.

————. *The Lost Notebooks of Loren Eiseley.* Ed. Kenneth Heuer. Boston: Little, Brown, 1987.

————. *The Night Country.* New York: Scribner's, 1971.

————. *The Star Thrower.* New York: Times Books, 1978.

————. *The Unexpected Universe.* New York: Harcourt, Brace & World, 1969.

Emerson, Ralph Waldo. *Nature.* Boston: J. Munroe, 1836.

Faulkner, William. *Go Down, Moses.* New York: Random House, 1942. Includes "The Bear," a classic story focusing on Ike McCaslin's mythical hunt of a great bear in the deep woods of Mississippi.

Finch, Robert. *Common Ground: A Naturalist's Cape Cod.* Boston: Godine, 1981.

————. *The Primal Place.* New York: Norton, 1983.

Fletcher, Colin. *The Man Who Walked through Time.* New York: Knopf, 1968. Hiking through the Grand Canyon.

————. *The Thousand-Mile Summer.* Berkeley: Howell-North, 1964. Hiking the Pacific Crest Trail through California.

Fremont, John Charles. *Report on the Exploring Expedition to the Rocky Mountains in the Year 1842 and North California in the Years 1843–1844.* Washington: U.S. Senate, 1845.

Frost, Robert. *The Collected Poems: Complete and Unabridged.* New York: Holt, Rhinehart & Winston, 1969.

Gilbert, Bil. *Our Nature.* Lincoln: U of Nebraska P, 1986. Essays on adventures in the American outdoors.

Gould, Stephen Jay. *Ever Since Darwin: Reflections in Natural History.* New York: Norton, 1977.

————. *The Flamingo's Smile: Reflections in Natural History.* New York: Norton, 1985.

————. *Hen's Teeth and Horse's Toes: Further Reflections in Natural History.* New York: Norton, 1983.

————. *The Panda's Thumb: More Reflections in Natural History.* New York: Norton, 1980.

Graves, John. *From a Limestone Ledge.* New York: Knopf, 1980. Observations of a Texas homesteader.

————. *Goodbye to a River.* New York: Knopf, 1960. A final canoe trip down the Brazos River before it is dammed.

————. *Hard Scrabble: Observations on a Patch of Land.* New York: Knopf, 1974.

Grinnell, George Bird. *The Passing of the Great West.* Ed. John F. Reiger. New York: Scribner's, 1972.

Gruchow, Paul. *Journal of a Prairie Year*. Minneapolis: U of Minnesota P, 1985.

―――. *The Necessity of Empty Places*. New York: St. Martin's, 1988.

―――. *Travels in Canoe Country*. Boston: Little, Brown, 1992. Essays on traveling through the Boundary Waters Canoe Area Wilderness in northern Minnesota.

Haines, John. *Living Off the Country: Essays on Poetry and Place*. Ann Arbor: U of Michigan P, 1981. An Alaskan homesteader reflects on his practice.

Hardy, Martha. *Tatoosh*. New York: Macmillan, 1946. A fire lookout in Washington in the 1940s.

Harwood, Michael. *The View from Hawk Mountain*. New York: Scribner's, 1973.

Hasselstrom, Linda. *Land Circle: Writings Collected from the Land*. Golden, CO: Fulcrum, 1991. A rancher-environmentalist in South Dakota.

Hay, John. *The Immortal Wilderness*. New York: Norton, 1987. Cape Cod nature writing.

―――. *Nature's Year*. Garden City, NY: Doubleday, 1961.

Helmricks, Constance. *Down the Wild River North*. Seattle: Seal, 1968. A mother and her two daughters boat down the Mackenzie River.

Hemingway, Ernest. *The Green Hills of Africa*. New York: Scribner's, 1935.

―――. *The Short Stories of Ernest Hemingway*. New York: Scribner's, 1938. See especially "Big Two-Hearted River," about trout fishing in Michigan's Upper Peninsula.

Hoagland, Edward. *The Courage of Turtles*. New York: Random House, 1970. One of the premier essayists reflects on life in the country and in New York City.

―――. *The Edward Hoagland Reader*. Ed. Geoffrey Wolff. New York: Vintage, 1979.

―――. *Notes from the Century Before: A Journal of British Columbia*. New York: Random House, 1969.

―――. *Red Wolves and Black Bears*. New York: Random House, 1976.

―――. *Seven Rivers West*. New York: Simon & Schuster, 1986. Fiction about wilderness life in the 1880s.

―――. *The Tugman's Passage*. New York: Random House, 1982.

―――. *Walking the Dead Diamond River*. New York: Random House, 1973.

Hoover, Helen. *A Place in the Woods*. New York: Knopf, 1969. Chicagoans move to the North Woods of Minnesota.

Hubbell, Sue. *A Country Year: Living the Questions*. New York: Random House, 1986. A beekeeper writes about homesteading in the Ozarks.

―――. *On This Hilltop*. New York: Ballantine, 1991.

Hudson, W. H. *Hampshire Days*. London: Longman, Green and Co., 1903. A turn-of-the-century English classic that influenced such later writers as Leopold.

Irving, Washington. *A Tour on the Prairies*. 1835; Norman: U of Oklahoma P, 1955.

Jeffers, Robinson. *Selected Poems*. New York: Random House, 1963. A California poet based near Big Sur.

Jefferson, Thomas. *Notes on the State of Virginia*. Paris: 1784–1785.

Jewett, Sarah Orne. *The Country of the Pointed Firs*. Boston: Houghton Mifflin, 1925. Fiction about a coastal Maine community and its close ties to the land and ocean.

Kalm, Peter. *Peter Kalm's Travels in North America*. 2 vols. Ed. Adolph B. Benson. New York: Wilson-Erickson, 1937.

Kerouac, Jack. *Desolation Angels*. New York: Putnam, 1960. Beat fiction on fire-lookout life.

———. *The Dharma Bums*. New York: Viking, 1958.

King, Clarence. *Mountaineering in the Sierra Nevada*. Boston: James R. Osgood, 1872.

Kinseth, Lance. *River Eternal*. New York: Viking, 1989. Postmodernist nonfiction about a river in Iowa.

Kline, David. *Great Possessions: An Amish Farmer's Journal*. San Francisco: North Point Press, 1990.

Krutch, Joseph Wood. *The Best Nature Writing of Joseph Wood Krutch*. New York: Morrow, 1970.

———. *The Desert Year*. New York: William Sloane, 1952.

———. *The Forgotten Peninsula*. New York: William Sloane, 1961.

———. *The Grand Canyon*. New York: William Sloane, 1958.

———. *The Great Chain of Life*. Boston: Houghton Mifflin, 1956.

———. *The Voice of the Desert*. New York: William Sloane, 1954.

LaBastille, Anne. *Beyond Black Bear Lake*. New York: Norton, 1987.

———. *Woodswoman*. New York: Dutton, 1976. Wilderness life in the Adirondacks.

Leopold, Aldo. *Aldo Leopold's Wilderness: Selected Early Writings by the Author of 'A Sand County Almanac.'* Eds. David Brown and Neil Carmony. Harrisburg, PA: Stackpole Books, 1990.

———. *Game Management*. New York: Scribner's, 1933.

———. *Round River: From the Journals of Aldo Leopold*. Ed. Luna Leopold. New York: Oxford UP, 1953.

———. *The River of the Mother of God and Other Essays by Aldo Leopold*. Eds. Susan Flader and J. Baird Callicott. Madison: U of Wisconsin P, 1991.

———. *A Sand County Almanac*. New York: Oxford UP, 1949. The most important work of nature writing of the 20th century.

Lewis, Meriwether, and William Clark. *The Journals of Lewis and Clark.* Ed. Bernard DeVoto. Boston: Houghton Mifflin, 1953.

Levin, Ted. *Backtracking: The Way of a Naturalist.* Chelsea, VT: Chelsea Green, 1987.

London, Jack. *The Call of the Wild.* New York: S. S. McClure, 1903. Popular stories set in the Arctic.

Lopez, Barry. *Arctic Dreams: Imagination and Desire in a Northern Landscape.* New York: Scribner's, 1986.

———. *Crossing Open Ground.* New York: Scribner's, 1988.

———. *Desert Notes: Reflection in the Eye of a Raven.* New York: Avon, 1976.

———. *River Notes: The Dance of Herons.* New York: Avon, 1979.

———. *Of Wolves and Men.* New York: Scribner's, 1978.

McCarthy, Cormac. *All the Pretty Horses.* New York: Knopf, 1992. Two young Texans seek a new frontier in Mexico in the 1940s. Stunning prose.

———. *The Crossing.* New York: Knopf, 1994. A young Texan tries to return a wolf to its natural habitat in the mountains of Mexico.

McGinnis, Joe. *Going to Extremes.* New York: Knopf, 1980. Reflections on the last frontier of Alaska.

Mackenzie, Alexander. *Exploring the Northwest Territory.* Ed. T. H. McDonald. Norman: U of Oklahoma P, 1966. The journal of the great explorer's voyage by bark canoe from Lake Athabasca to the Pacific Ocean in 1789.

McKinney, Sam. *Reach of Tide, Ring of History: A Columbia River Voyage.* Portland: Oregon Historical Society Press, 1987.

Maclean, Norman. *A River Runs through It and Other Stories.* Chicago: U of Chicago P, 1976. The title novella did for fly-fishing what the film *Deliverance* did for canoeing.

———. *Young Men and Fire: A True Story of the Mann Gulch Fire.* Chicago: U of Chicago P, 1992.

McPhee, John. *Assembling California.* New York: Farrar, Straus & Giroux, 1993.

———. *Basin and Range.* New York: Farrar, Straus & Giroux, 1981.

———. *Coming into the Country.* New York: Farrar, Straus & Giroux, 1977.

———. *The Control of Nature.* New York: Farrar, Straus & Giroux, 1989.

———. *Encounters with the Archdruid.* New York: Farrar, Straus & Giroux, 1971.

———. *The Pine Barrens.* New York: Farrar, Straus & Giroux, 1968.

———. *Rising from the Plains.* New York: Farrar, Straus & Giroux, 1986.

———. *The Survival of the Bark Canoe.* New York: Farrar, Straus & Giroux, 1975.

————. *In Suspect Terrain*. New York: Farrar, Straus & Giroux, 1983.

Madson, John. *Where the Sky Began: Land of the Tallgrass Prairie*. Boston: Houghton Mifflin, 1982.

Marshall, Robert. *Arctic Wilderness*. Berkeley: U of California P, 1956.

Matthiessen, Peter. *The Cloud Forest: A Chronicle of the South American Wilderness*. New York: Viking, 1961.

————. *At Play in the Fields of the Lord*. New York: Random House, 1965. A novel about a missionary in South America.

————. *The Snow Leopard*. New York: Viking, 1978. Following the biologist George Schaller in the Himalayas in search of a rare predator.

Melville, Herman. *Moby-Dick*. New York: Harper and Brothers, 1851. The greatest American novel about the greatest of themes: humans in search of the beast without and within.

Merwin, W. S. *The Rain in the Trees*. New York: Knopf, 1988. Poems with insights into ecology and natural history.

————. *Travels*. New York: Knopf, 1994.

Mills, Enos. *The Spell of the Rockies*. Boston: Houghton Mifflin, 1911. The founder of Rocky Mountain National Park celebrates his home.

Mitchell, John Hanson. *Ceremonial Time: Fifteen Thousand Years on One Square Mile*. Garden City, NY: Anchor Press/Doubleday, 1984.

————. *Living at the End of Time*. Boston: Houghton Mifflin, 1990.

Momaday, N. Scott. *The Way to Rainy Mountain*. Albuquerque: U of New Mexico P, 1969. Tribal legends and history, and autobiography of a pilgrimage to a sacred site of the Kiowa in Oklahoma.

Mowat, Farley. *People of the Deer*. Boston: Little, Brown, 1952.

————. *The Snow Walker*. Toronto: McClelland and Stewart, 1975.

Muir, John. *John of the Mountains: The Unpublished Journals of John Muir*. Ed. Linnie Marsh Wolfe. Boston: Houghton Mifflin, 1938.

————. *The Mountains of California*. New York: Century, 1894.

————. *My First Summer in the Sierra*. Boston: Houghton Mifflin, 1911. Muir's most lyrical, autobiographical book.

————. *Our National Parks*. Boston: Houghton Mifflin, 1901.

————. *Summering in the Sierra*. Ed. Robert Engberg. Madison: U of Wisconsin P, 1984.

————. *The Story of My Boyhood and Youth*. Boston: Houghton Mifflin, 1913.

————. *South of Yosemite: Selected Writings of John Muir*. Ed. Frederick R. Gunsky. Berkeley: Wilderness Press, 1968.

————. *A Thousand-Mile Walk to the Gulf*. Boston: Houghton Mifflin, 1916.

————. *Travels in Alaska*. Boston: Houghton Mifflin, 1917.

————. *The Yosemite*. New York: Century, 1912.

————. *John Muir: To Yosemite and Beyond*. Eds. Robert Engberg and Donald Wesling. Madison: U of Wisconsin P, 1980.

Murie, Adolph. *A Naturalist in Alaska*. New York: Devin-Adair, 1961.

Murie, Margaret. *Two in the Far North*. New York: Knopf, 1962.

Murie, Olaus. *Journeys to the Far North*. Palo Alto: Wilderness Society and American West Publishing, 1973.

Murie, Olaus, and Margaret E. Murie. *Wapiti Wilderness*. New York: Knopf, 1966.

Nabhan, Gary. *The Desert Smells Like Rain: A Naturalist in Papago Indian Country*. San Francisco: North Point Press, 1985.

————. *Enduring Seeds: Native American Agriculture and Wildlife Plant Conservation*. San Francisco: North Point Press, 1989.

————. *Gathering the Desert*. Tucson: U of Arizona P, 1985.

————. *Songbirds, Truffles, and Wolves: An American Naturalist in Italy*. New York: Pantheon, 1993.

Nearing, Helen, and Scott Nearing. *Living the Good Life: How to Live Sanely and Simply in a Troubled World*. New York: Schocken Books, 1954. A famous example of the simple life during the Depression.

Nelson, Richard. *The Island Within*. San Francisco: North Point Press, 1989. Life on an island off the Alaska coast.

————. *Make Prayers to the Raven: A Koyukon View of the Northern Forest*. Chicago: U of Chicago P, 1983. Anthropological study.

Norris, Kathleen. *Dakota: A Spiritual Geography*. New York: Ticknor and Fields, 1993.

Nuttall, Thomas. *A Journal of Travels into the Arkansas Territory, during the Year 1819*. Philadelphia: Thos. H. Palmer, 1821.

Oliver, Mary. *American Primitive*. Boston: Little, Brown, 1983. Won the Pulitzer Prize for Poetry.

————. *New and Selected Poems*. Boston: Beacon Press, 1992. Won the National Book Award for poetry.

————. *Twelve Moons*. Boston: Little, Brown, 1979.

————. *White Pine*. Boston: Little, Brown, 1994.

Olson, Sigurd. *Listening Point*. New York: Knopf, 1958. Reflections on homesteading in northern Minnesota.

————. *The Lonely Land*. New York: Knopf, 1961.

————. *Open Horizons*. New York: Knopf, 1969.

————. *Runes of the North*. New York: Knopf, 1963.

————. *The Singing Wilderness*. New York: Knopf, 1956.

Parkman, Francis. *The Oregon Trail*. 1849; New York: New American Library, 1950.

Patterson, R. M. *Dangerous River*. Toronto: Stoddart Publishing, 1954. Trapping and hunting along the South Nahanni River in the Northwest Territories 1927–1928.

Peacock, Douglas. *Grizzly Years: In Search of the American Wilderness.* New York: Henry Holt, 1990.

Peattie, Donald Culross. *An Almanac for Moderns.* New York: Putnam's, 1935.

———. *The Road of a Naturalist.* Boston: Houghton Mifflin, 1941.

Perrin, Noel. *First Person Rural: Essays of a Sometimes Farmer.* New York: Penguin, 1980.

———. *Second Person Rural: More Essays of a Sometimes Farmer.* Boston: Godine, 1980.

———. *Third Person Rural: Further Essays of a Sometimes Farmer.* Boston: Godine, 1983.

Pollan, Michael. *Second Nature: A Gardener's Education.* New York: Atlantic Monthly Press, 1991.

Powell, John Wesley. *The Exploration of the Colorado River and Its Canyons.* Washington: U. S. Government, 1875.

Pyle, Robert Michael. *Wintergreen: Listening to the Land's Heart.* New York: Scribner's, 1986. Essays on exploring southwestern Washington state.

Quammen, David. *The Flight of the Iguana: A Sidelong View of Science and Nature.* New York: Delacorte Press, 1988.

———. *Natural Acts: A Sidelong View of Science and Nature.* New York: Schocken, 1985.

Rawlins, C. L. *Sky's Witness: A Year in the Wind River Range.* New York: Henry Holt, 1993.

Rawlings, Marjorie Kinnan. *Cross Creek.* New York: Scribner's, 1942. Woman homesteader in Florida.

Roberts, David. *The Mountain of My Fear.* New York: Vanguard, 1968.

Rockland, Michael Aaron. *Snowshoeing through Sewers: Adventures in New York City, New Jersey, and Philadelphia.* New Brunswick, NJ: Rutgers UP, 1994.

Roosevelt, Theodore. *Wilderness Writings.* Ed. Paul Schullery. Salt Lake City: Gibbs M. Smith, 1986.

Russell, Andy. *Grizzly Country.* New York: Knopf, 1968.

Russell, Osborne. *Journal of a Trapper.* Lincoln: U of Nebraska P, n.d. An account of the author's explorations in the Rockies from 1834 to 1843.

Sarton, May. *Journal of a Solitude.* New York: Norton, 1973. Meditations on life on the Maine coast.

———. *Letters from Maine: New Poems.* New York: Norton, 1984.

Schullery, Paul. *Mountain Time: Man Meets Wilderness in Yellowstone.* New York: Simon & Schuster, 1984.

Seton, Ernest Thompson. *Ernest Thompson Seton's America.* Ed. Farida A. Wiley. New York: Devin-Adair, 1962.

Sevareid, Eric. *Canoeing with the Cree.* New York: Macmillan, 1935. The famous television correspondent and a companion canoe from Minnesota to Hudson Bay.

Silko, Leslie Marmon. *Ceremony.* New York: Viking, 1977. A novel about a Native American veteran returning to his reservation in the southwest after World War II.

Smith, John. *The General Historie of Virginia, New England & the Summer Isles, Together with the True Travels, Adventures, and Observations, and a Sea Grammar.* 2 vols. London: Michael Sparkes, 1624.

Snyder, Gary. *Axe Handles.* San Francisco: North Point Press, 1983.

————. *The Back Country.* New York: New Directions, 1968.

————. *Earth Household.* New York: New Directions, 1969.

————. *Left Out in the Rain: New Poems 1947–1985.* San Francisco: North Point Press, 1986.

————. *The Practice of the Wild: Essays by Gary Snyder.* San Francisco: North Point Press, 1990. An important collection on living a biocentric life.

————. *Riprap & Cold Mountain Poems.* San Francisco: Grey Fox Press, 1965.

————. *Turtle Island.* New York: New Directions, 1974. Won the Pulitzer Prize for poetry.

Stanwell-Fletcher, Theodora C. *Driftwood Valley.* Boston: Little, Brown, 1946. Husband and wife scientists homesteading in British Columbia.

Stegner, Wallace. *Angle of Repose.* Garden City, NY: Doubleday, 1971. Won the Pulitzer Prize for fiction. Homesteading and irrigation politics in the American west.

————. *The Sound of Mountain Water.* Garden City, NY: Doubleday, 1969. Essays on the American west and conservatism.

————. *Where the Bluebird Sings to the Lemonade Springs.* New York: Random House, 1992.

————. *Wolf Willow: A History, a Story, and a Memory of the Last Plains Frontier.* Toronto: Macmillan, 1962.

Steinbeck, John. *The Grapes of Wrath.* New York: Viking, 1939. Okies flee the dust bowl for California.

————. *The Log from the Sea of Cortez.* New York: Viking, 1951. Accompanying a marine biologist.

Stevens, Wallace. *The Complete Poems.* New York: Random House, 1952. One of the greatest American poets speculates on the nature of nature.

Sullivan, William L. *Listening for Coyote: A Walk across Oregon's Wilderness.* New York: Henry Holt, 1988.

Tanner, John. *The Falcon: A Narrative of the Captivity & Adventures of John Tanner.* 1830; New York: Penguin, 1994. Introduction by Louise

Erdrich. A young white boy captured by Indians in the late 1700s who spends most of his life among the Ojibwe.

Teale, Edwin Way. *Autumn across America.* New York: Dodd, Mead, 1956.

———. *Journey into Summer.* New York: Dodd, Mead, 1960.

———. *Life and Death of a Salt Marsh.* New York: Ballantine, 1971.

———. *North with the Spring.* New York: Dodd, Mead, 1951.

———. *Wandering through Winter.* New York: Dodd, Mead, 1965.

Thomas, Lewis. *The Lives of a Cell: Notes of a Biology Watcher.* New York: Viking, 1974.

Thoreau, Henry David. *Cape Cod.* Boston: Ticknor and Fields, 1865.

———. *Faith in a Seed: "The Dispersion of Seeds" and Other Late Natural History Writings.* Ed. Bradley P. Dean. Washington, D.C.: Island Press, 1993.

———. *Journals.* Vols. 7–20 of *The Writings of Henry David Thoreau.* Boston: Houghton Mifflin, 1906.

———. *The Maine Woods.* Boston: Ticknor and Fields, 1864.

———. *The Natural History Essays.* Ed. Robert Sattelmeyer. Salt Lake City: Gibbs M. Smith, 1980.

———. *Walden.* Boston: Ticknor and Fields, 1854.

———. *A Week on the Concord and Merrimack Rivers.* Boston: James Munroe and Company, 1849.

Van Dyke, John C. *The Desert.* New York: Scribner's, 1901.

Vickery, Jim Dale. *Open Spaces.* Minocqua, WI: NorthWord, 1991. Year-round adventures in the North Woods of Minnesota and Ontario.

Wallace, David Rains. *Bulow Hammock.* San Francisco: Sierra Club Books, 1988. Essays on Florida.

———. *The Dark Range: A Naturalist's Night Notebook.* San Francisco: Sierra Club, 1978. Nocturnal ramblings in California's Yolla Bolly Middle Eel Wilderness.

———. *Idle Weeds: The Life of a Sandstone Ridge.* San Francisco: Sierra Club, 1980.

———. *The Klamath Knot: Explorations of Myth and Evolution.* San Francisco: Sierra Club, 1983.

———. *The Turquoise Dragon.* San Francisco: Sierra Club, 1985. Eco-fiction focusing on northern California.

———. *The Untamed Garden and Other Personal Essays.* Columbus: Ohio State UP, 1986.

Walton, Izaak, and Charles Cotton. *The Compleat Angler.* London: T. Maxey, 1653; with Cotton's continuation, 1676.

Warner, William. *Beautiful Swimmers: Watermen, Crabs, and the Chesapeake Bay.* Boston: Little, Brown, 1976.

White, Gilbert. *The Natural History and Antiquites of Selbourne, in the County of Southampton*. London: Benjamin White & Son, 1788. The most important and most popular natural history work of the modern era.

Williams, Terry Tempest. *Pieces of White Shell: Journey to Navajoland*. New York: Scribner's, 1984.

———. *Refuge: An Unnatural History of Family and Place*. New York: Pantheon, 1991. A Utah naturalist and Mormon grapples with the high incidence of breast cancer in her family.

———. *An Unspoken Hunger: Stories from the Field*. New York: Pantheon, 1994.

Wilson, Alexander. *American Ornithology: or, the Natural History of the Birds of the United States*. 9 vols. Philadelphia: Bradford & Inskeep, 1808–1814.

Wood, William. *New England's Prospect*. London: I. Bellamie, 1634.

Wright, Billie. *Four Seasons North: A Journal of Life in the Alaskan Wilderness*. New York: Harper & Row, 1973.

Wright, Mabel Osgood. *The Friendship of Nature: A New England Chronicle of Birds and Flowers*. New York: Macmillan, 1894.

Zwinger, Ann. *Beyond the Aspen Grove*. New York: Harper & Row, 1970. Homesteading in Colorado.

———. *A Desert Country Near the Sea: A Natural History of the Cape Region of Baja California*. New York: Harper & Row, 1983.

———. *Run, River, Run*. New York: Harper & Row, 1975. Retracing John Wesley Powell's journey down the Green River.

———. *Wind in the Rock*. New York: Harper & Row, 1975.

Notes and References

In citing endnotes, to avoid distracting the reader, I have consolidated references and placed the superscript number at the end of the paragraph in the text.

1. Overview

1. See Allen Wallach, "Making a Picture of the View from Mount Holyoke," *Bulletin of Detroit Institute of Arts* (1990): 35–37. Edmund Burke, *A Philosophical Inquiry into the Origin of Our Ideas of the Sublime and Beautiful* (Oxford: Oxford UP, 1990), 36, 53. A good study of the sublime is Thomas Weiskel, *The Romantic Sublime* (Baltimore: John Hopkins UP, 1976).

2. See Oswaldo Rodriguez Roque, "Thomas Cole," *American Paradise: The World of the Hudson River School* (New York: Metropolitan Museum of Art, 1987), 126.

3. Wallach 35; Roque 127. Roderick Nash discusses polarities in *The Oxbow* in *Wilderness and the American Mind*, 3d ed. (New Haven: Yale UP, 1982), 81.

4. See Angela Miller, *The Empire of the Eye: Landscape Representation and American Cultural Politics, 1825–1875* (Ithaca: Cornell UP, 1993), 39–49.

5. Standard references on the role of landscape art in 19th-century American culture and the creation of tourist sites are Barbara Novak, *Nature and Culture: American Landscape and Painting 1825–1875* (New York: Oxford UP, 1980), 3–17; and

John Sears, *Sacred Places: American Tourist Attractions in the Nineteenth Century* (New York: Oxford UP, 1989), 4–5, 12–30, respectively.

6. For a concise history of pastoralism see Frank Kermode, introduction, *English Pastoral Poetry: From the Beginnings to Marvell* (New York: Norton, 1972), 20–28; and Raymond Williams, *The Country and the City* (New York: Oxford UP, 1973), 13–22. Marx is quoted in *The Pilot and the Passenger: Essays on Literature, Technology, and Culture in the United States* (New York: Oxford UP, 1988), xii–xiii.

7. Herbert Lindenberger, "The Idyllic Moment: On Pastoral and Romanticism," *College English* 34.3 (Dec. 1972): 337–38. H. Daniel Peck applies Lindenberger's theories to Thoreau in "The Crosscurrents of *Walden*'s Pastoral," *New Essays on Walden*, ed. Robert F. Sayre (Cambridge: Cambridge UP, 1992), 73–94. I am grateful to Professor Peck for informing me of his article, ideas from which are central to my analysis.

8. Like most other scholars of nature writing to date, I restrict my attention to nonfiction prose. This traditional focus has to do, I think, with the factual—i.e., nonfictional—orientation of the ancestors of nature writing: natural history, travel literature, and autobiography. To my knowledge, a book-length study of fictional nature writing has yet to be done; it would provide a much-needed perspective.

9. A good summary of the land-use practices of indigenous peoples of America prior to European discovery is Richard White, "Native Americans and the Environment," *Scholars and the Indian Experience: Critical Reviews of Recent Writing in the Social Sciences*, ed. William Swagerty (Bloomington: U of Indiana P, 1984), 179–204. For the northeast both before and after contact with Europeans, see William Cronon, *Changes in the Land: Indians, Ecologists, and the Ecology of New England* (New York: Farrar, Straus & Giroux, 1983). See also Richard White, "American Indians and the Environment," *Environmental History Review* 9.2 (Summer 1985): 101–3.

10. John Brinckerhoff Jackson, *Discovering the Vernacular Landscape* (New Haven: Yale UP, 1984), 3–8. Roderick Nash discusses a "spectrum" approach to types of landforms as well as definitions of wilderness in *Wilderness and the American*

Mind, 1–7. I should point out that I am aware of the claim made by Simon Schama (for one) in *Landscape and Memory* (New York: Knopf, 1995) that "it is difficult to think of a single such natural system that has not, for better or worse, been substantially modified by human culture. Nor is this simply the work of the industrial centuries. It has been happening since the days of ancient Mesopotamia. It is coeval with writing, with the entirety of our social existence. And it is this irreversibly modified world, from the polar caps to the equatorial forests, that is all the nature we have" (7). Is there in fact any wilderness left today (i.e., land that remains unaffected in any way by humans)? True, DDT residue has been found in the ice of the north pole, and a hole in the ozone layer above the south pole affects humans (not to mention other species) there, too. Still, we seek out places on the globe that at least present the appearance of being untouched—witness the scramble by mountaineers to climb one more unconquered peak, by botanists to discover one final "virgin" forest—and this quest for wildness is not without some significance, I think. Sometimes what *appears to be* is at least as vital and forceful as what actually *is*. Call it the reification of wilderness.

11. Henry David Thoreau, "Walking," *The Natural History Essays*, ed. Robert Sattelmeyer (Salt Lake City: Peregrine Smith, 1980), 112.

12. Rueckert's essay is part of a larger article, "Into and Out of the Void: Two Essays, "*Iowa Review* 9.1 (Winter 1978): 62–86. For a representative treatment by an ecocritic of contemporary literary theory, see Karl Kroeber, *Ecological Literary Criticism: Romantic Imagining and the Biology of Mind* (New York: Columbia UP, 1994).

13. The claim was made by Alan Lui in *Wordsworth: The Sense of History* (Palo Alto: Stanford UP, 1989), and it is quoted, discussed, and disputed by Jonathan Bate in *Romantic Ecology: Wordsworth and the Environmental Tradition* (London: Routledge, 1991), 18–19, 56. Other important discussions of ecocriticism are by SueEllen Campbell, "The Land and Language of Desire: Where Deep Ecology and Post-Structuralism Meet," *Western American Literature* 24.3 (Nov.

1989): 199–211; Glen Love, "Revaluing Nature: Toward an Ecological Criticism," *Western American Literature* 25.3 (Nov. 1990): 201–15; Glen Love, "Pastoral Theory Meets Ecocriticism," *Western American Literature* 27.3 (Nov. 1992): 195–207; and Michael Branch, "Ecocriticism: The Nature of Nature in Literary Studies," *Weber Studies* 11.1 (Winter 1994): 41–45. The most recent treatment—one that should prove to be a landmark—is by Lawrence Buell, *The Environmental Imagination: Thoreau, Nature Writing, and the Formation of American Culture* (Cambridge: Harvard UP, 1995). See particularly Buell's discussion "What Is an Environmental Text?" (6–14). An important contribution by an environmental historian to the debate between poststructuralists and ecocritics over the nature of reality and the reality of nature is William Cronon's "A Place for Stories: Nature, History, and Narrative," *Journal of American History* 78.4 (Mar. 1992): 1347–76. Finally, for a contemporary nature writer's perspective on the interiority and exteriority of landscape, see Barry Lopez, "Landscape and Narrative," *Crossing Open Ground* (New York: Scribner's, 1988), 61–71.

14. Michael Cohen, *The Pathless Way: John Muir and American Wilderness* (Madison: U of Wisconsin P, 1984), 275; Bate 5; Henry David Thoreau, *The Illustrated Walden* (Princeton: Princeton UP, 1973), 201. Other fine book-length studies that employ fieldwork are William Howarth, *Thoreau in the Mountains* (New York: Farrar, Straus & Giroux, 1982), which I discovered after encountering Cohen's work; John Elder, *Imagining the Earth: Poetry and the Vision of Nature* (Urbana: U of Illinois P, 1985); and Frederick Turner, *Spirit of Place: The Making of an American Literary Landscape* (San Francisco: Sierra Club, 1989). I like very much the anecdote related by Simon Schama in *Landscape and Memory* about "one of my best-loved teachers . . . [who] had always insisted on directly experiencing 'a sense of place,' of using 'the archive of the feet'" (24).

15. The standard work relating representations of nature in painting and literature is Barbara Novak, *Nature and Culture: American Landscape and Painting, 1825–1875* (New York: Oxford UP, 1980). I find useful as well the collection of litera-

ture and art compiled by William Conron, ed., *The American Landscape: A Critical Anthology of Prose and Poetry* (New York: Oxford UP, 1973).

16. See Brook Thomas, *The New Historicism and Other Old-Fashioned Topics* (Princeton: Princeton UP, 1991), 6–7; and H. Aram Veesher, ed., *The New Historicism* (New York: Routledge, 1989).

17. To my knowledge there is no full-scale study that traces both western and Asian attitudes toward nature. Good surveys of western attitudes are Clarence Glacken, *Traces on the Rhodian Shore: Nature and Culture in Western Thought from Ancient Times to the End of the Eighteenth Century* (Berkeley: U of California P, 1967); and Schama, *Landscape and Memory*. A recent work on Asia is *Nature in Asian Traditions of Thought: Essays in Environmental Philosophy*, eds. J. Baird Callicott and Roger T. Ames (Albany: SUNY P, 1989). Lawrence Buell discusses the myth of American exceptionalism with regard to American nature literature in *The Environmental Imagination* (77–82). Certainly, such Asian authors as Dōgen (*Mountain and Waters Sutra*, c. 1250) and Bashō (*A Haiku Journey*, 1689) can be seen as "nature writers." And important Americans in the tradition, like Thoreau (who incorporated Asian philosophies into *Walden*) and Gary Snyder (in a work such as *Riprap and Cold Mountain Poems* [San Francisco: Grey Fox, 1958], in which he provides translations of poems by the 8th-century A.C.E. Chinese writer Han-shan), were strongly influenced by nonwestern thinking. What is needed is some (unavoidably monumental) analysis of cross-pollenization in eastern and western, northern and southern ways of inter-acting with the nonhuman world.

18. William Beebe, *The Book of Naturalists: An Anthology of the Best Natural History* (Princeton: Princeton UP, 1988), 12–18. See also Clarence Glacken, *Traces on the Rhodian Shore* 3–6. Robert Downs discusses Aristotle as a natural historian in *Landmarks in Science: Hippocrates to Carson* (Littletown, CO: Libraries Unlimited, 1982), 25–28.

19. Beebe 19–23; Downs 40–51.

20. Williams 16. Williams goes on to point out that the speaker of the poem, Meliboeus, laments his eviction from his own

property: "Ah, when shall I see my native land again? after long years / or never?" (16), indicating the fragility and tenuousness of the pastoral dream even in its early stages. On the development of pastoralism, see also John Barrell and John Bull, introduction, *The Penguin Book of English Pastoral Verse* (New York: Penguin, 1982), 1–9; and Kermode 11–28.

21. A good discussion of John Ray can be found in Joseph Wood Krutch, "Prologue," *Great American Nature Writing* (New York: William Sloane, 1950), 15–18. See also Keith Thomas, *Man and the Natural World: A History of the Modern Sensibility* (New York: Pantheon, 1983), 167, 253; and Glacken 379–80.

22. On the Linnaean revolution, see Beebe 45–46; Downs 158–60; and Glacken 510–12. Insightful overviews of natural history in colonial America are provided by Philip Marshall Hicks, *The Development of the Natural History Essay in American Literature* (Philadelphia: U of Pennsylvania P, 1924), 11–13; Thomas Lyon, ed., *This Incomperable Lande: A Book of American Nature Writing* (Boston: Houghton Mifflin, 1989), 16–19; and Wayne Franklin, *Discoverers, Explorers, Settlers: The Diligent Writers of Early America* (Chicago: U of Chicago P, 1979). Stephen Greenblatt in *Marvelous Possessions: The Wonder of the New World* (Chicago: U of Chicago P, 1991) argues that the rhetoric of exploration and discovery of America served Europe's ideology of conquest. See *The Diario of Christopher Columbus's First Voyage to America 1492–93*, translated and transcribed by Oliver Dunn and James E. Kelly, Jr. (Norman: U of Oklahoma P, 1989).

23. Wood is quoted in Lyon 101. See Franklin 38–43 on Wood's style.

24. Gilbert White, *The Natural History of Selbourne* (New York: Penguin, 1977), 125; subsequent references appear parenthetically in the text. I have found the following studies to be useful analyses of White's writing: the introduction to the Penguin edition by Richard Mabey; David Allen, *The Naturalist in Britain: A Social History* (London: Allen Lane, 1976), 1–54; Donald Worster, *Nature's Economy: A History of Ecological Ideas* (New York: Cambridge UP, 1989), 3–25; Lucy Maddox, "Gilbert White and the Politics of Natural History," *Eighteenth Century Life* 10.2 (May 1986): 45–57; David Fussell,

"The Greening Eye: Gilbert White, the Picturesque and Natural History," *Critical Survey* 2.1 (1990): 14–20; Clarence Wolfshol, "Gilbert White's Natural History and History," *CLIO* 20.3 (1991): 271–81; and Frank Stewart, *A Natural History of Nature Writing* (Washington, D.C.: Island Press, 1995), 13–29.

25. Worster 3–25. On the "chain of being," see Glacken 481–82, 599–600; and Arthur O. Lovejoy, *The Great Chain of Being: A Study of the History of an Idea* (Cambridge: Harvard UP, 1948).

26. Rashleigh Holt-White, *The Life and Letters of Gilbert White of Selbourne*, 2 vols. (New York: Dutton, 1901), 2: 255.

27. Mabey viii. Frank Stewart also emphasizes White's importance in the tradition of nature writing, citing him as a long-time model "for what many people still associate with nature writing. Certainly, those who wrote about nature and landscape immediately after White, including Thoreau, were measured, in style and content, in accuracy and in humility, against the gentle curate of Selbourne" (xxi–xxii).

28. Thomas Jefferson, *Notes on the State of Virginia* (New York: Norton, 1972). See Charles A. Miller, *Jefferson and Nature: An Interpretation* (Baltimore: Johns Hopkins UP, 1993). On cultural nationalism and the celebration of nature in early America, see Larzer Ziff, *Writing the New Nation* (New Haven: Yale UP, 1991).

29. J. Hector St. John de Crèvecoeur, *Letters from an American Farmer and Sketches of 18th-Century America* (New York: Penguin, 1963). See Pamela Regis, *Describing Early America: Bartram, Jefferson, Crèvecoeur and the Rhetoric of Natural History* (DeKalb: Northern Illinois UP, 1992), 106–34.

30. William Bartram, *Travels* (New York: Dover, 1955). Two good studies that focus in part on natural history in America at the turn of the 18th century are William Smallwood, *Natural History and the American Mind* (New York: Columbia UP, 1941); and Hans Huth, *Nature and the American: Three Centuries of Changing Attitudes* (Berkeley: U of California P, 1957). Of the many treatments of Bartram, one I find particularly compelling for its interdisciplinary approach is Jerome F. Anderson et al., *Bartram Heritage Report* (Montgomery,

Alabama: Heritage Conservation and Recreation Service, U.S. Department of the Interior, 1978).

31. Williams 127–64; Paul Shepard, *Man in the Landscape: A Historic View of the Esthetics of Nature* (College Station: Texas A & M UP, 1967); Roderick Nash, *Wilderness and the American Mind.* Marjorie Hope Nicholson argues convincingly that the shift to romantic appreciation of wilderness was prefigured by 17th-century developments in *Mountain Gloom and Glory: The Development of the Aesthetics of the Infinite* (Ithaca: Cornell UP, 1959). The definitions of wilderness are quoted in Nash, above, 1–3. Leo Marx discusses the influence of the industrial revolution in America in *The Machine in the Garden;* on this subject, see also Jack Larkin, *The Reshaping of Everyday Life 1790–1840* (New York: Harper & Row, 1988), 1–61.

32. On Audubon see Joseph Kastner, *A Species of Eternity* (New York: Dutton, 1969), 207–39; and *Audubon Reader: The Best Writings of John James Audubon,* ed. Scott Russell Sanders (Bloomington: Indiana UP, 1986), 29–30. On the coining of the term *autobiography,* see Robert F. Sayre, ed., *American Lives* (Madison: U of Wisconsin P, 1995), 3. James Goodwin, *Autobiography: The Self-Made Text* (New York: Twayne, 1993), xvii, offers 1807 as the date when *autobiography* is first used.

33. An in-depth and readable overview of Darwin's thought is Loren Eiseley, *Darwin's Century: Evolution and the Men Who Discovered It* (New York: Doubleday, 1958). Charles Darwin, *The Voyage of the Beagle,* ed. Leonard Engel (New York: Anchor, 1962); and *The Origin of Species,* ed. J. W. Burrow (New York: Penguin, 1968). A recent reevaluation of Darwin is Jonathan Weiner's *The Beak of the Finch: A Story of Evolution in Our Time* (New York: Knopf, 1994). Haeckel's coining of the term *ecology* is discussed in Kroeber 22–23. Worster provides a sound history of the development of modern ecology in *Nature's Economy.*

34. See Smallwood 336–39; Kastner 305–19; Lyon 37–48; and Charlotte Porter, *The Eagle's Nest: Natural History and American Ideas, 1812–1842* (University: U of Alabama P, 1986), 132–57.

35. Ralph Waldo Emerson, *Emerson's Nature: Origin, Growth, Meaning,* 2d ed., eds. Merton M. Sealts Jr. and Alfred R.

Ferguson (Carbondale: Southern Illinois UP, 1979), 8, 15. The best study of Emerson is Sherman Paul's *Emerson's Angle of Vision* (Cambridge: Harvard UP, 1952). See also Paul, *Repossessing and Renewing: Essays in the Green American Tradition* (Baton Rouge: Louisiana State UP, 1976). On the link between the Puritans and Emerson, see Perry Miller, *Errand into the Wilderness* (Cambridge: Harvard UP, 1956). On Augustine as spiritual autobiographer, see Goodwin 87–91.

36. Emerson 32. The complex, often troubled relationship between Emerson and Thoreau is chronicled most recently in two biographies by Robert Richardson: *Henry David Thoreau: A Life of the Mind* and *Emerson: The Mind on Fire*, both published by University of California Press (Berkeley, 1986, 1995).

37. Lawrence Buell analyzes Thoreau's writing in the tradition of the excursion essay in *Literary Transcendentalism: Style and Vision in the American Renaissance* (Ithaca: Cornell UP, 1973), 188–207. Henry D. Thoreau, *Journal: Volume 1: 1837–1844* (Princeton: Princeton UP, 1981), 370.

38. See Nash 84–95 on Thoreau as a conservationist. For Thoreau's relationships with Indians, see Robert F. Sayre, *Thoreau and the American Indians* (Princeton: Princeton UP, 1977). Don Scheese, "Nature Writing: A Wilderness of Books," *Forest & Conservation History* 34.4 (1990): 204–8, discusses the emergence of modern nature writing in the 19th century.

39. See Nash 78–82 on the importance of the Hudson River school in helping to develop American conservation-consciousness. A recent source on the Hudson River painters is the exhibition catalog *American Paradise*. For a good discussion of Church's treatment of wilderness, see Franklin Kelly, *Frederic Edwin Church and the National Landscape* (Washington, D.C.: Smithsonian, 1988), 80–122. Thomas Cole, "Essay on American Scenery," *The American Landscape: A Critical Anthology of Prose and Poetry*, ed. John Conron, 571, 578.

40. Nash 82–83 and Huth 148–61 discuss the western phase of the Hudson River school. Albert Boime links western expansion and art in *The Magisterial Gaze: Manifest Destiny and*

American Landscape Painting c. 1830–1865 (Washington, D.C.: Smithsonian Institution P, 1991). See also Matthew Baigell, *Albert Bierstadt* (New York: Watson-Guptill, 1988), 8–14, 36. George Catlin's contribution to national park ideology and Yosemite as the first national park is taken up in Alfred Runte, *National Parks: The American Experience* (Lincoln: U of Nebraska P, 1987), 238–39; see also Runte, *Yosemite: The Embattled Wilderness* (Lincoln: U of Nebraska P, 1990). A work that consolidates much of the scholarship on Watkins and Yosemite photography is Peter Palmquist, *Carleton Watkins: Photographer of the American West* (Albuquerque: U of New Mexico P, 1983).

41. George Perkins Marsh, *Man and Nature: Or, Physical Geography as Modified by Human Action* (Cambridge: Harvard UP, 1965). The best study of the romantic explorers remains William H. Goetzmann, *Exploration and Empire: The Explorer and the Scientist in the Winning of the West* (New York: Norton, 1966). John Wesley Powell, *The Exploration of the Colorado River and Its Canyons* (New York: Dover, 1961); and Clarence King, *Mountaineering in the Sierra Nevada* (Philadelphia: Lippincott, 1963).

42. John Muir, *A Thousand-Mile Walk to the Gulf* (Boston: Houghton Mifflin, 1944). The best book-length studies of Muir are Linnie Marsh Wolfe, *Son of the Wilderness: The Life of John Muir* (Madison: U of Wisconsin P, 1945); Michael Cohen, *The Pathless Way: John Muir and American Wilderness;* and Frederick Turner, *Rediscovering America: John Muir in His Time and Ours* (San Francisco: Sierra Club, 1985). Muir is quoted in Cohen 126.

43. The phrase is from Peter M. Schmitt, *Back to Nature: The Arcadian Myth in Urban America* (Baltimore: Johns Hopkins UP, 1990). The best study of the "nature faker" controversy is by Ralph Lutts, *The Nature Fakers: Wildlife, Science and Sentiment* (Golden, CO: Fulcrum, 1990); see also Lisa Mighetto, "Science, Sentiment, and Anxiety: Nature Writing at the Turn of the Century," *Pacific Historical Review* 54.1 (Feb. 1985): 33–50.

44. The quotations are from John Burroughs, introduction, *Wake-Robin* (Boston: Houghton Mifflin, 1921), xii–xiii. A con-

cise summary of Burroughs's thought can be found in John Burroughs, *A Sharp Lookout: Selected Nature Essays of John Burroughs*, ed. Frank Bergon (Washington, D.C.: Smithsonian, 1987), introduction 9–64. See also Lyon 63–67.

45. W. H. Hudson, *Hampshire Days* (New York: Oxford UP, 1980). Raymond Williams discusses Jeffries and Hudson in *The Country and the City* 191–96, 254. On American nature writing between the wars, see Lyon 67–68. Henry Beston, *The Outermost House* (Garden City, NY: Doubleday, 1928); his work is discussed by Sherman Paul in *For Love of the World: Essays on Nature Writers* (Iowa City: U of Iowa P, 1992), 111–31. Sally Carrighar, *One Day on Beetle Rock* (New York: Knopf, 1944). Donald Culross Peattie, *An Almanac for Moderns* (New York: Putnam's, 1935) and *The Road of a Naturalist* (Boston: Houghton Mifflin, 1941).

46. To my knowledge there is no book-length study of Canadian nature writing. Northrup Frye focuses on it to some extent in *The Bush Garden: Essays on the Canadian Imagination* (Toronto: Anansi, 1971). Ernest Thompson Seton, *Ernest Thompson Seton's America: Selections from the Writings of the Artist-Naturalist*, ed. Farida Wiley (New York: Devin-Adair, 1954). R. M. Patterson, *Dangerous River* (Toronto: Stoddart, 1954). Theodora Stanwell-Fletcher, *Driftwood Valley* (Boston: Little, Brown, 1946). Farley Mowat, *People of the Deer* (Boston: Little, Brown, 1952).

47. See Worster 191–253 on ecology in the 20th century and Nash 206–8 on the creation of the Wilderness Society. A fine study of the dust bowl is Donald Worster, *Dust Bowl* (New York: Oxford UP, 1979).

48. Aldo Leopold, *A Sand County Almanac with Sketches Here and There* (New York: Oxford UP, 1949), 224–25. The most important book-length treatments of Leopold are Susan Flader, *Thinking Like a Mountain: Aldo Leopold and the Evolution of an Ecological Attitude Toward Deer, Wolves, and Forests* (Lincoln: U of Nebraska P, 1978); J. Baird Callicott, ed., *Companion to 'A Sand County Almanac': Interpretive and Critical Essays* (Madison: U of Wisconsin P, 1987); Thomas Tanner, ed., *Aldo Leopold: His Life and Legacy* (Ankeny, IA: Soil Conservation Society of America, 1987); Curt Meine, *Aldo Leopold: His Life*

and Work (Madison: U of Wisconsin P, 1988); and J. Baird Callicott, ed., *In Defense of the Land Ethic: Essays in Environmental Philosophy* (Albany: SUNY P, 1989).

49. Loren Eiseley, "The Judgment of the Birds," *The Immense Journey* (New York: Random House, 1957), 163; and *The Night Country* (New York: Scribner's, 1971). On Eiseley's life and writings, see Gale E. Christianson, *Fox at the Wood's Edge* (New York: Henry Holt, 1990).

50. Rachel Carson, *Silent Spring* (Boston: Houghton Mifflin, 1962). The best book-length study remains Paul Brooks, *Rachel Carson at Work: The House of Life* (Boston: G. K. Hall, 1985); see, too, Mary A. McCay, *Rachel Carson* (New York: Twayne, 1993). Lyon 80–82 and Stewart 160–87 discuss Carson as well.

51. Daniel Botkin, *Discordant Harmonies: A New Ecology for the Twenty-First Century* (New York: Oxford, 1990), 140–41.

52. On the role of 20th-century photography in preservation politics, see "Wilderness and the Camera's Eye" by Andrea Gray in *Wilderness* (Fall 1985): 12–17; and Nash 228–30. Ansel Adams, *An Autobiography* (Boston: Little, Brown, 1985), 303. A concise summary of Adams's contribution (as well as his own statement on the role of the artist in the preservation movement) can be found in *Celebrating the American Earth: A Portfolio by Ansel Adams* (Washington, D.C.: The Wilderness Society, n.d.).

53. Edward Abbey, *Desert Solitaire: A Season in the Wilderness* (New York: Simon & Schuster, 1968), and *The Monkey Wrench Gang* (Philadelphia: J. P. Lippincott, 1975). Good studies of Abbey are Garth McCann, *Edward Abbey* (Boise, ID: Boise State U Western Writers Series #29, 1977); Ann Ronald, *The New West of Edward Abbey* (Albuquerque: U of New Mexico P, 1982); and James Bishop, Jr., *Epitaph for a Desert Anarchist: The Life and Legacy of Edward Abbey* (New York: Atheneum, 1994). Terry Tempest Williams, *Refuge: An Unnatural History of Family and Place* (New York: Pantheon, 1991); and, particularly on the theme of civil disobedience, "A Patriot's Journal," *An Unspoken Hunger* (New York: Pantheon, 1994), 97–114. A recent history of radical environmentalism is Christopher Manes, *Green Rage: Radical Environmentalism and the Unmaking of Civilization* (Boston: Little, Brown, 1990).

54. Wendell Berry, *The Unsettling of America: Culture and Agriculture* (New York: Avon, 1977); *A Place on Earth* (San Francisco: North Point Press, rev. ed. 1983); *Farming: A Handbook* (New York: Harcourt, Brace, Jovanovich, 1970). The collection of essays assembled by Paul Merchant (ed.), *Wendell Berry* (Lewiston, ID: Confluence Press, 1991), provides a good introduction to Berry's work.

55. Kenneth T. Jackson, *The Crabgrass Frontier: The Suburbanization of the United States* (New York: Oxford UP, 1985). The phrase "undiscovered country of the nearby" is from John Hanson Mitchell, *Ceremonial Time: Fifteen Thousand Years on One Square Mile* (New York: Anchor, 1984), 7. Michael Pollan, *Second Nature: A Gardener's Education* (New York: Atlantic Monthly, 1991). Michael Aaron Rockland, *Snowshoeing through Sewers: Adventures in New York City, New Jersey, and Philadelphia* (New Brunswick, NJ: Rutgers UP, 1994), 6.

56. Annie Dillard, *Pilgrim at Tinker Creek* (New York: Harper & Row, 1974). Among the many fine studies of Dillard, I recommend Peter Fritzell, *Nature Writing and America: Essays upon a Cultural Type* (Ames: Iowa State UP, 1990), 217–83; Linda Smith, *Annie Dillard* (New York: Twayne, 1991); Scott Slovic, *Seeking Awareness in American Nature Writing: Henry Thoreau, Annie Dillard, Edward Abbey, Wendell Berry, Barry Lopez* (Salt Lake City: U of Utah P, 1992), 61–92; and James I. McClintock, *Nature's Kindred Spirits: Aldo Leopold, Joseph Wood Krutch, Edward Abbey, Annie Dillard, and Gary Snyder* (Madison: U of Wisconsin P, 1994), 88–108.

57. N. Scott Momaday, *The Way to Rainy Mountain* (Albuquerque: U of New Mexico P, 1969), 83. The oral traditions and published writings of Native Americans remain a little-treated subject in ecocriticism. See *The American Nature Writing Newsletter* (Fall 1994), an issue devoted to the topic, "Native Americans and Nature Writing," published by ASLE (Association for the Study of Literature and the Environment, headed by Scott Slovic and Cheryll Glotfelty of the English Department at University of Nevada, Reno).

58. Gary Snyder, *Turtle Island* (New York: New Directions, 1974); Barry Lopez, *Arctic Dreams: Imagination and Desire in a Northern Landscape* (New York: Scribner's, 1986); Gary Paul Nabhan, *The Desert Smells Like Rain: A Naturalist in Papago Indian County*

(San Francisco: North Point Press, 1982); Richard Nelson, *The Island Within* (San Francisco: North Point Press, 1989). Max Oelschlaeger is one of the few intellectual historians of wilderness to trace the idea back to Paleolithic times; see *The Idea of Wilderness* (New Haven: Yale UP, 1991), 1–30. On the recent discovery of the Chauvet cave art, see Jean Clottes, "Rhinos and Lions and Bears (Oh, My!)" *Natural History* (May 1995): 30–35.

2. Thoreau

1. Lawrence Buell, "The Thoreauvian Pilgrimage: The Structure of an American Cult," *American Literature* 61.2 (May 1989): 175. See also Buell's expanded treatment of this theme in *The Environmental Imagination: Thoreau, Nature Writing, and the Formation of American Culture* (Cambridge: Harvard UP, 1995), 311–38.

2. Two articles that trace the transformation of the Walden landscape are Kurt Kehr, "Walden Three: Ecological Changes in the Landscape of Henry David Thoreau," *Journal of Forest History* 27 (Jan. 1983): 28–33; and Gordon G. Whitney and William C. Davis, "From Primitive Woods to Cultivated Woodlots: Thoreau and the Forest History of Concord, Massachusetts," *Journal of Forest History* 30 (Apr. 1986): 70–81. The number of visitors to the pond comes from John Houvouras, "On Once-Wild Walden Pond," *Sierra* May/June 1989: 94–96.

3. On the cultural ritual of pilgrimage, I have drawn specifically on Elizabeth McKinsey, *Niagara Falls: Icon of the American Sublime* (Cambridge: Cambridge UP, 1985), 191–96. Although McKinsey discusses the problems confronting the tourist who journeys to view Niagara Falls for the first time, her theory and conclusion are applicable to Walden as well. See also John Sears, *Sacred Places: American Tourist Attractions in the Nineteenth Century* (New York: Oxford UP, 1989), 3–11; and, on pilgrimages generally, Victor and Edith Turner, *Image and Pilgrimage in Christian Culture* (New York: Columbia UP, 1978).

4. John Muir, *The Life and Letters of John Muir*, ed. William Frederick Bade, 2 vols. (Boston: Houghton Mifflin, 1924), 2: 268.

5. On Thoreau's early years and his search for a vocation, see Sherman Paul, *The Shores of America: Thoreau's Inward Exploration* (Urbana: U of Illinois P, 1958), 1–48; Walter Harding, *The Days of Henry Thoreau* (New York: Dover, 1962), 52–74; and Robert Richardson, *Henry Thoreau: A Life of the Mind* (Berkeley: U of California P, 1986), 3–42. The paraphrase of a Journal passage is from Henry D. Thoreau, *Journal Volume 1: 1837–1844*, ed. Elizabeth Hall Witherell et al. (Princeton: Princeton UP, 1981), 348.

6. Lyndon Shanley, *The Making of Walden* (Chicago: U of Chicago P, 1957). Henry D. Thoreau, *The Illustrated Walden* (Princeton: Princeton UP, 1973), 98; subsequent references to this work appear parenthetically in the text.

7. For background on Thoreau's life at Walden, see David Shi, *The Simple Life: Plain Living and High Thinking in American Culture* (New York: Oxford UP, 1985); his specific discussion of Thoreau and Therien can be found on pp. 144–47.

8. Shi 147–48. On Therien's identity, see Walter Harding, *The Variorum Walden* (New York: Twayne, 1962), fn. 9, 284.

9. Thoreau's posturing and defensiveness in relation to the rest of Concord are often discussed in Thoreau studies. Walter Harding provides perhaps the most pro-Thoreau stance in *The Days*; Richard Bridgman the most negative in *Dark Thoreau* (Lincoln: U of Nebraska P, 1982).

10. See Roderick Nash, *Wilderness and the American Mind* (New Haven: Yale UP, rev. ed., 1982) on the "straddling" theme (92–95). On Thoreau's alienation, see Leon Edel, *Stuff of Sleep and Dreams: Experiments in Literary Psychology* (New York: Harper & Row, 1982), 50–65.

11. Leo Marx, *The Machine in the Garden: Technology and the Pastoral Ideal in America* (New York: Oxford UP, 1964).

12. Marx 253.

13. Marx 220–22. See also H. Daniel Peck, "The Crosscurrents of Walden's Pastoral," *New Essays on Walden*, ed. Robert F. Sayre (Cambridge: Cambridge UP, 1992), 77–81; Alfred Werner, *Inness: Landscapes* (New York: Watson-Guptill, 1973), 24–25; and Richard Schneider, "Thoreau and

Nineteenth-Century American Landscape Painting," *ESQ* 31.2 (1985): 67–88.

14. Good discussions of the cutbank passage can be found in Paul 343–49; Marx 260–64; and Kevin Radaker, "'To Witness Our Limits Transgressed': The Scientific and Nationalistic Perspectives of Henry Thoreau and Frederic Church in Describing the Maine Wilderness," *Yearbook of Interdisciplinary Studies in the Fine Arts* 2 (1990): 455–56.

15. Marx helped popularize the notion of Walden as a "middle landscape" (246, 255–60). A fine recent essay on Thoreau's agricultural project is David Robinson, "'Unchronicled Nations': Agrarian Purpose and Thoreau's Ecological Knowing," *Nineteenth Century Literature* 48.3 (Dec. 1993): 326–40.

16. See Robert McIntosh, *Thoreau as Romantic Naturalist: His Shifting Stance toward Nature* (Ithaca: Cornell UP, 1974), 253–56.

17. Richardson, 248–52. Robert Sattelmeyer, *Thoreau's Reading: A Study in Intellectual History* (Princeton: Princeton UP, 1988), 148, 284–85. Donald Worster in *Nature's Economy: A History of Ecological Ideas* (Cambridge: Cambridge UP, 1977) discusses Leopold as a 20th-century ecologist (98–111). See Aldo Leopold, *A Sand County Almanac with Sketches Here and There* (New York: Oxford UP, 1949); and Wendell Berry, *The Unsettling of America: Culture and Agriculture* (New York: Avon, 1977). A good overview of sustainable agriculture is the collection of essays *Meeting the Expectations of the Land: Essays in Sustainable Agriculture and Stewardship*, eds. Wes Jackson, Wendell Berry, and Bruce Colman (San Francisco: North Point P, 1984).

18. See Robert F. Sayre, *Thoreau and the American Indians* (Princeton: Princeton UP, 1977), 77–84.

19. Shi discusses Thoreau's diet in the context of the simple life (144–50). See also Frederick Garber, *Thoreau's Redemptive Imagination* (New York: New York UP, 1977), 111–22.

20. Buell in *The Environmental Imagination* provides insightful close readings of this seldom-treated chapter (168–69, 245–48).

21. A good book-length treatment of Thoreau's use of travel literature is John Aldrich Christie, *Thoreau as World Traveler* (New York: Columbia UP, 1965).

22. The essay "Ktaadn" first appeared in *Union Magazine of Literature and Art,* a popular periodical of the day, and was later revised by Thoreau and posthumously published as part of *The Maine Woods* in 1864. Henry D. Thoreau, "Ktaadn," *The Maine Woods,* ed. Joseph Moldenhauer (Princeton: Princeton UP, 1972), 358; subsequent references to this work are cited parenthetically in the text. An excellent study of Thoreau as a sensitive respondent to the literary marketplace is Stephen Fink, *Prophet in the Marketplace: Thoreau's Development as a Writer* (Princeton: Princeton UP, 1992), 150–52.

23. On the composition of "Ktaadn," see Stephen Adams and Donald Ross, Jr., *Revising Mythologies: The Composition of Thoreau's Major Works* (Charlottesville: U of Virginia P, 1988), 64–65; Robert Sattelmeyer, "Historical Introduction, "*Journal Volume 2: 1842–48* (Princeton: Princeton UP, 1988), 461–62; and Robert Cosbey, "Thoreau at Work: The Writing of 'Ktaadn,'" *New York Library Public Library Bulletin* (Jan. 1961): 21–30.

24. See Adams and Ross 67–69; and John Jaques, "'Ktaadn'—A Record of Thoreau's Youthful Crisis," *Thoreau Journal Quarterly* 1.4 (Oct. 1969): 4–5.

25. Geographic and historical details of the climb can be found in John Worthington, "Thoreau's Route to Katahdin," *Appalachia* (June 1946): 3–14; and Robert Cosbey, "Thoreau on Katahdin," *Appalachia* (June 1961): 409–11.

26. Some representative samples of the wide range of interpretations of "Ktaadn" are John Blair and Augustus Trowbridge, "Thoreau on Katahdin," *American Quarterly* (Winter 1960): 508–17; Ronald Wesley Hoag, "The Mark on the Wilderness: Thoreau's Contact with Katahdin," *Texas Studies in Literature and Language* 24.1 (Spring 1982): 23–46; and John Tallmadge, "'Ktaadn': Thoreau in the Wilderness of Words," *ESQ* 31 (1985): 137–48.

27. On the definition of "landscape" as opposed to "wilderness," see J. B. Jackson, *Discovering the Vernacular Landscape* (New Haven: Yale UP, 1984), 3–8.

28. On Thoreau's transcendentalism in "Ktaadn," see Jonathan Fairbanks, "Thoreau: Speaker for Wilderness," *South Atlantic Quarterly* 70 (1971): 487–506; and Hoag 32–33. For the original draft of "Ktaadn" (i.e., his journal entries), see Henry D. Thoreau, *Journal Volume 2: 1842–1848*, ed. Robert Sattelmeyer (Princeton: Princeton UP, 1984), 270–349.

29. Ralph Waldo Emerson, *Nature* (Boston: J. Munroe, 1836), 8. On Thoreau's anthropocentrism versus biocentrism generally, see Roderick Nash, *The Rights of Nature: A History of Environmental Ethics* (New Haven: Yale UP, 1989), 36–38.

30. Paul refers to it as "most frenzied" (361); Tallmadge calls it the "metaphysical climax" (142–44).

31. See Fink 186–87 on Thoreau's sensitivity to the literary marketplace with specific reference to "Ktaadn"; and Harding, *Days*, on Thoreau's difficulties as a lecturer (228–30).

32. Karl Kroeber criticizes the English profession and especially the rarefied approaches of contemporary literary theory in *Ecological Literary Criticism: Romantic Imagining and the Biology of the Mind* (New York: Columbia UP, 1994). John P. O'Grady and I are in (rare) agreement in our interpretations of Thoreau when O'Grady writes: "No doubt Thoreau's experience on Mount Katahdin had a profound effect upon him, but it is not one of cowardly retreat to the pastoral, humanized landscape of Concord, as many non-mountain-climbing scholars would have it" (*Pilgrims to the Wild: Everett Ruess, Henry David Thoreau, John Muir, Clarence King, Mary Austin* [Salt Lake City: U of Utah P, 1993], 42).

33. The most cogent discussions of the lessons of the Katahdin experience for Thoreau are in Tallmadge (144–47), Hoag (33–38), and Fink (180–86).

34. Fink 180–86. A good study of the painter Frederic Church is Franklin Kelly, *Frederic Edwin Church and the National Landscape* (Washington, D.C.: Smithsonian, 1988); on Church's Maine experience, see specifically 67–74, and Radaker 460–69.

35. On the writing of "Walking," see Richardson 224–27 and Kenneth Egan, Jr., "Thoreau's Pastoral Vision in 'Walking,'" *American Transcendental Quarterly* 57 (July 1985): 21–30.

36. On the similar themes of "Walking" and *Walden*, see Henry David Thoreau, *A Year in Thoreau's Journal: 1851*, ed. H. Daniel Peck (New York: Penguin, 1994), 5–13. Lyndon Shanley, *The Making of Walden*, is the standard work on the composition of *Walden*. The Journal quotation is from Henry David Thoreau, *The Journal of Henry David Thoreau*, 14 vols., eds. Bradford Torrey and Frances H. Allen (1906; Salt Lake City: Gibbs M. Smith, 1984), 5: 459. Henry David Thoreau, "Walking," *The Natural History Essays*, ed. Robert Sattelmeyer (Salt Lake City: Peregrine Smith, 1980), 93; subsequent references to this work appear parenthetically in the text.

37. Henry David Thoreau, *The Journal of Henry David Thoreau*, ed. Bradford Torrey and Francis H. Allen, 14 vols. (1906; Salt Lake City: Gibbs M. Smith, 1984), 9:43. I offer a close reading of this passage in "Thoreau's Journal: The Creation of a Sacred Place," *Mapping American Culture*, eds. Wayne Franklin and Michael Steiner (Iowa City: U of Iowa P, 1992), 139–51.

38. Herbert Lindenberger, "The Idyllic Moment: On Pastoral and Romanticism," *College English* 34.3 (Dec. 1972): 345.

3. Muir

1. The quotation is from John Muir, *The Story of My Boyhood and Youth* (Madison: U of Wisconsin P, 1965), 8. Good coverage of Muir's early years, the conflict that developed between Muir and his father over religion, and Muir's attitude toward animals is provided in Linnie Marsh Wolfe, *Son of the Wilderness: The Life of John Muir* (Madison: U of Wisconsin P, 1945), 38; Ronald Limbaugh, "The Nature of John Muir's Religion," *The Pacific Historian* 29.2–3 (Summer/Fall 1985): 16–29; and Lisa Mighetto, "John Muir and the Rights of Animals," *The Pacific Historian* 29.2–3 (Summer/Fall 1985): 103–12.

2. The quotation is from John Muir, *A Thousand-Mile Walk to the Gulf* (Boston: Houghton Mifflin, 1944), 136–39. Frederick Turner glosses this important period of Muir's life in *Rediscovering America: John Muir in His Time and Ours* (San Francisco: Sierra Club, 1985), 131–57.

3. John Elder in "John Muir and the Literature of Wilderness," *Massachusetts Review* 22.2 (Summer 1981), identifies Muir's religion as "Christian pantheism" (385), but I will argue later that Muir's religious beliefs are best characterized as panentheism with an overlay of Christian imagery.

4. "For freshness of vision combined with ecological revelation, *My First Summer in the Sierra* is perhaps [Muir's] best book," Thomas Lyon claims in *John Muir* (Boise: Boise State Western Writers Series #3, 1972), 44. This point is reaffirmed by other commentators: see Gretel Ehrlich, introduction, *My First Summer in the Sierra* (New York: Penguin, 1987), vii–xvi; and Sherman Paul, *For Love of the World: Essays on Nature Writers* (Iowa City: U of Iowa P, 1992), 241, 252.

5. On Muir's arrival in California and his initial visit to Yosemite, see Wolfe 116; Turner 120–30, 163–64; Muir, *A Thousand-Mile Walk*, 186–88; and Stephen Fox, *The American Conservation Movement: John Muir and His Legacy* (Madison: U of Wisconsin P, 1985), 8–9.

6. John Muir, *My First Summer in the Sierra* (New York: Penguin, 1987), 26; subsequent references to this work appear parenthetically in the text.

7. On anthropocentrism versus biocentrism in Muir's thinking, see Max Oelschlaeger, *The Idea of Wilderness* (New Haven: Yale UP, 1991), 196–97; and Roderick Nash, *The Rights of Nature: A History of Environmental Ethics* (Madison: U of Wisconsin P, 1989), 39–42. The best study of the "nature faker" controversy in America at the turn of the century is Ralph Lutts, *The Nature Fakers: Wildlife, Science, and Sentiment* (Golden, CO: Fulcrum, 1990).

8. Richard Fleck, *Henry Thoreau and John Muir among the Indians* (Hamden, CT: Archon, 1985), remains the most substantial treatment of this issue to date. I am more critical of Muir's attitude toward Indians than Fleck is.

9. *Boyhood and Youth* 174. Alfred Runte discusses the natives' use of fire in Yosemite Valley as a form of game management, an important land-use practice Muir only mentions, in *Yosemite: Embattled Wilderness* (Lincoln: U of Nebraska P, 1990), 1–9. An excellent and concise summary of the Euramerican misinterpretation of Native American land use

is Samuel Wilson, "'That Wild Unmanned Countrey,'" *Natural History* (May 1992): 16–17.

10. Also critical of Muir in this passage is Michael Cohen, *The Pathless Way: John Muir and American Wilderness* (Madison: U of Wisconsin P, 1984), 185. For a counterinterpretation, see Fleck 39–41. On the extermination of Native Americans in California in the 19th century, see Leonard Dinnerstein et al., *Natives and Strangers: Blacks, Indian, and Immigrants in America* (New York: Oxford UP, 2d ed., 1990), 200.

11. Wolfe 27. In Muir's defense, it should be pointed out that his attitude toward Native American tribes he encountered later in Alaska is more open-minded, in part because they were not acculturated at the time. See John Muir, *Travels in Alaska* (1915; San Francisco: Sierra Club Books, 1988); and Frank Buske, "John Muir's Alaska Experience," *The Pacific Historian* 29. 2–3 (Summer/Fall 1985): 116.

12. I find the following articles useful and concise treatments of Muir's geological thinking: Bart O'Brien, "Earthquakes or Snowflowers," *The Pacific Historian* 29.2–3 (Summer/Fall 1985): 31–41; and Paul Sheats, "John Muir's Glacial Gospel," *The Pacific Historian* 29.2–3 (Summer/Fall 1985): 42–54. From 1874 to 1875, Muir published a series of articles about Sierra geology in a popular periodical, *Overland Monthly*; these were later published as a book, *Studies in the Sierra*, ed. William Colby (San Francisco: Sierra Club Books, 1949).

13. The best summary of the debate over the origins of Yosemite can be found in Michael Smith, *Pacific Visions: California Scientists and the Environment, 1850–1915* (New Haven, Yale UP, 1987), 65–101.

14. Loren Eiseley, *Darwin's Century: Evolution and the Men Who Discovered It* (Garden City, NY: Anchor, 1958), provides an insightful and readable account of the major influences on Darwin's thinking. The Whitney-Muir debate is taken up in O'Brien 31–41, Sheats 42–54, Smith 71–103, and Cohen 99–103 and 134–36.

15. Sheats 44–53. For journal passages on which this passage is based, see Robert Engberg and Donald Wesling, eds., *John Muir: To Yosemite and Beyond: Writings from the Years 1863 to 1875* (Madison: U of Wisconsin P, 1980), 52–54.

16. Gerald L. Carr, "Albert Bierstadt," *American Paradise: The World of the Hudson River School* (New York: Metropolitan Museum of Art, 1987), 288–90.

17. "Wind-swept slopes and total solitude" is from Herbert Lindenberger, "The Idyllic Moment: On Pastoral and Romanticism," *College English* 34.3 (Dec. 1972): 338. On Muir's anthropomorphic geology, see also Frank Stewart, *The Nature of Natural History* (Washington, D.C.: Island Press, 1994), 119–20; and Oelschlaeger 186–97.

18. On the degree and nature of Muir's transcendentalism, see Paul 262–64; Nash 40–41; and Daniel Weber, "The Transcendental Wilderness Aesthetics of John Muir," *The World of John Muir,* eds. Lawrence Murphy and Dan Collins (Stockton: U of the Pacific, 1981), 1–10. It should be pointed out that in his later Journal Thoreau makes various *private* pleas for the preservation of nature. See, for example, *The Journal of Henry David Thoreau,* 14 vols. (Salt Lake City: Gibbs M. Smith, 1984), 14: 303–7.

19. On Muir as a public figure and conservationist, see Nash 40–41; Fox 316–18; Donald Wesling, "John Muir and the Human Part of the Mountain's Destiny," *The World of John Muir,* eds. Lawrence Murphy and Dan Collins (Stockton: U of the Pacific, 1981), 58–63; Holway Jones, "John Muir, The Sierra Club, and the Formulation of the Wilderness Concept," *The World of John Muir,* eds. Lawrence Murphy and Dan Collins (Stockton: U of the Pacific, 1981), 64–78; and Michael Cohen, *The History of the Sierra Club, 1892–1970* (San Francisco: Sierra Club, 1988).

20. A concise summary of the Hetch Hetchy controversy is by Roderick Nash, *Wilderness and the American Mind* (New Haven: Yale UP, 3d rev. ed., 1982), 161–81.

21. The last two stanzas of Wallace Steven's poem, "The American Sublime," which I paraphrase, are as follows: "But how does one feel? / One grows used to the weather, / The landscape and that; / And the sublime comes down / To the spirit itself. / The spirit and space, / The empty spirit / In vacant space. / What wine does one drink? / What bread does one eat?" Wallace Stevens, *The Collected Poems of Wallace Stevens* (New York: Knopf, 1954), 131.

4. Austin

1. An insightful essay on Austin as a nature writer is Shelley Armitage, "Mary Austin: Writing Nature," *Wind's Trail: The Early Life of Mary Austin* (Albuquerque: Museum of New Mexico, 1990), 18–19. A good overview of Austin is Peter Wild, *Pioneer Conservationists of Western America* (Missoula, MT: Mountain Press, 1979), 81–91. Patricia Limerick in *Desert Passages: Encounters with the American Deserts* (Albuquerque: U of New Mexico P, 1985) redresses the neglect of deserts generally in studies of American attitudes toward nature, though (unaccountably) she fails to discuss Austin. A contemporary of Austin's who also helped transform perceptions of the desert was John C. Van Dyke; see, for example, *The Desert* (1901; Salt Lake City: Gibbs Smith, 1980).

2. Mary Austin, *The Land of Little Rain* (Albuquerque: U of New Mexico P, 1974), 5; subsequent references to this work appear parenthetically in the text.

3. Mary Austin, *Earth Horizon: Autobiography* (Albuquerque: U of New Mexico P, 1991), 51; subsequent references to this work appear parenthetically in the text as EH. The best biography of Austin is Esther Stineman, *Mary Austin: Song of a Maverick* (New Haven: Yale UP, 1989); on Austin's early years in Illinois, see 17–18.

4. On the popularity of nature at the turn of the century, see Peter M. Schmitt, *Back to Nature: The Arcadian Myth in Urban America* (Baltimore: Johns Hopkins UP, 1990). On Austin's college experience, see Stineman 22–25.

5. Stineman 211–14. David Wyatt examines the desert as surrogate mother in his chapter on Austin in *The Fall into Eden: Landscape and Imagination in California* (Cambridge: Cambridge UP, 1986), 69–76.

6. On the epidemic of neurasthenia in turn-of-the-century America and its gender implications, see Tom Lutz, *American Nervousness* (Ithaca: Cornell UP, 1991); and Carroll Smith-Rosenberg, *Disorderly Conduct* (New York: Oxford UP, 1985). An excellent study of how it affected one woman can be found in Jean Strouse, *Alice James, A Biography* (Boston: Houghton Mifflin, 1980). On the specific effects of neurasthenia on Austin, see Stineman 22–25.

7. Stineman 25–56. On Austin's years in California, see also T. M. Pearce, *Mary Hunter Austin* (New York: Twayne, 1965), 28–39.

8. The classic study of the myth of the American west as garden is Henry Nash Smith's *Virgin Land: The American West as Symbol and Myth* (Cambridge: Harvard UP, 1950). An update and a revision of the myth are provided by Limerick; see particularly her concluding chapter, "The Significance of Deserts in American History."

9. Austin, for example, wrote the introduction to *The Path on the Rainbow: An Anthology of Songs and Chants from the Indians of North America* (1918) and was invited to write the chapter on aboriginal literature for the *Cambridge History of American Literature* (1917–1921). Her *American Rhythm* (1923) interprets modernist poetry as a continuation in some ways of "Amerindian" oral traditions. See James Ruppert, "Discovering America: Mary Austin and Imagism," *Studies in American Indian Literature,* ed. Paula Gunn Allen (New York: Modern Language Association, 1983): 243–58. The key principles of ecofeminism are from Irene Diamond and Gloria Feman Orenstein, eds., *Reweaving the World: The Emergence of Ecofeminism* (San Francisco: Sierra Club, 1990), xi–xii. See also Greta Gaard, ed., *Ecofeminism: Women, Animals, Nature* (Philadelphia: Temple UP, 1993).

10. Mary Austin, *Lost Borders* (New York: Harper, 1909). Vera Norwood, *Made from This Earth: American Women and Nature* (Chapel Hill: U of North Carolina P, 1993), 46–52, 54–97. Edward Abbey, "Cliffrose and Bayonets," *Desert Solitaire: A Season in the Wilderness* (New York: Simon & Schuster, 1968).

11. On the relationship between Austin and Beale, see Stineman 32–35. Stineman provides an excellent close reading of *The Land of Little Rain* (70–80). Vera Norwood discusses Austin's reverence for all life in the desert in "Heroines of Nature: Four Women Respond to the American Landscape," *Environmental Review* 8.1 (Spring 1984): 41–44.

12. Two excellent studies of the "nature in harmony" paradigm in the history of science are Donald Worster, *Nature's Economy: A History of Ecological Ideas* (Cambridge: Cambridge UP, 1977); and Daniel B. Botkin, *Discordant Harmonies: A New*

Ecology for the Twenty-First Century (New York: Oxford UP, 1990).

13. Interestingly, Ralph Lutts makes no mention of Austin, popular writer though she was, in *The Nature Fakers: Wildlife, Science, and Sentiment* (Golden, CO: Fulcrum, 1990). James Work analyzes Austin's anthropomorphism in "The Moral in Austin's *The Land of Little Rain*," *Women and Western American Literature*, eds. Helen Stauffer and Susan J. Rosowski (Troy, NY: Whitston, 1982): 303.

14. Lawrence Buell takes up the issue of "escapism" in pastoral writing and the degree to which Thoreau is open to the charge of community neglect in *The Environmental Imagination: Thoreau, Nature Writing, and the Formation of American Culture* (Cambridge: Cambridge UP, 1995), 388–89. John O'Grady in *Pilgrims to the Wild: Everett Ruess, Henry David Thoreau, John Muir, Clarence King, Mary Austin* (Salt Lake City: U of Utah P, 1993) makes the claim that "Austin is the most sociologically insightful of all the nineteenth-century writers of the wild" (126). On the pursuit of simplicity in the United States, see David Shi, *The Simple Life: Plain Living and High Thinking in American Culture* (New York: Oxford UP, 1985).

15. Mary Austin, *The Land of Journey's Ending* (Albuquerque: U of New Mexico P, 1983), 246. Stineman discusses Austin's childhood religious influences (17–18); see also *Earth Horizon* 276–77, 282–83, 367–68.

16. On Austin's celebration of Native Americans, see Ruppert 243–58; Stineman 74–80; and Lois Rudnick, "Re-Naming the Land: Anglo Expatriate Women in the Southwest," *The Desert Is No Lady: Southwestern Landscapes in Women's Writing and Art*, eds. Vera Norwood and Janice Monk (New Haven: Yale UP, 1987), 10–26. Roderick Nash discusses the popularity of primitivism at the turn of the century in *Wilderness and the American Mind* (New Haven: Yale UP, 3d rev. ed., 1982), 141–60.

17. Winnenap is discussed as "The Medicine Man" in *Earth Horizon*, 276–77. On Native American demographics and the catastrophic decline in the population of the indigenous peoples of the Americas, see two works by Alfred Crosby: *The*

Columbian Exchange: The Biological Consequences of 1492 (West-port, CT: Greenwood, 1972), and *Ecological Imperialism: The Biological Expansion of Europe* (Cambridge: Cambridge, 1986). See also Henry Dobyns, *Their Number Became Thinned: Native American Population Dynamics in Eastern America* (Knoxville: U of Tennessee P, 1983).

18. Stineman 75–77. Some critics have accused Austin of roman-ticizing Native American culture; see, for example, Peter Wild, "The Dangers of Mary Austin's *The Land of Little Rain*," *North Dakota Quarterly* 56.3 (Summer 1988): 122–23; and Rudnick 25. The classic study of the romanticization of Indians by Euramericans is Roy Harvey Pearce, *Savagism and Civilization: A Study of the Indian and the American Mind* (Berkeley: U of California P, rev. ed. 1988).

19. Rudnick discusses Austin's feminist and environmental pro-jects separately but does not conjoin them as ecofeminism (16–22).

20. "The Walking Woman," *Lost Borders* (New York: Harpers, 1909), is the subject of much commentary by Austin critics; a number of them cite it as her finest work. See, for example, the excellent overview provided by Melody Graulich in the Afterword to *Earth Horizon* (373–94). On the relationship between Austin and Seyavi, see Stineman 53–56, 75–77; and Vera Norwood, "The Photographer and the Naturalist," *Journal of American Culture* 5.2 (Summer 1982): 5–6. For a suc-cinct summary of the concept of the "New Woman" at the turn of the century, see Margaret Culley, "The Context of *The Awakening*," *The Awakening*, ed. Margaret Culley (New York: Norton, 1976), 117–19.

21. Parallels between Austin and Seyavi are discussed in Rudnick 21–22; Norwood 1982, 2–3; Graulich 387–88; and Stineman 75–78.

22. Marjorie Pryse, in her introduction to *Stories from the Country of Lost Borders* (New Brunswick: Rutgers UP, 1989), which combines *The Land of Little Rain* and *Lost Borders*, discusses Jewett's influence on Austin (xv–xvi). A good discussion of "The Little Town of the Grape Vines" is Rudnick (19–23). I readily reaffirm Rudnick's claim that Austin's ideas "have

much in common with contemporary bioregionalist think-ing" (26).

23. On Austin's career as a conservationist, see Benay Blend, "Mary Austin and the Western Conservation Movement, 1900–1927," *Journal of the Southwest* 30.1 (Spring 1988): 12–34. On the role of women conservationists generally around the turn of the century, see Carolyn Merchant, "Women of the Progressive Movement, 1900–1916," *Environmental History Review* 8.1 (Spring 1984): 57–87.

24. Mary Austin, *The Land of Little Rain*, abridged version, with photographs by Ansel Adams (Boston: Houghton Mifflin, 1950). Mary Austin, *Taos Pueblo*, with photographs by Ansel Adams (San Francisco: Grabhorn, 1930). See Stineman (187–98) on the relationship between Austin and Adams. An interesting study of Austin and another important landscape photographer, Laura Gilpin, is Norwood (1982). On land-scape photography in the American west generally, see Weston Naef and James Wood, eds., *Era of Exploration: The Rise of Landscape Photography in the American West, 1860–1885* (New York: Metropolitan Museum of Art, 1975).

5. Leopold

1. The history of the land that Aldo Leopold purchased near the Wisconsin River in Sauk County is summarized briefly by Charles Bradley in "The Leopold Memorial Reserve," *Aldo Leopold: The Man and His Legacy*, ed. Thomas Tanner (Ankeny, IA: Soil Conservation Society of America, 1987), 161. For the argument that we are now living in a "postnat-ural" age, see Bill McKibben, *The End of Nature* (New York: Random House, 1989). Praise of *A Sand County Almanac* has been widespread. See, for example, Secretary of the Interior Steward Udall's remark in 1963: "If asked to select a single volume which contains a noble elegy for the American earth and a plea for a new land ethic, most of us at Interior would vote for Aldo Leopold's *A Sand County Almanac*" (quoted in Roderick Nash, *The Rights of Nature: A History of Environmental Ethics* [Madison: U of Wisconsin P, 1989], 63).

2. The best study of the relationship between conservation and hunting and fishing is John Reiger, *American Sportsmen and the Origins of Conservation* (Norman: U of Oklahoma P, 1985).

The definitive biography of Leopold is Curt Meine, *Aldo Leopold: His Life and Work* (Madison: U of Wisconsin P, 1988); on Leopold's early years, see 19–36. Aldo Leopold, *A Sand County Almanac and Sketches Here and There* (New York: Oxford UP, 1949), 121, 202; subsequent references to this work appear parenthetically in the text.

3. Meine 51–83. Stephen Fox in *The American Conservation Movement: John Muir and His Legacy* (Madison: U of Wisconsin P, 1985) discusses Pinchot's role in the conservation movement (110–30). See also Pinchot's autobiography *Breaking New Ground* (New York: Harcourt, Brace, 1947); and Harold Pinkett, *Gifford Pinchot: Private and Public Forester* (Urbana: U of Illinois P, 1970).

4. Aldo Leopold, "Foreword," *Companion to "A Sand County Almanac": Interpretive and Critical Essays,* ed. J. Baird Callicott (Madison: U of Wisconsin P, 1987), 282.

5. Good sources on Leopold's years in the southwest are David Brown and Neil Carmony, eds., "Aldo Leopold," *Aldo Leopold's Wilderness: Selected Early Writings by the Author of "A Sand County Almanac"* (Harrisburg, PA: Stackpole, 1990), 5–14; Susan Flader, *Thinking Like a Mountain: Aldo Leopold and the Evolution of an Ecological Attitude toward Deer, Wolves and Forests* (Lincoln: U of Nebraska P, 1974), 36–121; and Meine 87–228.

6. Meine 231–342; Flader 18–28. For a tribute to Leopold by one of his students, see Robert A. McCabe, *Aldo Leopold: The Professor* (Amherst, WI: Palmer Publications, 1987).

7. "Foreword" 287. Dennis Ribbens, "An Introduction to the 1947 Foreword [to *Great Possessions*]," *Companion to "A Sand County Almanac",* ed. Callicott 277–80.

8. In "The Husbandry of the Wild," *For Love of the World: Essays on Nature Writers* (Iowa City: U of Iowa P, 1992), Sherman Paul writes that the three parts of the *Almanac* "might also be designated *Thoreau, Muir,* and *Leopold,* for the participatory seasonal record, if not the family activity, recalls *Walden,* the double ply of adventure and conservation recalls any number of Muir's books (written in recollection), and Leopold, their successor, brings both forward in the uncompromising upshot of the conclusion . . ." (46).

9. On the composition of the *Almanac,* see Dennis Ribbens, "The Making of *A Sand County Almanac,"* ed. Callicott 91–109. Following Leopold's untimely death after the manuscript had been accepted for publication, a team of half a dozen friends and relatives revised and reorganized the book; Lawrence Buell points this out and calls for a "definitive edition of *Sand County Almanac* that distinguishes Leopold's own words from the published version." See Buell's *The Environmental Imagination: Thoreau, Nature Writing, and the Formation of American Culture* (Cambridge: Cambridge UP, 1995), 172.

10. Paul refers to Leopold's hunting as "folly" and criticizes his program of "game management" (41–42). For an eloquent defense of the spiritual aspects of hunting, see José Ortega y Gasset, *Meditations on Hunting* (New York: Scribner's, 1985).

11. On Leopold's biocentrism, see Nash 68–70; on Leopold's anthropocentrism, see Harold Fromm, "Aldo Leopold: Aesthetic Anthropocentrist," *ISLE* 1.1 (Spring 1993): 43–49. Buell discusses anthropomorphism and the pathetic fallacy generally in nature writing (182–218).

12. Robert Finch discusses Leopold's personal mythography in the introduction, *A Sand County Almanac* (New York: Oxford UP, 1987), xxii. James I. McClintock centers his discussion of Leopold on the theme of mythmaking, in *Nature's Kindred Spirits: Aldo Leopold, Joseph Wood Krutch, Edward Abbey, Annie Dillard, and Gary Snyder* (Madison: U of Wisconsin P, 1994), 23–45. Donald Worster discusses the prevailing attitude toward predators like wolves on the part of game management officials in the early 20th century in *Nature's Economy: A History of Ecological Ideas* (Cambridge: Cambridge UP, 1977), 258–90. Daniel B. Botkin offers a revisionist perspective on the deer and wolf scenario in the southwest, suggesting that there were other reasons (e.g., the effects of fire in producing more vegetation) for the increase in the deer population. See *Discordant Harmonies: A New Ecology for the Twenty-First Century* (New York: Oxford UP, 1990), 76–80.

13. Meine 453–59.

14. Aldo Leopold, *Game Management* (Madison: U of Wisconsin P, 1986), 3. Aldo Leopold, *Round River: From the Journals of*

Aldo Leopold, ed. Luna Leopold (New York: Oxford UP, 1993), 167.

15. The best treatment of Leopold's style is Robert F. Sayre, "Aldo Leopold's Sentimentalism: 'A Refined Taste in Natural Objects,'" *North Dakota Quarterly* 59.2 (Spring 1991): 112–25. For a view of Leopold as an "unsentimental" writer, see Frank Stewart, *The Nature of Natural History* (Washington, D.C.: Island Press, 1994), 155, 160. Buell provides an insightful gloss of Sayre's treatment of Leopold (386–87).

16. Leopold's critique of modern farmers anticipates that of Wendell Berry; see particularly "Margins," the last chapter of *The Unsettling of America: Culture and Agriculture* (New York: Avon, 1977). A good discussion of Leopold and farming is Curt Meine, "The Farmer as Conservationist," *Aldo Leopold: The Man and His Legacy,* ed. Thomas Tanner (Ankeny, IA: Soil Conservation Society of America, 1987): 39–52.

17. The best treatment of Leopold as a wilderness preservationist in the national context remains Roderick Nash, *Wilderness and the American Mind* (New Haven: Yale UP, 3d rev. ed., 1982). See also Craig Allen, "The Leopold Legacy and American Wilderness," *Aldo Leopold: The Man and His Legacy,* ed. Tanner 25–38.

18. I take issue with Buell, who claims that Leopold (in contrast to Thoreau) "had no interest in conducting a self-reliance experiment" (174). I find the difference between Thoreau and Leopold on this issue one of degree more than kind, since Leopold, like Thoreau, took great pride in making things (such as his own bows and arrows) for himself. On Leopold's anticipation of environmental history, see Donald Worster, "Transformations of the Earth: Toward an Agroecological Perspective in History," *Journal of American History* 76.4 (March 1990): 1087.

19. For an insightful reading of "Good Oak," and of the *Almanac* generally, see John Tallmadge, "Anatomy of a Classic," *Companion to "A Sand County Almanac,"* ed. Callicott 110–27.

20. See Nash, *The Rights of Nature* 63–74; and McClintock 23–45.

21. See Meine 329–31 on the genesis and composition of "Marshland Elegy." Peter Fritzell in *Nature Writing and*

America: Essays upon a Cultural Type (Ames: Iowa State UP, 1990) reads this sketch as a "divided picture of the natural world" (208), but I see Leopold achieving integration with the nonhuman environment here through his empathy for the cranes.

22. For another account by Leopold of the "raid" of the Flambeau River, see "The Ecological Conscience," *The River of the Mother of God and Other Essays by Aldo Leopold,* eds. Susan Flader and J. Baird Callicott (Madison: U of Wisconsin P, 1991), 338–46.

23. Significant commentary exists on the importance of the land ethic. I find the following treatments particularly useful: J. Baird Callicott, "The Conceptual Foundations of the Land Ethic," *Companion to "A Sand County Almanac,"* ed. Callicott, 186–217; Max Oelschlaeger, *The Idea of Wilderness* (New Haven: Yale UP, 1991), 205–42; and Nash, *The Rights of Nature.*

24. *Game Management,* 21.

25. See Bradley 161–64. For a thoughtful assessment of Leopold's legacy, see Wallace Stegner, "The Legacy of Aldo Leopold," *Companion to "A Sand County Almanac,"* ed. Callicott 233–45.

6. Abbey

1. Edward Abbey, introduction, *The Journey Home: Some Words in Defense of the American West* (New York: Dutton, 1977), xii. D. H. Lawrence, *Studies in Classic American Literature* (New York: Penguin, 1977), 58. Edward Abbey, preface, *Desert Solitaire* (Tucson: U of Arizona P, 1988), 13. In discussing Abbey, I refer to the first edition of this work (*Desert Solitaire: A Season in the Wilderness* [New York: Simon & Schuster, 1968]); subsequent references to it appear parenthetically in the text. Edward Abbey, introduction, *The Land of Little Rain* (New York: Penguin, 1988), vii–xiii. On Abbey as a nature writer (despite his protests to the contrary), see the insightful essay by David Morris, "Celebration and Irony: The Polyphonic Voice of Edward Abbey's *Desert Solitaire,*" *Western American Literature* 28.1 (May 1993): 21–32.

2. "The moral duty of the free writer is to begin his work at home: to be a critic of his own community, his own country,

his own government, his own culture," Abbey writes in "A Writer's Credo," *One Life at a Time, Please* (New York: Henry Holt, 1988), 161. One of the better early treatments of Abbey's writings, which focuses on his "full-blown rage," is the chapter on Abbey by Peter Wild in *Pioneer Conservationists of Western America* (Missoula, MT: Mountain Press, 1979), 185–97. On the flowering of modern environmentalism, see Roderick Nash, *The Rights of Nature: A History of Environmental Ethics* (Madison: U of Wisconsin P, 1989), 161–98; and Christopher Manes, *Green Rage: Radical Environmentalism and the Unmaking of Civilization* (Boston: Little, Brown, 1990).

3. Three works have been published posthumously: *Edward Abbey: A Voice Crying in the Wilderness: Notes from a Secret Journal* (Santa Fe: Rydall, 1989); *Hayduke Lives!* (Boston: Little, Brown, 1989); and *Confessions of a Barbarian: Selections from the Journals of Edward Abbey, 1951–1989,* ed. David Petersen (Boston: Little, Brown, 1984). Details on Abbey's early years come from Edward Abbey, "Hallelujah on the Bum," *The Journey Home,* 5.

4. Information on Abbey's college years is derived from several sources: Edward Abbey, "Anarchism and the Morality of Violence," master's thesis, University of New Mexico, 1959; Garth McCann, *Edward Abbey* (Boise: Western Writers' Series #29, 1977), 6–7; James Bishop, *Epitaph for a Desert Anarchist: The Life and Legacy of Edward Abbey* (New York: Atheneum, 1994), 79–120; and Gregory McNamee, "Scarlet 'A' on a Field of Black," *Resist Much, Obey Little: Some Notes on Edward Abbey,* eds. James Hepworth and Gregory McNamee (Salt Lake City: Dream Garden Press, 1985), 23–32.

5. On Abbey's life in the 1950s, see Bishop 147–54; and Frank Stewart, *The Nature of Natural History* (Washington, D.C.: Island Press, 1994), 195–96.

6. Abbey relates his version of the composition and publication of *Desert Solitaire* in the following works: Edward Abbey, introduction, *Abbey's Road* (New York: Dutton, 1979), xix; Edward Abbey, preface, *Beyond the Wall: Essays from the Outside* (New York: Holt, Rinehart, and Winston, 1984), xii–xiii; and Abbey, preface, *Desert Solitaire* 1988, 9–11.

7. Charmaine Balian, "The Carson Productions Interview," *Resist Much, Obey Little,* 59. Abbey, introduction to *The Journey Home,* xiv. The commentator quoted is Patricia Limerick, *Desert Passages: Encounters with the American Deserts* (Albuquerque: U of New Mexico P, 1985), 149. Thomas Lyon observes in his taxonomy of nature writing that the account of "Solitude and Backcountry Living" "tends to be much more radical and critical" than other types of the genre, and he places *Desert Solitaire* in this category; see *This Incomperable Lande: A Book of American Nature Writing* (Boston: Houghton Mifflin, 1989) 4–6.

8. See Aldo Leopold, "Conservation Esthetic," *A Sand County Almanac and Sketches Here and There* (New York: Oxford UP, 1949), 165–77. A wonderful treatment of this minimalist recreation theme as applied to the national parks is Joseph Sax, *Mountains without Handrails: Reflections on the National Parks* (Ann Arbor: U of Michigan P, 1980).

9. On nature writing as a seasonal account, see Lawrence Buell, *The Environmental Imagination: Thoreau, Nature Writing, and the Formation of American Culture* (Cambridge: Harvard UP, 1995), 219–51, 397–423. A fine essay on the artfulness of Abbey's work is Paul T. Bryant, "The Structure and Unity of *Desert Solitaire,*" *Western American Literature* 28.1 (May 1993): 3–19. Abbey's encounters with animals are discussed in Don Scheese, "*Desert Solitaire:* Counter-Friction to the Machine in the Garden," *North Dakota Quarterly* 59.2 (Spring 1991): 215–16; and James McClintock, *Nature's Kindred Spirits: Aldo Leopold, Joseph Wood Krutch, Edward Abbey, Annie Dillard, and Gary Snyder* (Madison: U of Wisconsin P, 1994), 74–79. Abbey's debt to Jeffers is discussed by McClintock (74–79) and Morris (22–24), and Abbey alludes to Jeffers when he forecasts the fall of democracy in *Desert Solitaire:* "It was all foreseen nearly half a century ago by the most cold-eyed and clear-eyed of our national poets, on California's shore, at the end of the open road. Shine, perishing republic" (132).

10. Scott Slovic in *Seeking Awareness in American Nature Writing: Henry Thoreau, Annie Dillard, Edward Abbey, Wendell Berry, Barry Lopez* (Salt Lake City: U of Utah P, 1992) goes so far as to claim that "the yearning simultaneously to control and to

surrender (or belong) to something beyond the self becomes the essential tension of the book" (96). For other discussions of Abbey's biocentric and neoprimitivist tendencies, see Stewart 199–201; and Paul Bryant, "Edward Abbey and Environmental Quixoticism," *Western American Literature* 24.1 (May 1989): 37–43, who argues that Abbey is even more extreme in his fiction than his nonfiction.

11. Raymond Benoit compares Abbey with Thoreau, Twain, Hemingway, and Faulkner in "Again with Fair Creation: Holy Places in American Literature," *Prospects* 5 (1990): 327–29. On Abbey's transformation of wilderness into sacred space, see also Belden Lane, *Landscapes of the Sacred: Geography and Narrative in American Spirituality* (New York: Paulist Press, 1988), 96–102.

12. The "sacrifice" of Glen Canyon Dam as a strategy of environmentalists to save Echo Park is discussed in Roderick Nash, *Wilderness and the American Mind* (New Haven: Yale UP, 3d rev. ed., 1982), 228–30.

13. Edward Abbey, *The Monkey Wrench Gang* (Philadelphia: Lippincott, 1975); and *Hayduke Lives!*

14. Preface to *Desert Solitaire* 1988, 12. See Scheese 221–24.

15. Abbey as a radical environmentalist and his influential legacy are discussed in Nash 1989, 189–98; Bishop 208–391; and Jack Loeffler, "Edward Abbey, Anarchism, and the Environment," *Western American Literature* 28.1 (May 1993): 43–49. For a treatment of the theory of ecotage see Michael Martin, "Ecotage and Civil Disobedience," *Environmental Ethics* 12.4 (Winter 1990): 291–310. A sharp critique of such activities is made by Martin Lewis in *Green Delusions: An Environmental Critique of Radical Environmentalism* (Durham, NC: Duke UP, 1992).

16. Edward Abbey, *Good News* (New York: Dutton, 1980). Abbey continued to profess his philosophy of radical environmentalism for the rest of his life; see, for example, "Eco-Defense," *One Life at a Time, Please,* 29–32.

17. Aldo Leopold, "Thinking Like a Mountain," *A Sand County Almanac,* 133. Ann Ronald discusses Abbey's vexation with

the national parks in *The New West of Edward Abbey* (Albuquerque: U of New Mexico P, 1982), 89–90.

18. Leo Marx, *The Machine in the Garden: Technology and the Pastoral Ideal in America* (New York: Oxford UP, 1964), 228.

19. Walt Whitman, "Song of Myself," *The Norton Anthology of American Literature*, 2 vols., ed. Nina Baym et al. (New York: Norton, 4th ed., 1994), 1: 2089. Other works on which Abbey collaborated with a photographer are *Appalachian Wilderness: The Great Smoky Mountains* (photos by Eliot Porter, New York: Dutton, 1970); *Cactus Country* (Alexandria, VA: Time-Life, 1973); *The Hidden Canyon: A River Journey* (photos by John Blaustein, New York: Viking, 1977); and *Desert Images* (with David Muench, New York: Chanticleer, 1981). On Abbey's disparagement of photography, see for example "A Walk in the Park," *Abbey's Road*, 113. Edward Abbey and Philip Hyde, *Slickrock* (Salt Lake City: Peregrine Smith, 1987), 20.

20. On landscape photography in the American deserts, see Weston Naef and James Wood, *Era of Exploration: The Rise of Landscape Photography in the American West, 1860–1885* (New York: Metropolitan Museum of Art, 1975); Mark Klett et al., *Second View: The Rephotographic Survey Project* (Albuquerque: U of New Mexico P, 1984); and Robert Adams, "Towards a Proper Silence: Nineteenth-Century Photographs of the American Landscape," *Aperture* 98 (Spring): 4–11.

21. On the details of Abbey's death and funeral arrangements, see Bishop 193–207; Edward Hoagland, "Standing Tall in the Desert," *New York Times Book Review* (7 May 1989): 44–45; Richard Manning, "Abbey's Clan Gathers to Rededicate Itself," *High Country News* (5 June 1989): 3; and Terry Tempest Williams, "A Eulogy for Edward Abbey," *An Unspoken Hunger: Stories from the Field* (New York: Pantheon, 1994), 73–78.

7. Dillard

1. Lawrence Buell, "American Pastoral Ideology Reappraised," *American Literary History* 1.1 (Spring 1989): 1–29. Dillard is quoted in Carla Hammond, "Drawing the Curtains: An Interview with Annie Dillard," *Bennington Review* 10 (Apr. 1981): 35.

2. Edward Abbey, introduction, *Abbey's Road* (New York: Dutton, 1979), xx. Abbey's "recommendation" of Dillard is discussed by James I. McClintock in *Nature's Kindred Spirits: Aldo Leopold, Joseph Wood Krutch, Edward Abbey, Annie Dillard, and Gary Snyder* (Madison: U of Wisconsin P, 1994), 88–89. Annie Dillard, *The Living* (New York: HarperCollins, 1992). On Dillard's habit of attention, see David Lavery, "Noticer: The Visionary Art of Annie Dillard, *Massachusetts Review* 21 (Summer 1980): 255–70.

3. Annie Dillard, *An American Childhood* (New York: Harper & Row, 1987), 15–85; subsequent references to this work appear parenthetically in the text. See also Linda Smith, *Annie Dillard* (New York: Twayne, 1991), 1–6.

4. Smith 5–9. Don Scheese, "Annie Dillard," *American Nature Writers,* ed. John Elder (New York, Scribner's, forthcoming 1996).

5. Annie Dillard, *Pilgrim at Tinker Creek* (Toronto: Bantam, 1974), 5, 12; subsequent references to this work appear parenthetically in the text. On the simple life, see David Shi, *The Simple Life: Plain Living and High Thinking in American Culture* (New York: Oxford UP, 1985). On individualism versus community in Dillard's work, see Gary McIlroy, *"Pilgrim at Tinker Creek* and the Social Legacy of *Walden,"* *South Atlantic Quarterly* 85 (Spring 1986): 111–22.

6. Annie Dillard, "Living Like Weasels, " *Teaching a Stone to Talk* (New York: Harper & Row, 1982), 12–13.

7. Ralph Waldo Emerson, *Emerson's 'Nature': Origin, Growth Meaning,* eds. Merton M. Sealts, Jr., and Alfred R. Ferguson (Carbondale: Southern Illinois UP, 1969, 2d ed.), 5. Wise discussions of Dillard's preoccupation with self-consciousness can be found in Scott Slovic, *Seeking Awareness in American Nature Writing: Henry Thoreau, Annie Dillard, Edward Abbey, Wendell Berry, Barry Lopez* (Salt Lake City: U of Utah P, 1992), 63–69; and Peter Fritzell, *Nature Writing and America: Essays upon a Cultural Type* (Ames: Iowa State UP, 1990), 235–62.

8. Annie Dillard, *Living by Fiction* (New York: Harper & Row, 1982). The case for Dillard as a postmodern nature writer is made by Suzanne Clark, "Annie Dillard: The Woman in Nature and the Subject of Nonfiction," *Literary Nonfiction:*

Theory, Criticism, Pedagogy, ed. Chris Anderson (Carbondale: Southern Illinois UP, 1989), 107–24.

9. Annie Dillard, *The Writing Life* (New York: Harper & Row, 1989), 26–31.

10. On Dillard's use of others' natural history in her nature writing, see Gary McIlroy, *"Pilgrim at Tinker Creek* and the Burden of Science," *American Literature* 59.1 (Mar. 1987): 80–82.

11. John Becker discusses the implications of the Heisenberg principle for Dillard in "Science and the Sacred: From *Walden* to *Tinker Creek,"* *Thought* 62 (Dec. 1987): 400–13; on this point, see also Fritzell 262–64. An illuminating treatment of Dillard in the context of the philosopher Alfred North Whitehead's belief in the "subjectivity" of all nature is John Elder, *Imagining the Earth: Poetry and the Vision of Nature* (Urbana: U of Illinois P, 1985), 170–80. The definition of nature writing comes from David Rains Wallace, "The Nature of Nature Writing, *New York Times Book Review* (22 July 1984): 1, 18.

12. The potentially antienvironmentalist aspects of *Pilgrim* are taken up by Elaine Tietjen, "Perceptions of Nature: Annie Dillard's *Pilgrim at Tinker Creek,"* *North Dakota Quarterly* 56.3 (Summer 1988): 101–13. On Dillard's anthropocentrism, see also Slovic 66–67.

13. The importance of "stalking" to Dillard's project of nature writing and her religious beliefs is explained by, among others, McClintock (94–96).

14. Henry David Thoreau, *The Illustrated Walden* (Princeton: Princeton UP, 1973), 318. The issue of theodicy and Dillard's quest for knowledge about the creator is taken up by Stan Goldman, "Sacrifices to the Hidden God: Annie Dillard's *Pilgrim at Tinker Creek* and Leviticus," *Soundings* 74.1–2 (Spring/Summer 1991): 195–213; Douglas Burton-Christie, "'A Feeling for the Natural World': Spirituality and Contemporary Nature Writing," *Continuum* 2.1 (Feb. 1992): 244–45; and Bruce Ronda, "Annie Dillard and the Fire of God," *The Christian Century* (18 May 1993): 483–86.

15. On Dillard's differences with the transcendentalists, see McIlroy, "Burden" 76–77; Becker 407–12; and Margaret

Loewen Reimer, "The Dialectical Vision of Annie Dillard's *Pilgrim at Tinker Creek* 24 (Spring 1983): 182–91. *Darwin: A Norton Critical Edition,* ed. Philip Appleman (New York: Norton, 1970), 125.

16. Dillard's debt to Darwin, though significant, is virtually ignored in the extensive critical commentary on her. See Dillard's own treatment of Darwin in "Life on the Rocks: The Galápagos," *Teaching a Stone to Talk: Expeditions and Encounters* (New York: Harper & Row, 1983), 110–31.

17. Smith discusses Dillard's religious beliefs thoroughly, including her panentheism (16–41). Critics categorize Dillard's religious views in different ways: for Dillard as mystical theologian, see Eugene Peterson, "Annie Dillard: With Her Eyes Open," *Theology Today* 43 (1986–87): 178–81; as conventional Christian, McClintock (89–91); and as "new age" Christian, Burton-Christie (229–52). On Dillard's preoccupation with the lesson of Job, see Becker 402–10.

18. Emerson 35. The movement of *Pilgrim,* with its action rising toward an ultimate revelation, is discussed by Sandra Johnson in *The Space Between: Literary Epiphany in the Work of Annie Dillard* (Kent: Kent State UP, 1992), 1–10. On the structure of the book, see also Smith 46–48.

19. Nature writers and their desire for encounters with the "shimmering force of the transcendent" are discussed by Burton-Christie 229–52. For nature writing as religious pilgrimage and the quest for and creation of sacred place, see the wonderful study by Belden Lane, *Landscapes of the Sacred: Geography and Narrative in American Spirituality* (New York: Paulist Press, 1988), particularly 3–33. Another good approach by a religious studies scholar is Catherine Albanese, *Nature Religion in America: From the Algonkians to the New Age* (Chicago: U of Chicago P, 1990), 163–71, which places Dillard in the Puritan tradition of preoccupation with evil.

20. On our contemporary "postnatural" world, see Bill McKibben, *The End of Nature* (New York: Random House, 1989). The notion of an "invisible" (mental) landscape is the theme of Kent Ryden, *Mapping the Invisible Landscape: Folklore, Writing, and the Sense of Place* (Iowa City: U of Iowa P,

1993). See also Barry Lopez and his discussion of "two land-scapes—one outside the self, the other within," in "Landscape and Narrative," *Crossing Open Ground* (New York: Scribner's, 1988): 61–71.

21. Wendell Berry, *Collected Poems: 1957–1982* (New York: North Point Press, 1984), 162.

8. Conclusion

1. A concise biography of Jeffers is James Karman, *Robinson Jeffers: Poet of California* (San Francisco: Chronicle Books, 1987).

2. Robinson Jeffers, *Selected Poems* (New York: Random House, 1965), 55. See Mercedes Monjian, *Robinson Jeffers: A Study in Inhumanism*. A good critical overview of Jeffers is Robert J. Brophy, *Robinson Jeffers* (Boise: Boise State University Western Writers Series #19, 1975). Lawrence Buell describes Jeffers's self-effacment as "desubjectification" in *The Environmental Imagination: Thoreau, Nature Writing, and the Formation of American Culture* (Cambridge: Harvard UP, 1995), 161–67.

3. On the etymology of "celebrate," see Robert Finch, "The Once and Future Cape," *Orion Nature Quarterly* 7.4 (Autumn 1988): 25.

4. Wallace Stegner, *Where the Bluebird Sings to the Lemonade Springs: Living and Writing in the West* (New York: Penguin, 1992), 201.

5. "Man . . . is the storytelling animal" is from Graham Swift's *Waterland* and is quoted in William Cronon, "A Place for Stories: Nature, History, and Narrative," *Journal of American History* 78.4 (Mar. 1992): 1347–76. Of course, other species pass on information about the space they inhabit, too, each in its own way. Swift is anthropocentric in his claim that humans are the *only* storytelling species.

6. See James Kunstler, *The Geography of Nowhere: The Rise and Decline of America's Man-Made Landscape* (New York: Simon & Schuster, 1993).

7. *The Journal of Henry David Thoreau*, 14 vols., eds. Bradford Torrey and Francis Allen (Salt Lake City: Gibbs Smith, 1984),

13: 170–71. I am grateful to Dan Peck of Vassar College for reacquainting me with this passage during an NEH Summer Institute in 1993. See Peck's own discussion of this passage in "Better Mythology: Perception and Emergence in Thoreau's Journal," *North Dakota Quarterly* 59.2 (Spring 1991): 33–44; he discusses Thoreau's epistemology generally in *Thoreau's Morning Work: Memory and Perception in* A Week on the Concord and Merrimack Rivers, *the Journal, and* Walden (New Haven: Yale UP, 1990).

Index

Abbey, Edward, 8, 35, 80, 91, 102, 106–119, 125; *Abbey's Road,* 120–121; "Anarchism and the Morality of Violence," 108; *Desert Solitaire,* 35, 80, 106–119; *Good News,* 115; *Jonathan Troy,* 108; *The Journey Home,* 108; *The Monkey Wrench Gang,* 35, 106

Adams, Ansel, 32–33; *Alkali Flat, Alabama Hills and Sierra Nevada in Distance,* 87–88; *El Capitan, Winter Sunrise, Yosemite Valley, 1968,* 32– 33; *Taos Pueblo,* 87

agriculture, 35–36, 46–48, 78, 97–98, 100

athropocentrism, 5, 17, 22–23, 28, 41, 44, 49, 54, 61, 62, 63–64, 66, 73, 78, 95–96, 109, 111, 113, 116, 125, 127, 134

antimodernism, 5, 47, 83

Apollo landing, 32

Arches National Monument, 108–109, 116

Aristotle, 13, 14, 37

Audubon, John James, 21

Audubon Society, 29

Augustine: *Confessions,* 23, 121, 130

Austin, Mary, 8, 28, 35, 68, 75–89, 90, 91, 96, 100, 109, 117, 119; *Earth Horizon,* 76, 77, 84; *The Land of Journey's Ending,* 82; *The Land of Little Rain,* 75, 77, 78–89, 107; "The Walking Woman," 85

autobiography, 6, 20–21, 22, 38

"back to nature" cult, 28–30, 76

Bailey, Florence Hyde, 28

Bartram, William: *Travels,* 19–20

Bate, Jonathan, 10

Battles, Jim: *South Lookout, Hawk Mountain,* 131

Beebe, William: *The Book of Naturalists,* 13

Berry, Wendell, 48; *Farming: A Handbook,* 36; "A Homecoming," 132; *A Place on Earth,* 35–36; *The Unsettling of America,* 35

Beston, Henry: *The Outermost House*, 30

Bierstadt, Albert, 25, 33; *Looking Up Yosemite Valley*, 70–71; *The Rocky Mountains*, 26

biocentrism, 5, 19–20, 22–23, 35, 41, 49, 54, 61, 62, 63–64, 66, 73, 78, 79, 80, 95–96, 109, 111, 112, 113, 116, 125

Boone and Crockett Club, 29

Botkin, Daniel, 32

Boy Scouts of America, 29

Brower, David, 33

Buell, Lawrence, 120

Buffon, Count Georges-Louis Leclerc de, 19

Burke, Edmund, 1

Burroughs, John, 28, 29

Carrighar, Sally: *One Day at Beetle Rock*, 30

Carson, Rachel: *Silent Spring*, 32, 107

Catlin, George, 27

Chauvet, France, cave art, 38

Church, Frederic: *Mount Ktaadn*, 58; *Twilight in the Wilderness*, 24–25

Clark, William, 19

Cohen, Michael: *The Pathless Way*, 10

Cole, Thomas: "Essay on American Scenery," 4, 25; *The Oxbow*, 1–5, 19, 41, 75

Coleridge, Samuel Taylor, 22

Columbus, Christopher, 15

Crèvecoeur, J. Hector St. John de: *Letters from an American Farmer*, 19

Cropsey, Jasper, 24

Darwin, Charles, 12, 69; *On the Origin of Species*, 21, 128; *The Voyage of the Beagle*, 21

Death Valley, 80, 87

Dillard, Annie, 8, 36, 120–130, 134, 135; *An American Childhood*, 121; *The Living*, 121; *Living by Fiction*, 125; *Pilgrim at Tinker Creek*, 36, 120–130; *The Writing Life*, 125

Earth Day, 32

Earth First!, 35, 115

ecocriticism, 8–10, 54

ecofeminism, 79, 84

ecology, 12, 21, 30–31

Eiseley, Loren: *The Immense Journey*, 31; *The Night Country*, 31

Emerson, Ralph Waldo, 10, 28, 54, 59, 124, 129; *Nature*, 4, 22–23, 42

environmental history, 7, 24, 99

environmentalism, 5, 31–33

exploration literature, 15, 27–28

Euramerican culture, 5, 12, 66–67, 83

Fabre, J. Henri, 126

fieldwork, in ecocriticism: 9–10; to individual authors' places: Abbey, 106–107; Austin, 87–89; Muir, 61–62, 73–74; Thoreau, 39–41, 52, 54–55, 56–57; in writers' works: Darwin, 21; Dillard, 125; White, 16, 17

Fink, Stephen, 54

Gilpin, Laura, 87, 118

Glen Canyon, 33, 35, 113–114

Gray, Asa, 22

Greylock, Mount, 55

Grinnell, George Bird, 28, 91

Harding, Walter, 40

Hetch Hetchy, 73

Hudson River school, 3–4, 24–25; *see also individual artists*, Landscape art

Hudson, W. H.: *Hampshire Days*, 30; *The Life of a Shepherd*, 30

Hyde, Philip: "Early Morning at Chesler Park," 118–119; *Slickrock*, 117

Indians. *See* Native Americans

industrial revolution, 4, 6, 18, 20, 24, 52

Inness, George: *Lackawanna Valley*, 45–46

Jackson, J. B., 7

Jackson, William Henry, 87, 118
Jeffers, Robinson, 111; "The Place for No Story," 133
Jefferson, Thomas: *Notes on the State of Virginia,* 19
Jeffries, Richard: *The Life of the Fields,* 30; *The Open Air,* 30
John Muir Trail, 61, 73–74

Katahdin, Mount, 11, 50–58, 61, 72
King, Clarence, 22, 69; *Mountaineering in the Sierra Nevada,* 28

landscape, 7–8, 9, 17, 32, 52, 53, 62, 78, 103, 131
landscape art, 10–11, 24–27, 87
Lawrence, D. H.: *Studies in Classic American Literature,* 107
Leopold, Aldo, 8, 31, 32, 90–105, 107, 109, 114, 115; *Game Management,* 91, 97, 103; *Round River,* 97; *A Sand County Almanac,* 31, 90–105
Lewis, Meriwether, 19
Lindenberger, Herbert, 4–5
Linnaeus, Carl, 14–15
Lopez, Barry: *Arctic Dreams,* 37
Lyell, Charles, 69

Marsh, George Perkins: *Man and Nature,* 27
Marx, Leo, 4, 44, 45, 116
Mojave Desert, 11, 75, 78, 79, 81, 87
Momaday, N. Scott: *The Way to Rainy Mountain,* 37
Monadnock, Mount, 55
Moran, Thomas, 25
Morgan, Lewis Henry, 22
Mowat, Farley, 30
Muir, John, 8, 28, 41, 61–74, 75, 81, 82, 91, 95, 96, 99, 100, 102, 106, 107, 109, 116, 129; *My First Summer in the Sierra,* 64–72; *The Story of My Boyhood and Youth,* 62, 66; *A Thousand-Mile Walk to the Gulf,* 28, 63–64, 66; *The Yosemite,* 73

Nabhan, Gary Paul: *The Desert Smells Like Rain,* 37

Nash, Roderick, 20
national parks, 26–27, 64, 73, 74, 106, 109
Native Americans, 5, 7, 20, 24, 28–29, 47, 64, 66–68, 78, 79, 80, 82–86, 87, 89
natural history, 6, 13, 14–24; 38: ancient forms, 13; in individual authors: Austin, 78, 82; Darwin, 21–22; Dillard, 126; Leopold, 91, 94, 99; Thoreau, 49; White, 15–18; and politics, 18–20; and Romanticism, 20–21; and transcendentalism, 22–24; and travel writing, 14–15
natural theology, 14, 16, 28, 37, 68, 120
"nature faker" controversy, 29, 66, 81
nature writing: evolution of, 11–38; and ancient Greek pastoralism, 13–14; "back to nature" cult, 28–30; and Darwin, 21–22; and ecology, 30–31; and nuclear age, 31–33; radical environmentalism, 34–35; and transcendentalism, 4, 22–24; and travel writing, 14–15; *see also individual nature writers*
Nelson, Richard: *The Island Within,* 37
New Historicism, 11
Norwood, Vera, 80

Olson, Sigurd, 91
O'Sullivan, Timothy, 87, 118
Owens Valley, 67, 68, 75, 78, 87, 89

panentheism, 64, 71, 128
pastoralism: ancient Greek, 13–14, 25; evolution of, 11–38; definition, 4; "hard" version, 7–8, 50, 62, 71, 77; "island experience," 5, 43, 56, 69–70, 71, 78, 93, 102, 110, 115; origins, 4; "soft" version, 7–8, 17, 50, 93, 123; in individual authors: Abbey, 107–119; Austin 75–89; Bartram, 19; Crèvecoeur, 19; Dillard, 120–130; Jeffers, 133–134;

Leopold, 90–105; Muir, 61–74; Thoreau, 41–60; and landscape art, 4; and nature writing, 6– 38; theory of containment, 5, 41, 60, 64, 78, 94

Patterson, R. M., 30

Peattie, Donald Culross: *An Almanac for Moderns;* 30; *The Road of a Naturalist,* 30

phenology, 16, 95

pilgrimage, 39–40, 58, 59, 129, 130, 131

Pinchot, Gifford, 91

Pliny the Elder, 126: *Natural History,* 13, 14, 37

Pollan, Michael: *Second Nature,* 36

Porter, Eliot: *The Place No One Knew,* 33

poststructuralism, 9

Powell, John Wesley, 113, 118: *The Exploration of the Colorado River and Its Canyons,* 27–28

progress, 5, 33, 47, 83, 94, 100

radical environmentalism, 5, 33–35, 107, 108, 109, 114–115, 119

Ray, John, 14, 16, 17, 120

recreation, 5, 61, 64, 72, 95, 116

re–creation, 5, 61, 64, 72, 95, 97, 116

Rockland, Michael Aaron: *Snowshoeing through Sewers,* 36

romanticism, 20–21

Roosevelt, Theodore, 29, 91

Rueckert, William: "Literature and Ecology," 8

Selbourne, 15–18

self-consciousness, 5, 123, 124–125, 133

Seton, Ernest Thompson, 29, 30, 91

Shepard, Paul, 20

Sierra Club, 29, 33, 73, 114

simple life, 42–43, 49, 82, 105, 123

Snyder, Gary: *Turtle Island,* 37

Stanwell–Fletcher, Theodora, 30

Stegner, Wallace: *Where the Bluebird Sings to the Lemonade Springs,* 134– 135

Stevens, Wallace, 74

sublime, 1–2, 26, 56, 62, 65, 70–71, 89, 104, 105, 107, 123

suburbs, 7, 36

Teale, Edwin Way, 37, 126

Theocritus, 4, 14

theodicy, 122, 128

Thoreau, Henry David, 4, 8, 10, 20, 22–24, 25, 28, 29, 35, 39–60, 65, 72, 73, 82, 89, 91, 99, 100, 102, 103, 107, 109, 115, 122, 123, 124, 128, 130; *Cape Cod,* 24; Journal, 23, 24, 42, 43, 55, 58, 60, 136; "Ktaadn," 41, 50–58; *The Maine Woods,* 24; "Resistance to Civil Government," 115; *Walden,* 10, 23, 39–50, 58, 60, 102, 111; "Walking," 8, 41, 58–60, 103; *A Week on the Concord and Merrimack Rivers,* 58

transcendentalism, 12, 22–24, 50, 51, 52, 53, 72, 128, 129; theory of correspondence, 23, 46, 47, 49, 55–56, 124

travel writing, 6, 14–15, 21, 23, 38, 50, 52, 61

Twain, Mark (Samuel Clemens), 113, 121

unconsciousness, 5, 123, 124–125

Van Dyke, John C., 118

Virgil, 4; *Eclogues,* 14

Walden Pond, 9, 11, 39–50, 51, 57, 78, 130

Washington, Mount, 55

Watkins, Carleton: *North and Half Domes from Sentinel Dome,* 27

Weed, C. L., 26

White, Gilbert, 15–18, 20, 21, 22, 24, 25, 29; *The Natural History of Selbourne,* 15–18

Whitman, Walt, 117

Whitney, Josiah, 68–69

Whitney, Mount, 62

wilderness: etymology, 20; in individual authors' works: Abbey, 109–119; Austin, 82; Bartram,

20; Crèvecoeur, 19; Dillard, 123; Leopold, 90, 101, 102, 103, 106; Muir, 61–74; Thoreau, 39, 41, 43, 46, 50–57, 58–60; White, 17; and pastoralism, 3–8
wilderness preservation, 30, 73, 92, 98, 100, 101
Wilderness Society, 30, 98
wildness, 8, 48, 59, 60, 101, 102, 103, 130
Williams, Raymond, 20; *The Country and the City*, 13

Williams, Terry Tempest: *Refuge*, 35
Wilson, Alexander, 21
Wood, William: *Prospects*, 15
Wordsworth, William, 10, 20, 22
Worster, Donald, 17

Yellowstone, 27
Yosemite Valley, 11, 26, 28, 62, 64, 65, 67, 68, 69, 72, 73, 106, 116

The Author

Don Scheese is an associate professor of English and Environmental Studies at Gustavus Adolphus College in St. Peter, Minnesota, where he teaches courses in American literature, nature writing, and environmental history. He received his Ph.D. in American Studies from the University of Iowa. He has published numerous articles on nature writing and environmental history and is currently working on a memoir based on his 10 seasons as a fire lookout for the United States Forest Service in Idaho.